Claiming the Center

Claiming the Center
Churches and Conflicting Worldviews

JACK ROGERS

Westminster John Knox Press
Louisville, Kentucky

Scripture quotations from the New Revised Standard Version of the Bible are copyright © 1989 by the Division of Christian Education of the National Council of the Churches of Christ in the U.S.A. and are used by permission.

Book design by Alec Bartsch
Cover design by Kim Wohlenhaus

First edition

Published by Westminster John Knox Press
Louisville, Kentucky

This book is printed on acid-free paper that meets the American National Standards Institute. Z39.48 standard. ∞

PRINTED IN THE UNITED STATES OF AMERICA

95 96 97 98 99 00 01 02 03 04 — 10 9 8 7 6 5 4 3 2 1

Library of Congress Cataloging-in-Publication Data

Rogers, Jack Bartlett.
    Claiming the center : churches and conflicting worldviews / Jack Rogers. — 1st ed.
        p.   cm.
    Includes bibliographical references.
    ISBN 0-664-25613-9 (alk. paper)
    1. Christianity—United States—History—20th century.
    2. Evangelicalism—United States—History—20th century.
    3. Presbyterian Church—United States—History—20th century.
    4. United States—Church History—20th century.   I. Title.
    BR526.R64   1995
    277.3'082—dc20   95-30148

Publisher's Note

The production of this book was assisted by a generous gift from Robert and Marea Stratton to the Presbyterian Publishing Corporation. Robert Stratton's commitment to Presbyterian publishing was evident throughout his forty-five years of service to the Presbyterian Publishing House and its predecessor organizations and culminated in this act of generosity.

The Strattons requested that their gift be used for the publication of a project important to the mission of the Presbyterian Publishing Corporation. We at Westminster John Knox Press believe that the issues explored by Jack Rogers in this book are significant for the Presbyterian Church (U.S.A.) and also for other mainline denominations. We are grateful to the Strattons for facilitating publication of this seminal work. We trust it will stimulate important discussions in many quarters.

To Matt, John, and Toby
with respect, admiration, and love

Contents

Acknowledgments

I wish to acknowledge the institutions listed below that gave me opportunity to lecture on elements of the materials contained in this book. In each case I learned things in the interaction with participants that helped me to progress in my thinking. For eight years, beginning in 1980, I concentrated on understanding the evangelical movement. From 1971 until 1988, I was on the faculty of Fuller Theological Seminary in Pasadena, California. The administration there was unfailingly generous in interpreting my times of research and lecturing in this area as part of my faculty responsibility.

Lectures on "Evangelicalism in America" were given as The Ransom-Butler Lectures at Wichita State University, November 1–3, 1981; at Loma Linda University, March 11, 1982; at New Orleans Baptist Theological Seminary in Louisiana, January 1983; as The Robinson Lectures at Erskine Theological Seminary, April 10 and 11, 1984; at the East Ohio School of Ministry of the United Methodist Church, August 15, 1984; at the Omaha Seminary School for Pastors, July 1987 and July 1988; and at The Chatauqua Institution, August 1987 and July 1989.

Since 1988, my primary focus has been on the mainstream churches. I am grateful to Dr. Robert Lynn, formerly vice president for religion of the Lilly Endowment, for appointing me to the evaluation team for Lilly's research projects on mainstream Protestantism in 1988 and 1989. That gave me the opportunity to become familiar with much of the research that was then beginning to be published on mainstream Protestantism. In the context of preparing my final evaluation for the Endowment, a colleague on the evaluation team suggested I apply for a grant to link my previous research and writing on evangelicalism with the new research on mainstream Protestantism. During part of the time that I was on the evaluation team, I was employed as associate for theological studies in the Theology and Worship Ministry Unit of the General Assembly Council of the Presbyterian Church (U.S.A.). The Reverend George Telford, director of that unit, recognized my need to honor the part-time commitment to the Lilly Endowment while beginning my new position.

Lectures combining research on evangelicalism with studies of mainstream Protestantism were given at Religion in American Life Week, The Chautauqua Institution, July 24, 1989; as The Greenhoe Lectures at Louisville Presbyterian Seminary, October 1989; at The Sierra Mission Area Synod School, at The College of Idaho, June 20–23, 1991; and at La Jolla Presbyterian Church, August 8–11, 1993; First Presbyterian Church, San Antonio, Texas, October 24–26, 1993; Kansas Pastors Seminar, January 24–28, 1994; Fresno Presbyterian Pastors Conference, September 2–4, 1994; San Clemente Presbyterian Church, September 23–25, 1994; The Presbytery of Nevada, November 5, 1994.

I am particularly grateful to the research team of Milton J Coalter, John M. Mulder, and Louis B. Weeks, who conceived and carried out the massive Lilly-funded study of American Presbyterianism through Louisville Presbyterian Theological Seminary. When I received a Lilly grant to do my own work in this area, I was in a period of transition, contemplating a move from the denominational staff in Louisville to San Francisco Theological Seminary. Thanks to Louisville Presbyterian Theological Seminary, where I was made a research faculty member and through which the grant was administered. I am grateful as well to Dr. Craig Dykstra, the current vice president for religion at the Lilly Endowment, for approving my request for a grant and this manner of administering it.

I need to say a special word of thanks to Dr. J. Randolph Taylor, former president of San Francisco Theological Seminary. It takes a special kind of grace to hire someone as vice president for Southern California with responsibility to begin a new program of theological education by extension and then agree that he should get six months' leave during the first year of that job. In doing that, Randy showed his full support of me as a scholarly member of the faculty, as well as an administrator, and I am grateful.

My colleagues at San Francisco Theological Seminary/Southern California, as well as all those on the Steering Committee in Southern California and on the faculty and staff in San Anselmo, deserve special thanks for carrying extra responsibility during my leave. I especially thank my administrative colleagues in Southern California: Drs. John Chandler, Cyris Moon, and Bear Scott, and our planning consultant, Ken Corr, Jr.

The School of Theology at Claremont has been wonderfully welcoming and supportive of our new Presbyterian seminary venture in Southern California. I wish, in addition, to thank President Robert W. Edgar, former dean Allan J. Moore, Dean Marjorie Suchocki, and director of the Library, Michael P. Boddy, for generously providing me a study in the STC library for one month each in the summers of 1992 and 1993 so that I could work without interruption on this book.

Dr. Margo Houts's painstaking concern for accuracy and her computer skills have been invaluable. She took time from her own doctoral studies in theology and drew on her experience as a legal secretary to prepare early drafts of this book.

My valued and extremely capable staff assistant, Mary Booker, accomplished the computer wizardry to radically change a manuscript designed on a sequential narrative into one that is organized on themes. She has gone well beyond the call of duty in preparing the final version of this manuscript for publication.

My friend, Dr. Ronald C. White, Jr., deserves special recognition. Luncheon conversations at the Huntington Library on mutual scholarly interests led to his giving major time to analyzing how to fix some of the organizational problems in earlier versions of this book. His editorial insights and his personal encouragement enabled me to undertake a full-scale revision that I had been reluctant to face.

I am always profoundly grateful to my wife, Sharon. She has moved with me from place to place, always making it the best place to be. In addition to her own demanding work as a speech and language therapist, preparing a manuscript in her own field, and pursuing advanced study of her own, she has unfailingly encouraged me. She really does believe that when I am reading a book, writing on the computer, or just sitting at my desk thinking, I am working.

My three sons, Matthew, John, and Toby, always express genuine interest in what their father is writing and doing. One of the most significant learnings from the Louisville Presbyterian study is that we have largely lost their boomer and buster generations for the church. I hope to continue to learn from and with them. Even though this book is primarily about the past, I hope that it may have some relevance to their future. I dedicate it to them with respect, admiration, and love.

Introduction

The center of mainstream Protestantism is strong. On every significant issue about 75 percent of Protestants are somewhere in the middle trying to make sense out of complex questions and to act responsibly in difficult circumstances. The function of a mainstream Protestant church is twofold: To root people in the biblical tradition and to enable them to cope with the modern world. Most mainstream Protestants want and need guidance in both those arenas, and when they get it, they think and act responsibly.

Reports in the media, and even attendance at a Presbyterian General Assembly, can give an opposite impression. The agenda and the arguments are dominated by conflict between the 15 percent on the ideological right and the 10 percent on the ideological left. The center is often leaderless and inarticulate. When the vote comes, however, the center most often prevails. Unfortunately, many Presbyterians and other mainstream Protestants have already withdrawn their financial and emotional support during earlier phases of the sometimes acrimonious discussion.

The thesis of this book is that the root cause of mainstream church decline is an internal conflict of worldviews. Good, intelligent, and devout people simply see reality differently. It is not that some people are smart and others stupid. Nor is it that some are virtuous and others wicked. It is rather that the worldview that some have adopted has caused them to see life in conservative terms, whereas others have acquired a worldview that gives a liberal interpretation of life. Most modern Americans, however, are neither conservatives nor liberals. They have been influenced both by conservative values and by liberal insights so that they are clustered somewhere in the center. That position is more difficult to articulate and apply because it is inherently more complex. It is also more adequate to describe and deal with the complexity that is reality. It was C. S. Lewis, I believe, who once commented that people want a simple religion, but real life isn't simple.

In the first chapter of *Claiming the Center* I introduce the concept of worldview. It is an overall, usually subconscious, perspective on reality learned from one's culture. It is the glasses that bring the vast array of our experiences into focus. It is the set of interpretative principles that enables one to make sense out of life. People in different countries have different cultures and thus different worldviews. But even within one country different subcultures exist that teach people differing interpretations of life.

Worldview is very similar to religion—so much so that some anthropologists identify worldviews as well as religion as they attempt to define the essence of a culture. At root, every religion is based on an ultimate religious worldview. It is a story that describes reality and our place in it. The Christian story is of a personal God who created a good world and good people. Tragically, and inexplicably, these human beings turned away from their Creator. God did not reject them, however, but came into the world in the person of Jesus Christ. Jesus' life, death, and resurrection provided the means to reconcile humans to God.

This ultimate religious worldview has been elaborated theologically, applied ideologically, and colored experientially. This elaboration, application, and coloring have occurred in particular historical and cultural contexts. Conflicts have arisen when people confused their ultimate religious worldview with the many culturally conditioned expressions of it.

In the Middle Ages and at the time of the Protestant Reformation, our conflicts were between theological elaborations of that worldview. Denominations grew up around these theological elaborations. Roman Catholics, Eastern Orthodox, and various Protestant groups fought with one another over what should be the appropriate theological elaboration of the Christian story. Often they denied the Christian commitment of others who differed with their theological elaboration.

In the 1960s, 70s, and 80s, we have been very conscious of conflicts between Christians over the ideological application of the Christian story. An ideology joins a religious worldview to a sociopolitical program. Ideological conflicts are fostered by transdenominational movements. So we have liberals, fundamentalists, charismatics, and so on, who sometimes feel they have more in common with people in other denominations than they do with those in their own who do not share their ideology. Often the Christian commitment of a person is judged by the stance that person takes on certain moral, social, and political issues.

In the 1990s we have become very sensitive to individual experiences related to race, gender, and sexual orientation. When the experience of one's individual particularity, or the common experience of a subculture, becomes the ultimate criterion of value, then conflicts with those of another race, gender, or sexual orientation can ensue.

Conflict occurs when people—Christian people—make their theological elaborations or ideological applications or experiential colorings the ultimate rather than the ultimate religious worldview itself. In Christian terms, conflict occurs when we put anything at the center except our commitment to God revealed in Jesus Christ.

In *Claiming the Center* I describe the form these conflicts have taken in what has traditionally been called mainstream Protestantism. I use the Presbyterian Church (U.S.A.) as an example both because that is my own tradition and I know it best and because the Presbyterian Church (U.S.A.) has become the most carefully researched church body in American history.

Claiming the Center describes the formation and evolution of an early American evangelical/mainstream worldview that developed during the first two centuries of the American experience. This worldview was composed of six motifs: separatism, election as God's chosen people, revivalism, common sense, moralism, and millennialism. This relatively homogeneous worldview functioned well for many until it was fractured in the mid-nineteenth century. Darwin's theory of evolution and the American Civil War were catalysts for the collapse of this common centrist worldview. Those who had identified this worldview with their ultimate Christian commitment were then thrust into a crisis of faith.

In the late nineteenth and early twentieth centuries, three conflicting ideological worldviews emerged in mainstream Protestantism. Fundamentalists held on to the principal motifs of the earlier evangelical/mainstream worldview while narrowing and rigidifying them. Those who became liberals or modernists reacted to their sense of betrayal by adopting worldview motifs directly counter to those of the earlier evangelical/mainstream worldview. The majority of mainstream Protestants remained in the middle, rethinking their worldview in more open and flexible terms but holding to the essentials of the Christian faith using the theological elaboration of their denomination.

Conflicts between fundamentalists and liberals marked mainstream Protestantism, and especially Presbyterianism, well into the 1930s. That conflict in Presbyterianism was managed but not resolved by decentralizing theological decision making to the regional presbyteries and away from the national church. Only a small group of fundamentalists withdrew (less than 1 percent of the membership). Liberals gained control of the denominational leadership by appealing to the moderates' sense of fairness and the need to follow constitutional procedures. It was generally believed that an explicit commitment to a shared polity would provide sufficient unity because the vast majority adhered to a common centrist theology and ideology.

In the decades since the 1930s, changes in American culture have been accompanied by ever more visible diversity in theology, ideology, and experience. In *Claiming the Center* I trace in six separate chapters the continuing influence of the six motifs of the early American evangelical/mainstream worldview I have just identified. Chapter by chapter, I describe the contemporary relevance of each specific motif and examine its historical setting, as well as recent conflicts that have surrounded each one. I then identify what I believe are the present tensions between those on the extremes to the right and to the left of each motif. Finally, I propose a contemporary centrist worldview that would allow each motif to function constructively for mainstream Christians.

In the process I deal with most of the well-known personalities and movements in society that have influenced mainstream Protestantism from within and from without. I am deeply concerned by the power that fundamentalists like Jerry Falwell and Pat Robertson exert in their appeals to a twisted and truncated form of the early American evangelical/mainstream worldview. I am equally concerned that the leadership of the mainstream denominations has been so fixated on the challenge of fundamentalism that it has uncritically accepted the liberal worldview countermotifs. The result has been that the majority of mainstream Protestants have withdrawn from the debate because they do not recognize a viable centrist alternative.

It is time for the moderate middle in mainstream Protestantism to claim the center. There is an ecclesiastical center that combines a commitment to personal evangelism and the transformation of society. There is an intellectual center that combines a commitment to the authority of scripture and its responsible interpretation. There is a moral center that combines a commitment to biblical moral law and compassionate pastoral application.

If the majority of Christians in the mainstream denominations do not claim the center and reassert their ecclesiastical, intellectual, and moral leadership, a fragmenting of the traditional mainstream Protestant churches may take place. That is something I cannot calmly contemplate. Schism based on differing ideological worldviews is a sin. Any schism at this time will be ugly and disabling for all parties involved well into the next century. Most important, still ringing in my ears is the insightful comment of my most influential seminary professor: "If Christ is divided, who bleeds?"

My treatment of these issues is certainly open to questioning and critique. That these are critical issues is surely beyond debate. My hope is that *Claiming the Center* will contribute to a deeper and hopefully defining discussion that will strengthen the center in Presbyterianism and mainstream Protestantism in the decades to come.

JACK ROGERS
PENTECOST 1995

1 | Worldview: A Source of Conflict

By the indwelling of the Holy Spirit all believers being
vitally united to Christ, who is the Head, are thus united
one to another in the Church, which is his body.

—The Westminster Confession of Faith IX, 4

FOCUS: A worldview, learned from our culture, guides our interpretation of reality. At the root of any worldview is an ultimate religious perspective. That perspective is elaborated theologically, applied ideologically, and colored by our experience. When people confuse these additional levels of worldview with the ultimate religious root, they make disagreements at other levels more important than they should be in a way that destroys Christian community.

During the formative years of early American culture, six denominations were recognized as "mainstream": Episcopal, Congregational, Presbyterian, Methodist, Baptist, and Disciples of Christ. Most members of these denominations and others in the dominant culture shared an ideological worldview. This ideology was rooted in religion, informed by theology, but functionally offered guidance as to how to think and behave in American culture.

Mainstream Americans shared a worldview containing motifs of separatism, election as God's chosen people, revivalism, common sense, moralism, and millennialism. This relatively homogeneous worldview functioned well until the mid-nineteenth century, when it was fractured by the Civil War and by Darwin's theory of evolution. This fracture created a

1

crisis of faith for those who had identified their American ideological worldview with the Christian faith.

Three conflicting ideological worldviews emerged in the late nineteenth century. Liberals or modernists adopted worldview motifs directly counter to those of the earlier evangelical/mainstream worldview. Fundamentalists narrowed and rigidified the earlier worldview while making it their own. Centrists, those in the moderate middle, held to the essentials of the Christian faith but became culturally more flexible and progressive in their ideological worldview. Pentecostalism, with its own worldview, arose outside the mainstream early in the twentieth century.

I believe that the principal cause of "mainstream" church decline is an internal conflict between worldviews. In large measure the membership and the leadership of the formerly mainstream churches have sharply differing views of the nature of the church, ways of knowing truth, and codes of moral conduct. This is destructive when each group assumes that its ideological worldview is the only authentic application of the Christian faith.

Hope for reconciliation and renewal lies in both leaders and members claiming the center and reconstituting a common worldview. This begins by patiently returning to a common affirmation of the root religious worldview that is more fundamental than any ideological application. Recognizing that those who differ with us accept the same religious worldview could enable us to build together on a foundation of Jesus Christ, the head of one body.

Worldview Analysis

Everyone has a worldview. We learn it from our culture. It is an overall, usually subconscious, perspective on reality. Philosopher of religion Ninian Smart asserts that "worldview analysis" is a main task of the modern study of religion. It is a cross-cultural and cross-disciplinary task.[1] Carrying out a worldview analysis may help us constructively to function in the period in which we are living, which some scholars have described as "one of the most significant periods in all of American religious history."[2]

Church historian Martin Marty calls a worldview "the mental furnished apartment in which one lives."[3] This worldview is a set of assumptions about reality shared by a community of people. It provides the overall framework of a group's basic beliefs.[4] It is a people's total response to their universe.[5]

Our culture teaches us the worldview by which we respond to reality. Culture, for anthropologists, represents the total nonbiologically transmitted heritage of the human race.[6] Humans are in culture as fish are in water.[7] We may critique it, but we cannot escape it.[8] Normally, culture provides the unconsciously accepted worldview glasses through which we view our environment.[9] When we are conscious of our own perspective we can certainly clarify and modify it.[10] But we must first be conscious that we have a particular and learned point of view.

Worldview is similar to religion.[11] Some anthropologists even identify worldview and religion.[12] One factor that makes worldview so powerful is that people often uncritically confuse religion with a worldview they have learned from their culture.

Worldviews contrast with one another on a horizontal plane. Worldviews also can and often do have layers of elaboration, application, and coloring in varying settings.

An Ultimate Religious Worldview

A genuinely religious worldview operates at the *ultimate religious* level, dealing with foundational questions.[13] This religious level of worldview explains the human condition and our place in the universe.[14] At this level the choice is between different world religions (and ideologies such as Marxism or Humanism when they take on an ultimate, religious dimension). For example, is reality ultimately governed by a being, God, or by a force, Karma? Each religion answers these ultimate questions by telling a story that embodies its view of reality.

The Christian story is of a good, personal God who created a good world with its own integrity, distinct from God's own being. An inexplicable and tragic fall from this original goodness alienated the world and its human inhabitants from God. This personal God continued to love creation and to communicate with its people. Finally, God came in a personal manifestation in Jesus of Nazareth to overcome the alienation between God and humanity by living righteously, suffering an unjust death, and rising to overcome the power of evil. The world and its people now have a revelation of God in scripture and the presence of the Spirit of Christ, which provide opportunity for a new relationship with God and with others. The final restoration of wholeness will come in a divine intervention in and culmination of human history and the creation of a new heaven and earth.

A Theological Elaboration

A theology is a way of elaborating the ultimate religious story in a particular historical and cultural context. Usually in their origins, denominations developed a *theological* perspective that explained the purpose and function of this particular group in its own time and culture. There are therefore Roman Catholic, Eastern Orthodox, and many Protestant theological elaborations of the basic Christian story.

In its historical origins the functioning denomination as a Christian subculture fit closely with, for example, its Reformed, Anabaptist, Lutheran, or Anglican theology. A denominational theology elaborated the Christian story in such a way as to enable people of a particular Christian subfamily to interpret life in a particular manner. A denomination usually developed official doctrinal statements in the form of creeds, confessions, or articles that embodied its elaboration of the ultimate religious worldview.

Conflicts among denominations in the medieval and Reformation eras came at the level of the theological elaboration of the worldview story. Because in their origins denominations articulated theologies as a means of expressing their distinctive being, conflicts were articulated in theological terms. Each group attempted to assert its own version of the Christian story as the definitive expression of that story. Often people treated those with a different theological expression of the Christian story as non-Christians because they confused their elaboration of the ultimate Christian story with the story itself.

An Ideological Application

Fundamentalist and liberal worldview applications operate at a different worldview level from either the theological elaboration or the ultimate story. They operate at the level of *ideology.*[15] An ideological application tries to answer the question of how a Christian can be an American in a particular culture in a world where there are other nationalities with their own cultures and subcultures. It joins a religious worldview and its theological elaboration to a sociopolitical program. People's religious commitments are judged by their stance on moral, social, and political issues. An ideological worldview is what motivates people to act in the body politic.

Religious worldviews and their theological elaborations do not give specific answers to all questions raised in contemporary culture. Thus another level, that of an ideological application, develops. These ideological worldviews are the result of transdenominational movements that apply the

Christian story to new situations that the older denominational theological elaborations no longer seem to fit.

The difficulty comes when people identify the various levels and make them one. Then ultimate religious and theological sanction is given to views that are culturally developed attempts to understand the particular, relative, American cultural situation and to place ourselves in a transdenominational religious community with a sociopolitical program.

Worldview conflicts of the 1960s, 1970s, and 1980s manifested themselves as ideological conflicts engendered by transdenominational movements. They cut across the lines of denominations and their official theologies. Recent conflicts were between groups who had applied a worldview to a set of issues that defined it as a religious community. Thus the conflicts are among liberals, fundamentalists, charismatics, evangelicals, and all the variety of subgroups within these broad ideological communities.

Applying the Christian story to particular issues tends to define who belongs to a community at this transdenominational level. For example, some conservatives have difficulty believing that anyone could be a Christian and tolerate abortion. Some liberals have difficulty believing that anyone could be a Christian and not seek to redistribute the world's material wealth for the sake of the poor. In each case, the ideological application of the ultimate religious story becomes the level at which the Christian community is defined. Conflicts of worldview are played out as conflicts over particular issues and values.

In the 1980s Jerry Falwell uncritically identified the Moral Majority's aims with those of the Reagan White House. In the 1990s Pat Robertson's Christian Coalition, with 1.5 million members, has replaced the defunct Moral Majority as the leading voice of the Religious Right. In January 1995, Coalition Executive Director Ralph Reed announced plans to provide one million dollars and full volunteer support to promote GOP House Speaker Newt Gingrich's Contract with America.[16] It may be that the Coalition expects in return that the GOP will expand its agenda to include the priorities of the Religious Right such as limiting abortion, permitting a constitutional amendment on public-school prayer, and curtailing rights of homosexuals.[17] Some conservatives assert that if the Republican Party does not embrace these issues then a third political party could emerge for the 1996 elections.[18] Such is the power of an ideological worldview that identifies the Christian cause with particular legislative objectives.

Experience

The culturally developed ideological worldview is colored by a person's individual *experience*. People test their religious, theological, and ideological frameworks in the crucible of their concrete everyday experience. For example, a person's ultimate religious worldview may be that of the Christian, biblical story. Theologically, that person might fit in the Reformed tradition. Conceptually, that worldview may be interpreted through a belief system in accord with an American conservative ideology. The person may belong to a mainstream church. But if that person happens to be racially an African American, concrete daily experience will modify and reshape her or his theological and ideological views so that they may, in at least some respects, differ from the theological and ideological worldviews of other Reformed, conservative, mainstream American Christians.

In the 1990s our worldview conflicts are increasingly couched in terms of our individual experience. The experience of race, gender, and sexual orientation are the lines along which conflicts often take place. This experiential coloring of our worldview takes precedence over our transdenominational ideology, our denominational theology, and in some cases over the ultimate Christian story. When that happens the experience of one's individual particularity, or participation in a subculture of common experience, becomes ultimate. Then meaningful conversation with those who do not share in that individual experience becomes difficult, if not impossible.

Confusion of Levels

Worldview analysis can help us deal with the conflicts that differing worldviews engender. When tensions occasioned by these differences run high, there is the danger that people opposed to each other at the theological, ideological, or experiential level will doubt that they actually share the same ultimate religious commitment. The theological elaboration, ideological application, or experiential coloring of a religious worldview can replace the religious worldview of a person if that person treats the elaboration, application, or coloring as of ultimate importance. That is why a recognition and clarification of the meaning and function of worldviews at various levels is important. It offers positive hope for reconciliation and renewal in the mainstream denominations.

If people in a denomination can recognize that they do share the same ultimate religious commitment to the Christian, biblical story, then they have a common basis on which to build. On that foundation they can explore and work toward a common theological elaboration and appreciate their differing ideological and experiential perspectives. Together they can build a functional worldview that enables them commonly to interpret their reality as twentieth-century Americans.

Mainstream Decline: Conflict of Worldviews

I believe that the root cause of mainstream church decline is the internal conflict of worldviews. In large measure, the governing body leadership and the congregational membership of the formerly mainstream churches have different views of reality. Good, intelligent, and devout people see things differently. The two groups appear to each other to have decidedly different understandings of the nature of the church, ways of knowing the truth, and codes of moral conduct. When they do not acknowledge and deal with the worldview issue, they continually misunderstand and offend one another.

One example is the continuing tension between the denominational leadership of the Presbyterian Church (U.S.A.) (PC(USA)) and the Presbyterian Lay Committee (PLC). The moderator of the 1994 General Assembly, Robert Bohl, appointed a Committee on Reconciliation. At a meeting on November 30, 1994, the vice-chair of the PLC presented an issues paper. "This is not an adversarial document," he said. "I don't see how any reasonable person could disagree with it." In a disbelieving response, the executive director of the General Assembly Council (GAC), James Brown, declared that the language of the issues paper "is grounded in polarity." Brown charged, "This is denunciation and I'm incredulous that you could present this as healing and unifying."[19]

The one party sees his presentation as so reasonable that no one could disagree, and the other party is incredulous and hears denunciation. That is the kind of misunderstanding that arises when people proceed from different worldviews.

Genuine reconciliation and renewal in the PC(USA) require that a majority of both leaders and members claim the center and reconstitute a common contemporary worldview. This can be done. Each side in the conflict sees an important aspect of reality. The need is for a working synthesis. The congregational side emphasizes the need to ground people in the biblical and confessional tradition. The governing body side stresses the need to enable people to cope creatively with modernity. The function of a mainstream church is to enable people to carry out both these tasks.

On the one hand dominantly conservative denominations concentrate on grounding people in their understanding of the church, their view of biblical interpretation, and their commitments to behavioral norms. On the other hand primarily liberal denominations stress flexible structures, openness to new ideas, and experimentation with new lifestyles.[20] The mainstream denominations began to fragment when the governing body leadership increasingly elaborated a liberal worldview and the congregational membership clung to a conservative worldview. Instead of a dynamic synthesis of these two perspectives to form a mainstream worldview, they became more and more estranged and were perceived as polar opposites. The result has been suspicion, distrust, and fragmentation within the large mainstream denominations.

I am not arguing that a conservative worldview is preferable to a liberal worldview. I am asserting that in the last half-century a liberal worldview has prevailed among the leadership of the mainstream denominations. These denominations have therefore become imbalanced to the left, just as at some earlier periods they were imbalanced to the right.[21] Church leaders must claim the center and achieve a workable balance that the majority in the church can own.

An Enduring Early American Perspective

For most of American history there have been general working agreements on the function of the church, the nature of truth, and the norms of morality. We have a relatively short history as a nation. An early American religious worldview is still imprinted in our psyches. It is a way of looking at the world that still, subconsciously, makes sense to most Americans. We can more effectively reshape our worldview if we understand its early American origins and become conscious of its pervasive power in our culture.

The Influence of Falwell and the Right

One example of the continuing power of the early American worldview in contemporary culture is provided by Jerry Falwell. I discovered this in 1981 when I was invited to give the Ransom-Butler Lectures at Wichita State University. When I asked the religion department chair what she wanted me to do she said: "Explain Jerry Falwell to us." Falwell's claim that the Moral Majority had elected Ronald Reagan President had aroused interest. Few knew much about Falwell or his views. I did not want to devote three lectures to Falwell. Thus I read his published manifestos and asked: What gives this person influence with a significant portion of the American populace? Falwell's influence can be traced to his use of six recurring themes of the early American worldview: separatism, election as God's chosen people, revivalism, common sense, moralism, and millennialism. The 1995 Republican majority in the House of Representatives, led by Newt Gingrich, the Speaker of the House, relied on the support of Pat Robertson's Christian Coalition, which continued Falwell's worldview themes.

These worldview motifs were not restricted to Falwell's fundamentalism. They also seemed pervasive in the culture of American evangelicalism with which I was familiar as a professor at Fuller Theological Seminary. Leadership in mainstream Protestant churches, however, seemed to adhere to a contrasting set of worldview countermotifs. While the media were fascinated with evangelicalism in the 1970s and fundamentalism in the 1980s, the Lilly Endowment was pouring millions of dollars into research on why the mainstream Protestant churches were declining in membership and influence. A quarter of a million dollars was given to research on American Presbyterianism as a case study of a mainstream denomination in decline. Both in the mainstream Protestantism research and in that on Presbyterianism there was an apparent internal conflict between the early American worldview motifs and modern countermotifs. The PC(USA) serves as my primary illustration.

Countermotifs in the Mainstream

Countermotifs of ecumenical unity, internationalism, denominational control, the need for interpretation, pluralism of values, and the well-being of people here and now seemed to form a modern ideological worldview that was deliberately contrasted with the early American worldview of separatism, election as God's chosen people, revivalism, common sense, moralism, and millennialism. The relatively homogeneous early American worldview seemed to persist as a working perspective for many mainstream religious Americans. It was also clear that a worldview composed of counterthemes exercised a powerful influence on many, especially within the leadership of the mainstream denominations. The presence of these contrasting, powerful, but usually unconscious worldviews was a source of continuing destructive conflict. I will now sketch in greater detail the development of these conflicting worldviews and their role in the mainstream denominations.

Worldview Parallels

In this book I identify themes in the American experience from the colonial period to the present that appear to be the motifs of some religiously oriented worldviews. Some of these worldview motifs have become important in the contemporary American political, social, and religious scenes. Milton Coalter, John Mulder, and Louis Weeks, in *The Re-Forming Tradition,* assert that "the current situation for American Presbyterians and mainstream Protestants bears more similarity to the late eighteenth and early nineteenth centuries than it does to the period immediately after World War II."[22] They argue that "like the Revolutionary and early national periods of American history, the late twentieth century is an era of the reforming and redefinition of American Presbyterianism and American religious life."[23] An analysis of the worldviews of these two eras shows some remarkable similarities.

To be a Christian in early America meant to look at life in a particular way. Christian beliefs were incorporated into and interpreted by the cultural assumptions of the majority male, Anglo-Saxon, Protestant, Puritan culture. "Christian" and "American" were generally synonymous concepts in the unreflective worldview of most Christians in the majority culture in early America.

The Mainstream: A Brief History

The Colonial Establishment

During the colonial period, from the founding of Jamestown in 1607 until the adoption of the Constitution in 1789, three denominations came to form the unofficial religious establishment in early America—Episcopalians, Congregationalists, and Presbyterians.

The Episcopalians were the established church in England. For many, prior to the American Revolution, they still carried that mantle of mainstream authority, especially in Virginia and the South. The Congregationalists in the Massachusetts Bay Colony claimed never to have separated from the Church of England. They were the strongest, most prosperous, and best organized of the Puritan groups. They became a legally established religion in the New England colonies, where they were dominant. The Presbyterians had come nearest to succeeding in their efforts to make the Church of England Puritan. Anglicans had shared roots in the Reformed tradition. Both by conviction and for the sake of expediency, the Congregationalists, and even the Baptists, adopted a form of the Presbyterians' newest doctrinal platform, the Westminster Confession of Faith. By showing themselves thus to be contemporary and ecumenical, these groups hoped to fend off potential intrusion from England. The dominant Congregationalists also adopted a modified form of Presbyterian government for ecclesial relationships beyond the local level. Presbyterians dominated in the middle colonies.

Episcopalians, Congregationalists, and Presbyterians together represented an establishment not just of faith but of political and territorial power. There was also, not surprisingly, an antiestablishment. The separatist Puritans who settled in Plymouth saw themselves as pilgrims, having no firm home in this world. They represented the lower socioeconomic groups who then and later felt excluded from the middle- and upper-class establishment churches. Roger Williams's radical separatism represented those who had given up on all the established churches and desired a radical reformation in which God would make a totally new beginning.

Especially if we add Anne Hutchinson and the Quakers in New England, we can see these antiestablishment groups as precursors of later independent and Pentecostal churches that sprang from and ministered to the marginalized groups in American society—the poor, those with less education, and the racial ethnic minorities. The differences were less ones of doctrine than of culture. The marginalized naturally trusted more to their own individual experience of God than to the systems of theology and government of the establishment churches from which they felt excluded. The significant diversity in culture, race, and theology among the religious groups in early America foreshadowed the even greater diversity of the twentieth century.[24]

At the same time, the membership of an informal church establishment came largely from the middle and upper classes of the community. That pattern and its counterpart of other churches representing the less educated and less affluent has continued throughout most of American history. The breakdown of a more rigid class stratification in church membership and the call from women and racial ethnic persons for full participation in all of the churches is part of what has created a need for re-forming churches descendant from the Puritan establishment.

The informal, evangelical/mainstream establishment was an elite group. When America's political founders were writing a constitution and Presbyterians were forming the first American General Assembly in the 1780s, only 5 to 10 percent of the population formally belonged to a church.[25] Presbyterians, for example, numbered only twenty thousand in

1790.[26] Early Americans were religious, but they were not joiners, a characteristic that continues today.[27]

Opening the Frontier

The opening of the frontier and mushrooming population growth made revivals the best means of bringing religion to people. During the first half of the nineteenth century the American population grew from five to thirty million. The Protestant percentage of the population dropped dramatically, however. In 1790, approximately 95 percent of the population was Protestant, but by 1860 only 60 percent was so identified.[28] Outreach was needed.

As people pushed across the Appalachians and opened the frontier, the Episcopalians, Congregationalists, and Presbyterians were too structured in their East Coast establishment status to take the lead. Instead, the Methodists, the Baptists, and the Disciples of Christ, who did not require educated clergy, sent out their circuit riders, authorized lay preachers, and soon became the dominant church bodies on the American frontier.[29] Their rough-and-ready egalitarianism suited the needs of the individualistic democracy that was forming.[30] By 1850, over 70 percent of the Protestants in America belonged to these three denominations.

Thus, six denominations—Episcopalian, Congregationalist, Presbyterian, Methodist, Baptist, and Disciples of Christ—formed the Protestant mainstream in the first two hundred and fifty years of America's existence.[31] In the nineteenth century they were dubbed the "Evangelical United Front." Their members shared the early American religious/cultural worldview. They shared a common intellectual and moral perspective. And they assumed that what they believed was true for all right-thinking American people.

The word "mainline," applied to these denominations, apparently was coined at a later period when a principal means of transportation in the city of Philadelphia was the railroad, the "main line" of which ran from downtown out through the affluent suburbs where many of the churches in these denominations were located.[32] The denominations, composed mostly of upper middle class people, were called "mainline." Now skeptics and critics refer to these denominations as "dead-line," or "sideline," or "old-line."[33] These churches were "mainstream" in an earlier era in the sense that they were perceived as dominant Protestant religious bodies which were highly influential in shaping American culture.[34] Most non-Catholic, American Christians in the majority Anglo-Saxon culture thought of themselves as both evangelical and mainstream up to the mid-nineteenth century. Even Lutheran and Dutch Reformed bodies that would now be considered mainstream were initially excluded from that designation.[35] So long as they spoke European languages and embraced Continental customs, they were thought to be not quite American. While this working consensus as to who was mainstream was placid on the surface, inner contradictions would erupt by the mid-nineteenth century.

It is important to note at the outset that there is a difference between ultimate religious beliefs and culturally derived worldviews despite how intimately they may be intertwined. Native Americans, African Americans, and women, for example, could accept the basic biblical message of Christianity and still not be accepted in so called Christian society. It mattered more to those in power that one shared their ideological worldview than that one had a genuine Christian commitment.

From the earliest colonization at least until the 1830s, America's self-understanding was that it was overwhelmingly a Protestant Christian nation.[36] There was a Protestant establishment of six churches—Episcopal, Congregational, Presbyterian, Baptist, Methodist, and Disciples of Christ—that were central institutions. American society was deeply grounded in Anglo-Saxon and, for the most part, Calvinistically derived traditions. This churchly tradition, despite various experiences of disestablishment, exercised a cultural hegemony, a preponderant influence, down to the 1960s.[37]

The Six Motifs of the Early American Worldview

In this book I look at each of the six motifs that formed the early American worldview, which still has power in American culture: separatism, election as God's chosen nation, revivalism, common sense, moralism, and millennialism. I call this the early American evangelical/mainstream worldview to indicate that cultural groups which later were pulled apart and often appeared antagonistic—evangelical movements and mainstream churches, for example—once shared a worldview that helped to form a relatively cohesive religious/cultural community.

Puritanism as indigenized in America yielded three of these motifs.

1. *Separatism.* Some from conviction and others by force of circumstance affirmed that it was legitimate to leave one church and to

found another, just as they had found it legitimate to leave one country and found another.

2. *Election as God's chosen people.* Americans were convinced that they were God's elect with a special destiny to save the world and bring in the reign of God. The American Revolution was a manifestation and validation of this special calling.

3. *Revivalism.* Revivalism became the approved and accepted means of personal and social change. Individuals were brought to Christian commitment or renewal of life. The structures of society were changed for the better by changed people.

These three motifs have become general American assumptions. They are often expressed by the leadership of evangelical movements, but both statistical surveys and anecdotal evidence suggest that they are as surely embedded in the unconscious of many members of mainstream denominations.

After the individual colonies united to form a new nation, they assimilated new presuppositions about life that were characteristic of their unique national experience. The nation was being formed in the cultural context of eighteenth-century Enlightenment excitement. This was the era when modern secular society was formed. People turned from dependence on religious authority to trust in what human reason and will could accomplish. The state ceased to be regarded as a divinely given institution and began to be viewed as a social contract between human beings for mutual benefit.

American Christians, as well as Americans who rejected the Christian faith and evangelical/mainstream culture, accepted and assimilated Enlightenment attitudes. Most Christians adapted unconsciously, although some made their commitment consciously. But the adaptation to and assimilation of the prevailing culture was made.

Three further motifs were added to the early American worldview in the eighteenth century.

4. *Common Sense philosophy.* By midcentury, Scottish Common Sense philosophy guided people to organize nature according to Newton's laws and to read the Bible as if it had been written directly to them in their culture.[38]

5. *Moralism.* Most Americans presumed that there were absolute moral laws which all people knew and were obligated to obey.

6. *Millennialism.* Most Americans believed that the *millennium,* the establishment of God's thousand-year reign, was coming soon.

Balancing Counterthemes

Prior to the mid-nineteenth century, in America these six motifs formed a relatively coherent, widely held worldview. During the first two centuries of American existence, these themes did not become divisive because they were balanced by subordinate counterthemes. The initial *separatism* theme was balanced by the experience of American churches that sought formal or informal expressions of *ecumenical unity.* The notion that America was God's chosen nation was modified by a form of *internationalism* expressed in the sending of overseas missionaries. Revivalism by independent individuals and agencies founded by groups of like-minded Christians was balanced by the development of *denominational control* in which denominational boards and agencies managed everything from establishing new congregations to providing social services. The dominant epistemology of common sense, which claimed that the truth was obvious, was continually modified through the recognition, by some, of the relativism of knowledge and the *need for interpretation* of complex phenomena and ideas. Eighteenth-century moralism, which tended to think that all moral questions had clear and unambiguous answers, was balanced by the awareness, at least in educational circles, of a *pluralism of values* in which the exceptions, complexities, and imponderables were probed and appreciated. Finally, the heavenly, future orientation fostered by millennialism was softened by equally sincere concerns for the *well-being of all here and now* in a Christianized world.

Collapse of the Evangelical/Mainstream Worldview

Breaking the Balance

The period in which American mainstream Protestantism was formed extended from the mid-eighteenth through the mid-nineteenth century.[39] In the mid-nineteenth century, the balance of themes and counterthemes in the early American evangelical/mainstream worldview was disrupted. Two major cultural shifts evidenced this disruption.

One factor was the Civil War, in which evangelical/mainstream Americans in the North and South realized that they no longer interpreted the Bible alike. Nor did they share the same deep values on the crucial issue of slavery. The second factor was Darwin's theory of evolution.

Evangelical/mainstream Americans were forced to respond to a new method of thinking about reality. They had to choose between the old method, which assumed divine order, design, and constancy, and the new method, which was agnostic and assumed natural selection and constant change. For many, after the Civil War and Darwinism, the early American worldview built on an indigenized Puritanism and an assimilated Enlightenment appeared to be incompatible with the new cultural and scientific worldview.

A Crisis of Faith

Many mainstream church members in the majority culture in America were unreflectively committed to the evangelical/mainstream worldview and identified it with the Christian faith until the mid-nineteenth century. The collapse of this consensus led to a fragmentation of the American religious worldview that continues to the present. For people who identified the early American worldview with the Christian faith, the collapse of this cultural consensus became a crisis of faith. These people divided into two opposing camps.

One group became known as liberals or modernists. They had accepted an identification of the evangelical/mainstream worldview with the Christian faith. In their opinion, that worldview had now been shown to be untenable. They therefore felt obliged to adopt the new scientific worldview and to revise the Christian faith to fit it.[40] After the 1860s, people who came to be called liberals or modernists embraced the counterthemes of ecumenical unity, internationalism, denominational control, relativism that necessitated interpretation, pluralism of values, and well-being in the world here and now. These motifs formed a new alternative liberal/modernist ideological worldview.[41]

A second group acquired the label "fundamentalists" or "conservatives." They also had identified the evangelical/mainstream worldview with the Christian faith. Now they felt obliged to hold on to that earlier worldview lest they lose their Christian faith. To remain Christian they had to become old-fashioned (or early-modern), at least in their religion, even if they accommodated to modern life in other ways. At this point the main themes of the earlier evangelical/mainstream worldview became the property of the fundamentalists.[42] Fundamentalists rejected the counterthemes embraced by the modernists and stiffened their commitment to the earlier dominant themes of separatism, God's chosen nation, revivalism, common sense, moralism, and millennialism. In a narrow and

16

rigid form this became the alternative fundamentalist ideological worldview.[43]

A third group comprised the majority of Christian people. They realized that their earlier worldview, though commonly held, was not identical with their Christian faith. They were able to hold on to the essentials of the historic Christian faith and at the same time to change their cultural attitudes and values. They could, for example, accept evolution as a valid scientific theory but regard Genesis as dealing with theology, not geology.

These people could properly be called the moderate middle or centrists. They held fast to the doctrinal essentials of an evangelical/mainstream position, but they were not completely committed to its cultural limitations. They formed the working majority in most of the mainstream churches in the period from after the Civil War until the 1930s. They were doctrinally conservative but culturally, politically, and socially flexible.

They tended to be moderates and inclusivist churchpersons who rejected what they considered the extremes of both the left and the right.[44] The majority of Protestant Christians in America struggled to maintain some kind of balance between the themes and counterthemes of the early American worldview. This centrist majority also recognized that the Christian faith was not to be identified with any culture-specific elaboration of its worldview.

Compared to this centrist majority, the extremes of liberalism and fundamentalism were each more culture-specific and each more clear, because they were more one-sided. Therefore, the worldview extremes tended to be more clearly and forcefully articulated. The moderate, centrist majority tended to appear ambiguous in expressing its worldview, partly because this worldview was more comprehensive and thus more complex and less clear than that of the extremes to the right and left.

Members of the moderate middle formed the core of leadership in the mainstream churches to the end of the nineteenth century. Early in the twentieth century, however, the liberals took over that leadership role. Controversies since the 1930s have been shaped by struggles between liberals in the leadership of the mainstream denominations and conservatives who take an antiestablishment stance. The majority in the moderate middle have generally been leaderless and inarticulate. The exceptions have been moments of extreme crisis where moderates, fearing that great damage has been done to the church, temporarily assume leadership but then relinquish this role until the next crisis. The salutary response to the Re-Imagining controversy in 1994-1995 was such a moment.

A fourth group, Pentecostals, appeared in the early twentieth century. Pentecostalism had roots in colonial revivalism and in the perfectionism of the early nineteenth-century Holiness movement, but Pentecostals were not part of the mainstream. Culturally, this experience-oriented religion was developed by those who were marginalized by mainstream society—African Americans, women, and blue-collar workers. They tended to stand apart from and not be involved in the theological and cultural struggles that fragmented the former evangelical/mainstream movement.[45] But indirectly their presence and their perspective affected the mainstream churches, especially through the charismatic movement beginning in the 1960s.

Attempts to Reconstitute a Consensus

The themes and counterthemes of the original evangelical/mainstream worldview continued to reappear in refashioned forms. In the 1940s and 1950s, neo-orthodoxy for the mainline and neo-evangelicalism for the parachurch movements recaptured a semblance of balance in worldview themes but left the deep ideological fault lines in place. That apparent stability lasted less than three decades.

Social strife beginning in the 1960s prompted a proliferation of new theologies and a politicization of the mainline churches. The 1970s saw the reemergence of a many-faceted evangelical movement and the little-noticed roots of a resurgent fundamentalism. Then in the 1980s we experienced the politicization of American conservative religion. Jerry Falwell and the Moral Majority recapitulated a rigidified form of the earlier evangelical/mainstream worldview. President Reagan acted as the patriarch of the conservative clan, telling the early American worldview story in a way that encouraged and emboldened formerly withdrawn religionists to enter the political realm. The worldviews of Pentecostal and charismatic believers were exhibited and exaggerated in the histrionics of Jim Bakker and Jimmy Swaggart and the presidential campaign of Pat Robertson.

The rise of religious and political conservatism was accompanied by a steady downward slide of mainstream religion in both membership and cultural leadership. In the 1980s, while fundamentalists exerted political energy and Pentecostals and charismatics dominated the media's attention, mainstream church leaders seemed stuck in the strategies of the 1960s. All the while their children walked out the back door of the church, holding liberal values but seeing no need for acting them out in the context of the church.

All this leads to conclusions that argue that attention to the matter of worldview can help us respond constructively to our current situation. I contend that the contemporary conflict of worldviews has its roots in the disruptions of the mid-nineteenth century. I contend further that the often unrecognized longings for a return to a unified evangelical/mainstream worldview on the part of many is one explanation for the "striking similarity" of the situation of American Presbyterianism and mainstream Protestantism "to that of their counterparts of the formative period two hundred years ago."[46] If Coalter, Mulder, and Weeks are right, and I think they are, in that "what was formed then is now being re-formed," then we would do well to pay heed to the powerful force for unification or fragmentation that our worldviews can provide.

Movements and Churches

This book focuses on worldview conflicts at the theological and ideological levels with an eye toward the coloring that experience gives. Belief systems embodied in movements such as fundamentalism, liberalism, and Pentecostalism have had a powerful impact on all the organized expressions of Protestant Christianity in America. The former mainstream denominations have all been reshaped by these movements. The theological belief systems and ideological worldviews have in turn been molded and modified by the general movements in American culture. It is difficult to discern what is authentically religious and what may be unreflectively American. Something has happened over the three hundred years of American religious history that is worth reviewing.

A Final Word about Method

Focusing on American mainstream Protestantism, with Presbyterianism as a prime example, is one way to illustrate some trends. I have chosen to begin with the formation of these so-called mainstream denominations in the colonial period. I attempt to discern the ideological worldview that developed in the interaction between the religion that immigrants brought with them and their American experience in the New World. From this interaction of religion and culture came what I have called the evangelical/mainstream worldview. I then examine the motifs of this ideological worldview as they are rent and reshaped by interaction with other powerful cultural forces over time. I examine various religious movements within Protestantism as they provide a context to understand changes in the mainstream. None of this history is offered for its own sake, nor do I attempt to present a comprehensive historical picture. Rather, I use historical references as illustrations that enable us to understand the roots of the current cultural context in which the evangelical/mainstream worldview has persisted and continues to change.

Distinguishing Religion and Worldview

I am not arguing that only the six motifs I have identified are definitive of the early American worldview. I am rather suggesting that something like these are strands of an ideological worldview that is still enormously influential on American people. I would encourage others to do a similar "worldview analysis." I am at bottom arguing that there is a difference between an ultimate religious worldview and an evangelical/mainstream American ideological worldview. I am also asserting that it is dangerously easy to confuse or conflate them.

This book attempts to distinguish between the rudiments of authentic religious faith and the equally powerful belief systems represented by often uncritically held ideological worldviews which enable people to attempt to make sense of life. It warns of the ever present danger of identifying a particular American ideological worldview with the divine will, especially when applied to particular political programs. It probes some of the interrelations of American belief systems, denominational structures, racial and ethnic identities, and the ultimate worldviews deep in our psyches.

I am vulnerable at almost every point to the critique of specialists. I welcome that correction as I continue to learn. The criticism of specialists in particular concerns does not, however, relieve one of the responsibility to attempt a synthesis. As a Presbyterian, a mainstream Protestant, I need to understand what is happening to and through my church. I must take responsibility for its internal renewal and for its public role. A first step toward that responsibility is understanding who we are in the present ecclesiastical and societal context. One way to do that is to examine the function of particular worldview motifs as they have appeared in our history. These motifs continue to form a context for our contemporary discussion of the nature of the church, how we know the truth, and how we ought to behave. For the sake of forwarding discussion, I am willing to risk proposing a contemporary centrist worldview application that would reconnect the early American worldview motifs with their countermotifs to provide a more balanced and whole view of reality.

Most mainstream Protestants fit ideologically somewhere in a broad center. Studies by the PC(USA) research agency repeatedly show a bell-shaped curve of Presbyterian attitudes on most controversial issues. There is a far-right perspective of about 15 percent. There is also a far-left one of never more than 10 percent. About 75 percent of Presbyterians are somewhere in the middle, struggling to find an appropriate balance. We make a serious mistake when we allow those on the ideological edges to set the terms for discussion. I try in subsequent chapters to articulate a possible contemporary centrist position on the six motifs that formed the early American evangelical/mainstream worldview. We need to deal with these motifs because they are so deeply rooted in our American cultural experience. Neither those on the far right nor those on the far left can articulate an adequate worldview option for the majority in the mainstream.

My goal is twofold: that we might better understand our problems, and that together we might move beyond them to solutions. The United States needs mainstream churches that perform the dual function of grounding people in the biblical tradition and of enabling them to cope with modernity. To accomplish that function will require claiming the center and re-constituting a common contemporary worldview.

2 | Separatism: Can We Have Unity in Diversity?

I therefore, the prisoner in the Lord, beg you to lead a life
worthy of the calling to which you have been called, with
all humility and gentleness, with patience, bearing with one
another in love, making every effort to maintain the unity
of the Spirit in the bond of peace.

—Ephesians 4:1–3

FOCUS: Is there any possibility of genuine unity within a mainstream
church in the midst of its dizzying diversity? In order to answer that
question we must first understand the strength of separatism. Separatism is an ingrained American attitude. We cannot have unity in the
church today unless we understand that our country and our churches
can maintain unity while incorporating diversity.

To understand the instinct to separate and start over we must first look at
the history of Puritan immigration to this country and the history of splits
and reunions within American Presbyterianism. For some there has also
been a strong tendency to make unity a primary value. The conflict between these two values is one we are still struggling with today. Hidden
within the history of our divisions and reconciliations is the seed of the solution to how we can find unity in diversity.

The present context of the conflicts in our mainstream churches is
found in the fundamentalist-modernist controversy that convulsed the
mainstream churches in the 1920s. Presbyterians especially must understand it because we still live with the consequences of decisions made in
1927 not to discuss theology but to make polity the solution to our struggles over diversity and unity. The role of the conservative and liberal

23

parties in setting the agenda for the church is instructive. Even more important is to discover the latent but usually unused potential of the moderate middle to set policy for the denomination.

Persons whose worldview is shaped by the ideal of separatism have made news and deeply influenced both our church and our national life in the 1970s and 1980s. An example is Francis Schaeffer, a fundamentalist whose influence during the Reagan administration continues to the present. Others whose worldview is marked by a profound commitment to unity continue to make headlines and to shape our denominational discourse. For example, Presbyterians played a central role in the Parliament of the World's Religions in 1993.

I will show that the current conflict between the values of conviction and civility has deep historical roots. Fundamentally different worldviews, perceptions of reality, and commitments to values must be reconciled if we are to develop a contemporary centrist worldview that will enable us to have unity in diversity in the church and in our communities.

The Contemporary Relevance of Separatism

Membership Loss

Between 1965 and 1985, the Presbyterian Church lost 25 percent of its membership; other mainstream groups showed comparable losses. If we leave aside the Northern Baptists, who allow dual membership of congregations belonging to the large African-American Baptist denominations, five denominations that had formed the American mainstream establishment—Episcopal, Congregational, Presbyterian, Methodist, and Disciples of Christ—suffered a net membership loss of 5.2 million people during years when the U.S. population rose by 47 million.[1]

In the 1930s the Presbyterian Church lost less than one percent of its membership in a schism that formed a denomination called the Presbyterian Church in America, later changed to the Orthodox Presbyterian Church (OPC). We are still oriented to that schism. Resistance to the kind of fundamentalism the OPC stood for has justified the liberal worldview of denominational leaders, while support of church members for the kind of Old School Calvinism the OPC espoused has encouraged further schisms.

In the early 1970s the Presbyterian Church in the United States (PCUS), the former Southern Presbyterian Church, lost 260 congregations and some 250,000 members in a split that formed the Presbyterian

Church in America (PCA). Those separating from the PCUS did so in defense of the culture of the old South and in conscious continuity with the theology and worldview of those who had separated from Northern Presbyterianism in the 1930s. They cited doctrines like the inerrancy of scripture and heroes of the faith such as J. Gresham Machen, who led the OPC split. They were committed not only to a theology of Old School Calvinism but also to a worldview that saw separatism as a virtue.[2]

In the former Northern Presbyterian stream, the United Presbyterian Church in the U.S.A. (UPCUSA) lost some sixty congregations in the years 1979–1981. Many of these went into the Evangelical Presbyterian Church (EPC), a denomination formed from this schism. Many reasons for the separation were cited, but all seemed rooted in a sense that the members of the new EPC had a different worldview that was manifested in a different concept of the church, a different approach to interpreting the Bible, and a different attitude to moral questions. This worldview valued separation as a means to purifying the church.[3]

The Continuing Threat of Separatism

As recently as 1994, schism seemed possible in the PC(USA), the body in which the former PCUS and the former UPCUSA had united in 1983. Reaction to an ecumenical conference held in Minneapolis in November 1993, entitled "Re-Imagining God . . . the Community . . . the Church," evidenced that opposing worldviews were still operative. Allegations were made, especially in the *Presbyterian Layman,* that essential tenets of the Reformed tradition and the Christian faith had been denied or trivialized at this World Council of Churches sponsored event, part of an "Ecumenical Decade: Churches in Solidarity with Women."[4] Some two hundred and fifty congregations, two presbyteries, and one synod withheld funds from the General Assembly. More anger and agitation were apparent than at any time since the PCA split in the South in the 1970s.

Fortunately, the PC(USA) did not split in 1994. But the threat of potential schism still hangs in the air as the church waits to see what further action regarding ordination of gay and lesbian persons will come in 1996. At a 1994 conference of Presbyterian church leaders, some acknowledged that little discussion of the issue was going on in some regions in response to a General Assembly mandate to study the matter. One leader averred that in his region the only discussion was on what form the schism would take.

There is ample anecdotal evidence that separatism as a solution to problems in the church is still part of the worldview of many Christians. We need to understand the roots of this worldview motif and its role in our contemporary context if we are adequately to cope with its consequences.

The Historical Setting of Separatism

Puritan Immigration

The Protestant Reformation of the sixteenth century in Europe often led to the establishment of national churches. Lutheranism prevailed in Germany, and Reformed (Calvinistic) churches took root in what is now Switzerland and in The Netherlands.[5] England presented a different pattern, for England had a national church *before* it had a Reformation.[6] Henry VIII's quarrel with the pope over his desired divorce from Catherine of Aragon led to Henry declaring himself Supreme Head of the Church of England in 1531.[7]

Puritanism began as a movement by those who wished to "purify" the as yet unreformed Church of England from the remnants of what they saw as Roman Catholic "popery."[8] That struggle marked the English church and the English nation. The century of greatest Puritan activity, the 1560s to the 1660s, was also the century of the colonization of America.[9] As the fortunes of various Puritan groups rose and fell in England, America offered a fresh opportunity to create a truly reformed church and state. Many institutions of the English-speaking world were shaped by the Puritan spirit of reform.[10]

When examining Puritanism, one finds that Presbyterianism represents a special case. The basic thrust of Puritanism in the 1640s was to reform the Church of England in a Presbyterian direction governmentally and in a Calvinistic direction theologically. A Presbyterian, Puritan-dominated Parliament called the Westminster Assembly into being in 1642 to accomplish those aims.

Original English Puritanism in its Presbyterian form was emphatically and in principle against separation from the established church. Historical circumstances have caused us to read the history of Presbyterianism through the eyes of later nonconformists with whom the Presbyterians, after their ejection from the state church, had to make common cause. However, the single most influential person in the development of the Westminster Confession of Faith, Edward Reynolds, exemplified a deeply rooted principle of English Presbyterianism by conforming to the Elizabethan prayer book rather than separating from the established church in 1660 when many of his Presbyterian colleagues were ejected from the church for faithfulness to other principles they held dear.[11]

During a century of struggle in England, varieties of Puritanism appeared depending on the extent of reform they required. Some forms of Puritanism would have been content with minimal reform, while others demanded radical change in the church. Thus, groups that came to America were identified as Anglican Puritans, Separatist Congregational Puritans, Non-Separating Congregational Puritans, Radical Separatist Puritans (Baptists and Quakers), and Presbyterian Puritans, to name only the principal varieties. Representatives of each of these groups of Puritans immigrated to North America as each in turn failed fully to accomplish their desired reforms in England. In the New World, English Puritanism gradually transformed into an American evangelical/mainstream Protestantism.[12]

In America the varieties of Puritanism shared several motifs that together constituted the American/Puritan evangelical worldview. The first motif was separatism. All the Puritan groups began with the notion of reforming the Church of England from within. All had been forced to leave England under various degrees of external pressure or internal frustration. All became separatist by circumstance even if not by conviction. Puritans now lived in a new land far from the English church, with which they could not practically communicate on routine matters.

Presbyterian Splits and Reunions

Some Presbyterians came to the New World during the 1640s and drifted to areas settled earlier by the Dutch Reformed. New Amsterdam, for example, became New York when the English settled there in 1664. The essential reason that Presbyterians did not come sooner and in larger numbers is that, until 1662, the Presbyterians believed that they had a chance to succeed in accomplishing their goals within the Church of England.

Two groups of Presbyterians were in tension from the very beginning: (1) the English and Welsh, and (2) the Scots and Irish. They embodied, in a primitive form, the diversity that was to provide both strength and conflict for Presbyterians from that time forward. Their differences presaged the conflicts that would later sometimes lead to schism in the Presbyterian Church and other mainstream denominations.

In 1706, under the leadership of an Irishman, Francis Makemie, these diverse groups were brought together into the first presbytery in America.[13]

But this ethnic and attitudinal diversity, though slight by contemporary standards, foreshadowed both the dynamism and the difficulties that would characterize the mainstream denominations. The struggle to maintain one body in which a variety of perspectives could be expressed was to mark the nature of the mainstream denominations.

The English and Welsh contributed what came to be known as New Side, or later, New School, values. They focused on the needs of the congregation, and they were quite willing to cooperate with agencies outside the church for the sake of meeting people's needs in the community. They utilized laypeople in ministry. They had a functional rather than formal notion of ministry; whoever could get the job done was allowed to lead. They relied on revivals to quicken people's hearts and to reshape their lives. A genuine religious experience was more important to them than precise formulations of doctrine. We can recognize in these values those that are dear to many contemporary Presbyterian pastors and members of congregations.

The Scots and Irish emphasized traditional values on the Scottish model. Their emphases came to be known as those of the Old Side and, later, the Old School. The Old Side was much more concerned about church government and the organization of the church into larger governing bodies, favoring the church developing its own agencies to meet community needs. The Old Side was equally concerned about having a professional and highly educated ministry and focused also on precise polity and confessional statements. The values of this group have been reflected primarily in the attitudes of Presbyterian governing body leaders, especially at the General Assembly level.

At times, one party or the other felt that their emphases were no longer being valued and their needs were not being met. As a result, splits between the two occurred. In 1741, the New Side and the Old Side split over the style and consequences of the revivals known as the Great Awakening. Again, in 1837, the New School and the Old School split over church union with the Congregationalists, which had been in effect for some time, and over the issue of slavery, which was mounting in importance.

Reunions and reconciliation occurred when both sides were assured that their differing emphases would be acknowledged and allowed to function. Wise people found formulas for enabling the two sides to recognize the values in each other's differences. The New Side/Old Side split was healed in 1758, and the New School/Old School division in 1869. Both sides came together and were willing to live with the tensions when each realized that it was limited by its own one-sidedness and needed the emphases of the other in order to embody the wholeness exemplified in Christ.

The Recent Context of Conflicts over Separatism

The Fundamentalist-Modernist Conflict in the 1920s

The tension between unity and diversity was stretched to the breaking point in mainstream churches in the 1920s. On May 21, 1922, a Baptist, Harry Emerson Fosdick, preached a sermon in the First Presbyterian Church in New York City titled "Shall the Fundamentalists Win?" Fosdick had been carrying on a debate with William Jennings Bryan in the *New York Times* over teaching evolution in the public schools.[14] Clarence Edward Macartney, pastor of the Arch Street Presbyterian Church in Philadelphia, answered Fosdick with the sermon "Shall Unbelief Win?" in which he accused Fosdick of naturalism. At Macartney's urging, the Presbytery of Philadelphia overtured the General Assembly to condemn the teachings expressed in Fosdick's sermon and to ensure orthodoxy in the pulpit of First Presbyterian of New York.

In 1923, William Jennings Bryan, three-time U.S. presidential candidate and a Presbyterian elder, was narrowly defeated as the conservative candidate for moderator of the General Assembly. Bryan and Macartney were successful in getting the General Assembly to instruct the Presbytery of New York to take corrective action regarding First Presbyterian and report back in 1924. Also in 1923, J. Gresham Machen, professor of New Testament at Princeton Seminary, published *Christianity and Liberalism*. Machen called liberalism "un-Christian" and "unscientific" and declared: "A separation between the two parties in the Church is the crying need of the hour."[15]

In 1924, the liberals responded. Shailer Mathews, dean of the University of Chicago Divinity School, published *The Faith of Modernism*, an indirect answer to Machen. Mathews seemed to share with Machen the basic premise of the incompatibility of their two systems: "If Christianity is essentially only what the seventeenth century thought it, a theological system inherited from the past, the charge that Modernism is unchristian is logically sound."[16]

Both Machen and Mathews were proceeding from ideologically oriented worldviews. The former held a form of the early American evangelical/mainstream worldview, while the latter espoused a form of the liberal/modernist worldview. They perceived these ideological worldviews to be mutually exclusive, but erroneously identified their ideological worldviews with the ultimate religious worldview that encapsulates the essential Christian story.

THE FIVE ESSENTIAL AND NECESSARY DOCTRINES

One catalyst for the sharp conflict within Presbyterianism was the imposition of an extraconfessional doctrinal test. In 1910 the Presbyterian General Assembly adopted a five-point declaration of "essential and necessary doctrines" that all candidates for ordination had to affirm. They were: (1) the inerrancy of scripture; (2) the virgin birth of Christ; (3) Christ's substitutionary atonement; (4) Christ's bodily resurrection; and (5) the authenticity of biblical miracles. The order of this five-point creed-within-a-creed is not inconsequential. The inerrancy of scripture, buttressed by Scottish Common Sense assumptions, was the cornerstone of the edifice of conservative theology that had been championed by Old Princeton Seminary. The five articles were reaffirmed by the General Assemblies of 1916 and 1923.[17]

Other groups picked up the five points and adapted them to their use. Often, point 2 became the deity of Christ rather than his virgin birth. Some forms listed Christ's premillennial second coming as point 5. By the 1920s these points were known as the "five fundamentals" and had become a rallying cry for fundamentalists across a broad spectrum.[18]

In January of 1924, 20 percent of the ministers in the Presbyterian Church signed the Auburn Affirmation, which contended that the five fundamentals, reaffirmed by the denomination in 1923, were theories that went beyond the facts to which scripture and the Westminster Confession committed them.[19]

THREE PARTIES WITHIN PRESBYTERIANISM

By 1924 three political groups within the Presbyterian Church were clearly identifiable. Theological liberals believed in an inclusive church (containing all who wished to belong). They were a minority but had some influential leaders. Directly opposed to them were the exclusivists, doctrinal fundamentalists who by now were arguing for an exclusivist church containing only those who agreed with the five fundamental points as formulated in 1910. The largest group, and politically the most important, was those who were theologically conservative but who were inclusivists for the sake of the peace, unity, and mission of the church.[20] Few of the combatants were conscious of the extent to which a conflict not just of theologies but of theological worldviews was at stake.

At the General Assembly of 1924, William Jennings Bryan nominated Clarence Edward Macartney as the exclusivist candidate for moderator. Opposing Macartney was Charles R. Erdman, professor of practical theology at Princeton. Evidence that worldview was more at issue than theology was that the theologically orthodox Erdman failed to satisfy the fundamentalists because he was an inclusivist churchman.

Macartney won a narrow victory and appointed Bryan vice-moderator. Fosdick was invited to join the Presbyterian Church, with the implication that if he did so he would be tried for heresy. Understandably, Fosdick refused and subsequently resigned from First Presbyterian. John D. Rockefeller built Riverside Church as a place for Fosdick to preach.[21]

At the General Assembly of 1925, Erdman, who had been working for reconciliation, was elected moderator. In response, the exclusivists pushed through a measure that would allow the General Assembly to review the ordination of ministerial candidates who would not affirm the "five points." Henry Sloane Coffin, a leading liberal, spoke for the Presbytery of New York in declaring the action unconstitutional and announcing that the presbytery would not abide by it. The stage was set for a denominational split along the Old School–New School lines. Erdman left the chair and proposed the formation of a special theological commission to study the spiritual state of the church. Both Coffin and Bryan seconded the motion.[22]

THE TURNING POINT

The turning point in the fundamentalist-modernist controversy came not in a church convocation but later in the summer of 1925 in a courtroom in Dayton, Tennessee.[23] In the spring of 1925, an obscure legislator in the Tennessee House of Representatives, John Washington Butler, introduced a measure prohibiting the teaching of evolution in the public schools of the state. A lecture by William Jennings Bryan titled "Is the Bible True?" had been distributed to the members of the legislature while the bill was being considered. The bill passed both houses of the legislature and was signed by the governor, who also indicated that he had no intention of enforcing it.[24]

What had likely been a political act to appease the voters in Tennessee led to a famous trial because of the interest of outsiders in the principles involved. The American Civil Liberties Union (ACLU) announced that it would finance a test case to challenge the constitutionality of the law. John Scopes, a young biology teacher in Dayton, Tennessee, was persuaded to be the defendant in the case. The trial gained further attention when the World's Christian Fundamentals Association (WCFA) asked William Jennings Bryan to assist the prosecution. At that point, the most famous criminal lawyer in America and an opponent of organized religion, Clarence Darrow, volunteered his services, without fee, to the defense.[25]

Bryan won the case. Scopes was declared guilty and fined one hundred dollars. But fundamentalism paid a high price for its victory. Its militant defense of a literally interpreted Bible lost the battle for public approval. Four days after the trial, Bryan died. Even in death the press heaped scorn on him. Fundamentalism, which had claimed to represent the common sense of all humankind, was now an object of ridicule. The elaborate attempt to defend pre-Darwinian concepts of science in the name of scripture was no longer generally acceptable. People, including most Christians, were tired of militant argumentation, especially when it proved ineffective.[26]

The Next Stage: Theological Decentralization

After the Scopes trial, Christians tended to move in one of two directions. Centrists and liberals in the mainline churches longed for peace, patched over their differences, and resumed their commitment to get on with the work of the church. Evangelical centrists were able to work with liberals despite their theological differences because their worldview was closer to that of the liberals, even though their theology was quite different. Fundamentalists who could not tolerate a modernist worldview and who could no longer control their denominations withdrew. They formed new denominations, new educational institutions, and created parachurch agencies.

The Presbyterian Church, again, exemplified these trends. In 1926, the Special Theological Commission issued an interim report declaring that "the Christian principle of toleration" was deeply embedded in the denomination's constitution.[27] In 1927, in their final report, they declared that no one, not even the General Assembly, had the right to single out specific doctrines and declare them to be "essential and necessary." Only cases in the church courts could so define doctrine. Conservative control over the church's doctrinal stance was broken by decentralization of theological decision making to the presbyteries.[28]

Unfortunately, this decision dealt with neither the theological nor the worldview issues. Rather, the church as a whole chose not to discuss theology just at a time when it was moving toward a more centralized bureaucratic form of administration, the corporate denomination. As a result, polity rather than theology became the mechanism for dealing with controversies in the church. Lefferts Loetscher, the late Princeton Seminary historian of Presbyterianism, noted in 1954:

> If the Church now has no means of authoritatively defining its faith short of the amending process—which could hardly function in the midst of sharp controversy—ecclesiastical power is seriously hindered for the future from preventing more radical theological innovations than those discussed in the "five points."[29]

Loetscher in 1954 hoped that the "group mind" of the church would provide a consensus view when controversy arose. Because the church did not consciously deal with the theological or worldview issues at stake in the fundamentalist-modernist controversy, by the 1960s the group mind began to erode. Events of the 1970s through the 1990s only caused further fragmentation.[30] After the 1927 decision, people assumed that differing, localized interpretations of the confession and scripture were possible if sanctioned by local polity.[31] (The neo-orthodoxy consensus from the 1930s into the 1960s obscured the difficulty of decentralized theological decision making. When neo-orthodoxy lost its dominance in the late 1960s, the problems of the 1927 decision became more apparent.)

Moderates moved to end the control of the fundamentalist party. In 1929, the General Assembly approved a reorganization of the governmental structure of Princeton Seminary so that the exclusivists could no longer control it. Machen and three other faculty members left to form Westminster Theological Seminary in Philadelphia. Among the fifty-two students enrolled at Westminster for the first semester were Carl McIntire and Harold John Ockenga, soon to become prominent conservative leaders.[32] Westminster Seminary was committed to continue the theological and worldview tradition of Old Princeton prior to its reorganization.

33

Presbyterian Reconfiguration in the 1930s

SEPARATISTS

Soon after founding Westminster Seminary, Machen acted to counter what he felt was the influence of liberalism in the Presbyterian Church's mission program. He organized the Independent Board for Presbyterian Foreign Missions and became its president. The General Assembly declared this competition with a denominational agency unconstitutional and ordered all Presbyterians to withdraw from the Independent Board. Machen refused, was tried, and on March 29, 1935, was suspended from the ministry of the Presbyterian Church.[33] The Old Princeton churchmen were no longer in control of the denomination. They were everywhere on the defensive.

Politically, Machen had made a tactical mistake. He conceived of a conflict between two parties, fundamentalists and liberals, one of which had to win. But the majority of votes in the church were held by those in the moderate middle.[34] The ecclesiastical situation changed as the liberals learned to cooperate with doctrinal conservatives who were, nonetheless, denominational loyalists. Machen disliked these moderates most of all. He inveighed against their "indifferentism" and called them "theological pacifists."[35]

Machen was incapable of dealing with the new context of American Protestantism because he was completely captive to the earlier evangelical/mainstream worldview. For Machen the truth was obvious to all persons. It consisted of unalterable historical facts to which he had direct access in scripture. The doctrinal facts were organized in creeds that gave a comprehensive view of the system of truth. The church was a voluntary gathering of individuals who agreed to this system of doctrinal truth. Individual conversion and change in society came about as persons conformed themselves to these obvious truths. Apologetics, or the defense of the Christian system of truth, was the principal task of the church. When leaders in the church ceased to insist on a precise agreement with the doctrinal facts, as Machen understood them, the solution for Machen was to separate.[36]

LIBERALISM

Meanwhile, the liberal wing of American Protestantism was taking new shape. Henry Sloane Coffin was elected president of Union Theological

Seminary in 1926. He was responsible for the appointments of Reinhold Niebuhr and Paul Tillich to the seminary faculty. Both his and the institution's liberalism underwent reformulation from the 1930s through the 1950s. But, in the confrontation with Machen, Coffin represented a clear commitment to the central values of liberalism: God was an immanent presence within people and the world. There was no normative value to doctrines organized into creeds. There were no obvious facts, in Machen's sense, available in the Bible. Scripture was an expression of the evolving religious experience of the human race. And creeds were only "man's attempt in the best thought and language at his command to express his religious experience."[37]

The church, for Coffin, was "the company of those who share the purpose of Jesus and possess His Father's Spirit for its accomplishment."[38] The purpose of Jesus was to bring in God's kingdom of love and peace. Change in individuals and society came about, therefore, as people opened themselves to the Spirit of Christ and worked together for common ends. Coffin was willing to include fundamentalists in the church, but in 1925 he threatened to separate if fundamentalists were allowed to limit the freedom of liberals.

Changes in the New School–Old School Alignments

The fundamentalist-modernist controversy caused a realignment in the traditional party divisions within Presbyterianism. Prior to the onset of modernity in the mid-nineteenth century, Presbyterians had conflicts and sometimes divided along New Side–Old Side and New School–Old School lines. The Old Side/Old School party was committed to strict confessional and governmental standards. The New Side/New School folk were more interested in personal religious experience and attendant social reform.

Once Machen and his followers withdrew or were forced out of the denomination, the Old School party with its concern for strict adherence to confessional and governmental standards was no longer a viable political force. The Old School people had lost governmentally, and now church polity was used against them because inclusivism became a tenet of Presbyterian government.

The traditional New School group that remained, had, however, divided into two discernible parties. One was the liberal inclusivists, who carried on the social activism of the New School. They were theologically moderate to liberal and felt that an essential characteristic of the church was its acceptance of persons holding varying perspectives. They believed that Presbyterian Church government guaranteed the inclusion of all persons willing to join the church with the minimum confession of faith that Jesus Christ is Lord. A strict adherence to the procedures of Presbyterian government was the means to ensure pluralism in the church's membership and openness to a liberal program of social witness. This part of the former New School party was made up of constitutional pluralists.

These liberal inclusivists had learned to use polity to forward their cause. Henceforth concern for social reform and ecclesiastical pluralism went together. This liberal inclusivist party learned to institutionalize their concerns through church polity.

The other part of the former New School party was made up of the evangelical moderates, who carried on the New School's revivalistic concern for personal religious conversion. Evangelicals or pietists, like Erdman, were tolerant and inclusive regarding church membership, even though they were doctrinally more orthodox than the liberals. These pious but tolerant people, whom Machen despised, made up the moderate middle. They were theologically conservative but committed to include in the church all who would abide by its constitutional procedures. They believed that following the due process of Presbyterian government was the way to ensure both doctrinal orthodoxy and church unity. They were constitutional evangelicals.

What eventually held the constitutional evangelicals in the church was a commitment to the process of Presbyterian government. These constitutional evangelicals made up the moderate majority in the church. But they tended to eschew involvement in the affairs of the higher governing bodies and preferred to work through the local congregation.

In the 1930s Clarence Edward Macartney typified a stance that many Presbyterian evangelicals would continue to take. He was torn between his commitment to the doctrinal essentials for which Machen stood and his commitment to the denomination and its rich tradition. He stayed in the PCUSA but lost his enthusiasm for working through the denominational structure.

In 1939, Macartney wrote an article in the *Christian Century* series "How My Mind Has Changed in This Decade," in which he professed his continued allegiance to the "grand particularities" of the Christian faith. He expressed gratification that toward the end of the 1930s, many liberals, like Coffin, were moving toward the doctrinal center, but noted that for him, the incipient pluralism of the Presbyterian Church as a whole made it less effective as a witness to the truth. Macartney stated:

> Therefore, I value less the whole ecclesiastical structure, and feel that more and more for the true witness to the gospel and the Kingdom of God we must depend upon the particular local church, the individual minister and the individual Christian. Between such believers and such Christians there is indeed a real church unity.[39]

Macartney set the pattern for generations of subsequent evangelicals. They remained tacitly loyal to the mainstream denominations but found their mission and fellowship primarily in the local congregation and with like-minded believers in special interest groups inside the church and in parachurch organizations outside it.

The moderate middle, therefore, continued to be relatively inarticulate and inept in church controversies. The few remaining fundamentalists and the dominating liberal social activists tended to set the terms of debates in the denomination.[40]

A TIGHTENED POLITY

Presbyterians were also in accord with the general spirit of the times in the United States. The burgeoning of new areas of knowledge, the influx of immigrant groups, and the proliferation of governmental bureaucracies required political control to prevent centripetal forces from fragmenting the nation. Governmental control expanded in society and in the church. In both arenas the purpose was to maintain unity as pluralism increased.

As the Presbyterian Church broadened theologically, it tightened governmentally. Between the extreme conservatives and the extreme liberals there was a clear clash of worldviews. For Machen, the church was defined as a body of beliefs around which adherents gathered. For Coffin, the church was an organic community of diverse persons who shared the spirit of Jesus and were committed to applying that spirit in society.

Those in the moderate middle hoped to have it both ways. When the Special Theological Commission of the General Assembly gave its interim report in 1925, it asserted that "toleration does not involve any lowering of standards."[41] The Commission went on to argue that "Presbyterianism is a great body of belief, but it is more than a belief; it is also a tradition, a controlling sentiment. The ties which bind us to it are not of the mind only; they are ties of the heart as well."[42]

While affirming a parity of mind and heart, belief and tradition, the direction laid down in 1926 gave a practical priority to polity. The limits of doctrine had henceforth to be established "either *generally,* by amendment to the Constitution, or *particularly,* by Presbyterial authority, subject to the constitutional right of appeal."[43] The stage was set for several decades of reducing most theological disputes in the church to matters of proper interpretation of polity. The church was most often viewed not as an association of the doctrinally pure but as a diverse people committed to good management. Those competing views of reality were difficult to reconcile.

William Joseph Weston correctly observed that the liberal inclusivists wrested control of the denomination away from the conservative exclusivists because "the liberals learned to be constitutional pluralists, and on that basis were able to win the equally constitutional moderates away from their historic alliance with the doctrinal conservatives."[44]

The situation in the Presbyterian Church in the 1930s illustrates the further fragmentation of the earlier evangelical/mainstream worldview. It also demonstrates how persons holding different ideological worldviews can form alliances when there are agreements at another level. In this case the more important agreements were the assumptions by both the constitutional conservatives and the constitutional liberals that they each were Christians at the deepest level of the heart (the ultimate religious worldview), and that their own ideological vision of the truth would be best served by adherence to constitutional procedures of church government.

FUNDAMENTALIST SPLINTERING

In October 1935, one faculty member and a majority of the board of Westminster Seminary, including Macartney, resigned rather than endorse the aggressive ecclesiastical separatism of Machen and the faculty majority. The General Assembly of 1936 heard four judicial cases appealing censures of members of the Independent Board. In each of the cases the Assembly upheld the censure imposed by lower judicatories.

Within nine days of these judicial decisions, Machen and some of his most vocal followers formed a new denomination, the Presbyterian Church of America. (The name was changed in 1939 to the Orthodox Presbyterian Church. Interestingly, the original name was claimed in the 1970s by a separatist group that left the PCUS.)

Machen's movement was soon fragmented when, in 1937, Carl McIntire and some others broke ranks and formed the Bible Presbyterian Synod. Faith Theological Seminary in Philadelphia became their training school. The stated reasons for this division were McIntire's desire to maintain premillennialism, total abstinence from alcoholic beverages, and a more congregational form of government as church distinctives. Machen died a few weeks after the McIntire defection while on a trip to North Dakota trying to persuade the few churches of his denomination to stay together.[45]

The process of division that Machen began continued, with the splinter groups becoming ever smaller and more militant. Faith Seminary was divided by a group who founded Covenant Seminary in St. Louis. This group created the Reformed Presbyterian Church, Evangelical Synod. Later, Covenant Seminary divided and a small group founded Biblical Seminary in Hatfield, Pennsylvania.[46] Francis Schaeffer illustrated the separatist mentality. He was a student at Westminster who left with the splinter group to form Faith and later joined the dissident group that formed Covenant.

The separating group represented less than one percent of the membership of the PCUSA.[47] Nonetheless, the experience of schism shook the composure of the Presbyterian Church. In the 1930s, other mainline denominations experienced the withdrawal of fundamentalist groups, some of whom formed new, more homogeneous denominations. Frequently, these new splinter groups splintered repeatedly as leaders vied with each other to enforce purity in doctrine and practice.

Tensions between the Right and Left

Resurgent Separatism on the Right

Although most mainstream Christians had never heard of him, Francis Schaeffer was a fundamentalist leader who embodied the ideal of separatism that exerted great influence in the churches and the nation from the 1960s through the 1980s. Schaeffer exemplified the power of the early American evangelical/mainstream worldview in its most separatist form.

As recently as 1995, *Christianity Today* identified Schaeffer as the chief architect of the New Religious Right and the pro-life movement.[48] Over three million copies of his twenty-two books have been sold. His five-volume complete works, subtitled *A Christian Worldview*, have gone through multiple printings.[49] At Schaeffer's death in 1984, President Reagan proclaimed him "one of the greatest Christian thinkers of our century."[50]

Schaeffer was a guest at dinner parties of Republican members of Congress, and his books were discussed by Senate wives in their weekly Bible study.[51]

What was the basis of Schaeffer's teaching? His theology was that of Old Princeton Seminary prior to 1930. He had developed a contemporary style for communicating the method of antithesis that he imbibed at Westminster Seminary in 1935. Machen taught that Christianity and liberalism were two different and opposed religions. Cornelius Van Til, who had left the Princeton Seminary faculty with Machen in 1929, taught Schaeffer apologetics, that is, how to defend the Christian faith. Van Til's method was to presume the Christian system of thought (in its Old Princeton form) and then to show the inadequacy of his opponent's presuppositions.[52]

Schaeffer taught and practiced the method of antithesis that rejected any compromise with his opponent's view—"ecclesiastically and in evangelism."[53] Separatism was therefore a central principle for him. Schaeffer left Westminster in 1937 when McIntire led a split to found Faith Seminary. In 1941, McIntire formed the American Council of Christian Churches (ACCC) to fight the "impure" Federal Council of Churches. Schaeffer was a part of the ACCC from the beginning. As a pastor in St. Louis, Schaeffer split with Child Evangelism Fellowship when its national board would not allow him to collaborate only with ACCC churches. He then formed his own Children for Christ, Inc., as a separatist organization. In 1947, he became a missionary to Europe sponsored by the Independent Board of Foreign Missions, founded by Machen. There he helped McIntire found the International Council of Christian Churches (ICCC) to fight the newly created World Council of Churches in 1948. Simultaneously, Schaeffer attacked neo-orthodoxy as a counterfeit of true Christianity. He charged the neo-orthodox with "mental gymnastics" and "black magic in logic." When Karl Barth replied to a paper Schaeffer had sent him, Schaeffer referred to Barth's theology as "insanity"[54] because in Schaeffer's view it was based on existentialism that was pure subjectivism without any objective authority.

Schaeffer served the ICCC and several other fundamentalist organizations in Europe until 1953, when he broke with the Independent Board in a dispute over organizational authority. In 1953 he came to the United States on an eighteen-month tour of speaking and fund-raising. During this time, he received an honorary doctorate from now-defunct Highland College in Long Beach, California. He returned to Switzerland in 1954, determined to operate independently. In 1955, the Schaeffers formed L'Abri as an independent "faith" mission and church. The following year, Schaeffer's third denomination, the Reformed Presbyterian Church, Evangelical Synod, broke with the ICCC, and Schaeffer's close relationship to McIntire ended in acrimony.[55]

Schaeffer was little known outside conservative religious circles in the United States until, on January 11, 1960, *Time* ran a story about him titled "Mission to the Intellectuals." It was reminiscent of *Time's* designation in 1951 of Reinhold Niebuhr as "the high priest of Protestantism's young intellectuals." This time the "intellectuals" were American college-age people tramping through Europe trying to find themselves. Some of them landed at L'Abri (French for "the shelter"), a study and communal living center in Huemoz, Switzerland, founded by Schaeffer and his wife, Edith. One such young person was the *Time* writer's daughter, who was converted to Christianity there.[56]

Schaeffer exemplified in his thought and practice all six motifs of the evangelical/mainstream worldview in a rigidified fundamentalist form. He adhered to (1) separatism, (2) revivalism, (3) moralism, and (4) premillennialism, all on the basis of (5) Scottish Common Sense, which taught that the truth was obvious. What brought him national influence was in part his adherence to the other motif of the early American worldview: (6) America is God's chosen nation.

Replayed Inclusivism on the Left: The Parliament of the World's Religions in 1993

The worldview motif of separatism in Schaeffer's thinking was abhorrent to those with a liberal worldview. The countermotif of ecumenical unity remained a noble ideal for many among the leaders of mainstream Protestantism. But in 1993 unity was much more difficult because the participants were much more diverse than at the original Parliament of the World's Religions in 1893. The 125 different religious groups that met in Chicago on August 28–September 5, 1993, would have amazed the participants at the original Parliament. In addition to representatives of Buddhism, Christianity, Hinduism, Islam, and Judaism, neo-pagan groups with names such as the Fellowship of Isis, the Covenant of the Goddess, and Lyceum of Venus of Healing were there.[57]

No attempt was made to deal with theology or creeds. The goal was to deal with ethical, especially ecological, issues and to lower the tensions in a world where more than two-thirds of the armed conflicts have religion as a motivating factor.[58] Despite the withdrawal of support by some Greek

Orthodox and Jewish groups who found some of the other participants' presence offensive, the Parliament was remarkably harmonious and demonstrated a diversity of religious life in the United States that would have been unthinkable even thirty years ago.[59]

Most representatives signed a final statement called "Toward a Global Ethic." Its primary author was Swiss Roman Catholic theologian Hans Küng. The declaration calls on people to respect all life, individuality, and diversity so that every person is treated humanely. Nowhere in the document is the word "God" mentioned, since that would have excluded the Buddhists, who do not believe in a divine being.[60] The declaration, in the mind of its author, represents a "paradigm shift" toward a "global consciousness." Küng said: "We had to answer questions that Jesus or Moses never thought about. We are at a transformation of consciousness with regard to nature. Nobody thinks anymore as we thought 30 years ago."[61] Küng concluded on a revivalist note: "We have learned that a better global order cannot be created or enforced by laws, prescriptions and conventions alone . . . . The minds and hearts of women and men must be addressed."[62] Some of the participants felt that the tone of the statement was too Western and too Christian. It was therefore proposed to endorse the text only as a provisional statement *toward* a global ethic. Apparently 95 percent of the assembly endorsed the statement with that understanding. The statement affirmed "that a common set of core values is found in the teachings of the religions, and that these form the basis of a global ethic. We affirm that this truth is already known, but yet to be lived in heart and action."[63]

Energy for the liberal/modernist worldview, especially in its motif of ecumenical unity, has largely shifted to non-Protestant groups if the Parliament of the World's Religions is indicative. Less than one hundred and fifty Protestant Christians registered for the event. Of these, about twenty were members of the PC(USA). Some of them played a central role. David Ramage, former president of McCormick Theological Seminary, served as chairperson of the thirty-seven-member Board of Trustees that spent five years planning the event. Four Presbyterians (three staff persons and a former moderator of the General Assembly) were among the 225 participants in the Assembly of Religious and Spiritual Leaders that formulated responses to the issues raised at the Parliament.[64] Few evangelical Christians or Orthodox Jews were present.[65] The liberal countermotif of ecumenical unity, so important to mainstream church leadership, nevertheless did not seem to stir much response in the Protestant mainstream church membership.

42

The worldview contrast between Schaeffer and Küng and their conservative and liberal adherents could hardly be sharper. On the one hand, Schaeffer's approach was founded on exclusivism and separatism. He expounded a contemporary version of a two-centuries-old worldview and exerted an extensive influence on exclusivist movements with significant religious and political power in contemporary society.

On the other hand, Küng articulated an inclusivism that is generally accepted in liberal religious and secular society. He confidently announced that no one thinks as we used to think even thirty years ago. Schaeffer and the movements he had initiated are either unknown to Küng or he appears unable to take them seriously. Presbyterian and other mainstream religious leaders generally share Küng's worldview. Large numbers of mainstream church members continue to be influenced by Schaeffer and those who share his worldview. How can we cope with such a deep division within the churches and our communities?

Creating a Contemporary Centrist Worldview of Unity and Diversity

Civility and Conviction in the Center

The tension between diversity and unity is often exemplified by the choice between the values of civility and conviction. For many, civility exemplifies the ecumenical commitment to continuing conversation and inclusivism. To these same people, an emphasis on conviction can raise the specter of separatism.

While I served on the national staff of the Presbyterian Church I was asked to be one of two speakers on the topic "A Theology of Pluralism." The other speaker was one of the leading theologians in the Presbyterian Church. He and I were friends and had worked together. As our inviting body desired, he took a strong stance for pluralism and I an equally strong stance against it.

For my friend, the principal theological task of the church is the affirmation and defense of pluralism. He argued that pluralism must be defended wherever there is a threat to it. We are mainstream insofar as we model pluralism.

I argued that diversity is enriching when it is an accompaniment to a basic unity. Diversity keeps unity from being uniformity. A commitment to diversity that embraces inclusion of persons of all races, genders, and cultures is enriching when it accompanies a unity of ecclesiology,

43

theology, and morality. Diversity becomes destructive when it changes into a pluralism that affirms diversity for its own sake as a basic value. That affirmation opens the door to diversity of basic values and commitments that fragments the essential unity of the church.

The more that we talked and others entered the discussion, the clearer it became that we each feared a different set of consequences. My colleague in dialogue emphasized *civility*. He feared that if the conversation stopped, violence would begin. He had grown up in a subculture dominated by fundamentalism. Conviction, in his experience, could too easily slide over into arrogance and authoritarianism.

I emphasized *conviction*. I feared that in the subculture of the PC(USA) at that moment we had become so muddleheaded in our embrace of pluralism that we were in danger of losing touch with a centering clarity of conviction. I too had chilling experiences with fundamentalism. But, at the moment, the fundamentalists were not dominating the leadership of the Presbyterian Church. Our present danger, and one documented by recent sociological studies, was rather that we might slide over into an amorphous identification with secular society.

Although our emphases were different, we agreed that a mainstream church should ideally model a balance of civility and conviction. When my eldest son, Matthew, graduated from Princeton University he, along with all seniors, was given a quarter page in the yearbook in which he could put anything he chose. I was naturally interested to see what message he had conveyed to his class. He published three quotations. The first was from Martin Luther: "Here I stand. I can do no other."[66] That represents conviction. The second was from Oliver Cromwell: "I beseech you in the bowels of Christ, think it possible you may be mistaken."[67] That statement embodies civility. The third was from Reinhold Niebuhr on the children of light and the children of darkness. It indicates that there will always be people who will choose in different directions, some placing their accent on civility and some on conviction.[68]

Clearly a mainstream church must have a balance of conviction and civility. Conviction provides unity. Civility allows for diversity. Conviction applies to essentials of faith and practice. Civility describes the process of dialogue by which we determine essentials and nonessentials and incorporate the enrichment of diversity. Conviction affirms the ultimate religious worldview, the basic Christian story. Civility opens us to many possible theological elaborations, ideological applications, and experiential colorings of that basic story.

It is possible to have a balance of conviction and civility if we keep them in the proper order and apply them to the appropriate subjects. We begin with the conviction that we belong to a sovereign God revealed in Jesus Christ. That same God calls us to civility in all that we think and do.

Applying Conviction and Civility

Our ability to have unity in the midst of our diversity in the church depends on our willingness to synthesize a new worldview from two previously opposing worldview motifs—separatism and ecumenical unity. First we will have to maintain a balance between conviction and civility. Second, we will need the courage to make conviction primary. Not just conservatives are currently calling for the primacy of conviction. In the *Christian Century*, Carl Dudley has articulated both the problem and a positive proposal.

> Many middle-class mainline churches have elevated pluralism from a descriptive condition to a primary tenet of faith. As a central belief, an "ism," pluralism is sterile. Theologically, pluralism is related to belief in the same way that works are related to faith in Jesus Christ. Although we are saved by grace through faith ("lest anyone should boast," Eph. 2:9), we see the consequences of faith in the inclusive community.

A contemporary centrist worldview would respond to the question, Can we have unity in diversity? with a resounding yes! We can emulate in contemporary terms the stance of the original English Puritans. We are committed to the church. Separation from it is unthinkable. We would leave only if driven away. And as loyal members of the church, we will continue to work from within for its reform and renewal in a Calvinistic direction theologically, and in a Presbyterian direction governmentally. That is what is meant by the nifty Latin phrase, Ecclesia reformata, semper reformanda. "Reformed, and always willing to be reformed," as the Book of Order says, "according to the Word of God and the call of the Spirit."[69]

3 | Election as God's Chosen People: What Is the Church?

> There is one body and one Spirit, just as you were called to the one hope of your calling, one Lord, one faith, one baptism, one God and Father of all, who is above all and through all and in all.
>
> —*Ephesians 4:4–6*

FOCUS: Deeply rooted in the American psyche is the notion that we are God's chosen people. That notion affects our understanding of both the church and the nation. Within the constitutional documents of the PC(USA) are two different, sometimes conflicting, and unresolved notions of the nature and function of the church. In some confessional documents the church is an ark of salvation, protecting individuals from the world. In other confessions the church is an agent of social change, involving the individual in the world. Some parts of the book of government make the church a nurturer of individual piety through preaching, sacraments, and discipline. Other parts of the book of government present a corporate view with mission in the world and inclusivism of all people as the primary marks of the church. We need to understand these competing worldviews embedded in our constitutional documents in order to understand present conflicts between those who differ deeply and yet feel themselves authentically Presbyterian.

The involvement of the church in the world was given special prominence in the late nineteenth and early twentieth century by two powerful social movements. The first was the social gospel. The second was the institutionalization of the social gospel in ecumenical councils of churches. We cannot understand the present pull these movements have, especially on the leadership of the mainstream churches, unless we understand this history.

The contemporary context of these conflicts can be understood more clearly in two ways. One is by observing the changes in mainstream denominational organization at the national level that reflect changing understandings of the nature of the church. Another is by looking at one case study: the history of the Presbyterian Church since the reunion of 1983 and its attempts to restructure without dealing with the fundamentally different worldviews of (1) those for whom the church is primarily the local congregation and (2) those for whom the church is primarily the higher governing bodies.

Presbyterian conflicts reflect those in the larger mainstream Protestant community between a public and a personal view of the church. A new understanding of the role of the denomination in contemporary society is needed if we are to have a creative and functioning worldview of a mainstream church that serves betwixt and between fundamentalist sectarianism and liberal inclusivism.

The Contemporary Relevance of the Worldview Motif of Election as God's Chosen People

From the late eighteenth to the late nineteenth century, churches in the United States were organized as constitutional confederations. They had no national staff or program. The Presbyterian General Assembly's purpose was to provide a framework for debating issues that had proved to have wider than local concern.

During the late nineteenth and the early twentieth century, the churches adopted the organizational model of corporate bureaucracy. Denominations provided goods and services to their constituents, such as Sunday school materials, pensions for clergy, home and overseas missionaries, and social welfare activities. At the height of the corporate model in the 1950s, the journal *Presbyterian Life* had more subscribers than *Newsweek*. Denominations developed large professional staffs to manage these enterprises. A General Assembly became the equivalent of a corporate stockholders' meeting. The delegates came to see if the staff had been doing a good job and to set corporate policy.

In the 1960s, the corporate model began to break down. The national church leadership adopted a liberal worldview that saw changing the unjust structures of society as the primary task of the church. The Presbyterian Church diminished its commitment to planting new churches, withdrew many overseas missionaries, ceased to produce denominational church school literature, and abandoned Presbyterian national youth ministries. These popular goods and services were abandoned, usually in favor of some cooperative ecumenical effort.

Denominational leaders took uncompromising stands on controversial social issues and shifted denominational resources to support these stands. As those resources diminished, they relied on policy statements to justify continuing desired programs. The organization moved to the model of a regulatory agency. The Presbyterian General Assemblies of the 1980s became negotiating sessions where special interest groups came to lobby for their cause. Their effort was to get regulations made that required conformity to a particular social policy.[1]

To understand how such changes occurred, we need to understand the colonial origins of the exclusivist worldview motif of election as God's chosen people and its nineteenth- and twentieth-century inclusivist countermotifs expressed in the social gospel and ecumenism.

The Historical Setting of Election as God's Chosen People

The early Americans believed that in a special way they were the elect, God's chosen people.[2] In this they were simply retaining a conviction that English Puritans had held since the sixteenth century. The first English Bible translator, William Tyndale, saw England, like ancient Israel, as a covenant nation.

For American Puritans, the English national church had failed its covenant obligation by refusing to reform. New England Puritans considered America a sacred place of refuge where they could finally realize the ideal of a covenant people in church and nation. Those fleeing from other oppressive Old World regimes in later generations understandably shared that vision. In 1654, Edward Johnson (1598–1672), known as the First Citizen of Woburn, Massachusetts, published *Wonder-Working Providence of Zion's Saviour in New England.* He wrote: "This is the place where the Lord will create a new Heaven, and a new Earth in, new Churches, and a new Commonwealth together."[3] This view was widely held through the eighteenth and nineteenth centuries.

As the nineteenth century gave way to the twentieth, two powerful movements made their mark on American society and especially on the mainstream churches. One was the social gospel; the other was the ecumenical movement.

The Social Gospel

The social gospel grew within the context of profound political and social changes in late-nineteenth-century America. It also became the theological expression of the humanitarian movement called Progressivism associated with the political eras of Theodore Roosevelt and Woodrow Wilson.[4] Leaders of the social gospel utilized the methods of the new social sciences to implement strategies of social change.[5]

The unique insight of this movement was that human misery is rooted not only in the individual's sin but also, and perhaps primarily, in the sinful structures of society.[6] Its leaders wanted to move beyond individualism to deal with society as an organism and the church as an ecumenical body.[7] At its roots, however, the social gospel was a religious movement. Its leaders wished to add to the traditional concern to change individuals, the concern to establish the kingdom of God. Walter Rauschenbusch, its leading exponent, said that it was "not a matter of getting individuals to heaven, but of transforming the life on earth into the harmony of heaven."[8] Theology and sociology were united in the oft-repeated slogan of the movement: "The Fatherhood of God and the brotherhood of man."

The social gospel embodied the motifs of the modernist worldview. According to Rauschenbusch, "We have a social gospel. We need a systematic theology large enough to match it and vital enough to back it."[9]

There was never an official organization for promoting the social gospel, yet it penetrated the mainstream Protestant establishment churches and the large African-American denominations founded during this period. Its incorporation into the institutions of American life occurred through the actions of the Federal Council of Churches of Christ (FCCC) established in 1908. The official historian of the FCCC declared: "On the one hand it established church federation on a recognized and national basis and on the other hand it gave official ecclesiastical form to the Social Gospel."[10] The social gospel gave the FCCC a reason for being, and the FCCC gave the social gospel a medium of institutional expression.

World War I proved to be the occasion for the consolidation of power within the mainstream churches by the leaders of the social gospel movement. In this period two central commitments of liberal/mainstream Protestantism came together and were given institutional expression: ecumenism and social reform. During this same period the gap began between leaders and members of the mainstream churches; this gap would widen dramatically in the 1960s. One aspect of that gap was the discernible shift in emphasis on the part of mainstream church leaders from personal evangelism to direct reform of the structures of society.[11]

Ecumenism

Leaders of the social gospel movement wanted to establish the kingdom of God. What would that kingdom look like? The model for the present-day church, they assumed, was surely the undivided church at the time of Christ. Denominations represented the sin of schism. The goal of the social gosepl movement was to return the church to pristine wholeness. One consequence of this attitude was the modern ecumenical movement, which developed from the late nineteenth century until just after World War II. Its proponents called it the great new fact of the twentieth century. It changed the character of the Christian community worldwide.[12]

Organic ecclesiastical unity proved to be an unattainable ideal. Denominational leaders soon settled for some form of federation among the existing denominations.[13] In the United States, the energies of the social gospel and the ecumenical movement were fused in the creation of the FCCC in 1908. From its outset, the FCCC, like its successor in 1950, the National Council of Churches, envisioned itself as the sole representative of the mainstream Protestant establishment. It intended to be not only the voice of the mainstream churches but the conscience of the nation.[14]

The FCCC's stated purposes were to "manifest the essential oneness of the Christian churches of America" and "to secure a larger combined influence" for them in all matters "affecting the moral and social condition of the people."[15] At its first meeting the FCCC accepted as its own a "social creed of the churches" that had originated with the social gospel activists in the northern Methodist Church. The FCCC's uncritical acceptance of the social gospel, from the beginning, alienated a large proportion of the laypersons in its member churches. When the evangelical/mainstream community divided during the fundamentalist-modernist controversy, the FCCC evidenced its sympathies for the liberal, social activists.[16]

Both the social gospel and the ecumenical movement were concrete expressions of the liberal/modernist worldview. The conflict between the early American evangelical/mainstream worldview motifs and these modern countermotifs caused tensions in the churches and the body politic from the beginning of the twentieth century. They burst into open antagonism in a way that divided churches and the nation in the 1960s.

Church leaders, whose principal concern was changing the structures of society, and pastors and church members, whose concern was dealing with individual human sin, had difficulty understanding one another. This was further complicated in the reunited PC(USA) after 1983 since two conflicting worldviews regarding the nature of the church were present in the constitutional documents of the denomination. Rather than being synthesized into one whole, they became diverse elements to which factions with conflicting worldviews appealed.

Conflicting Marks of the Church in the Constitution

THE BOOK OF CONFESSIONS AND THE CHURCH'S MISSION

Conflict over the nature and mission of the church is built into the constitutional documents of the PC(USA). Opposing groups can legitimately appeal to the constitution to support their views. *The Book of Confessions* contains two different views of the nature of the church.

The sixteenth- and seventeenth-century confessions depicted the church as an ark of salvation. The primary functions of this church are to bring people to salvation—a right relationship with God—and to guide them in living the Christian life. The Second Helvetic Confession declares: "The Church is an assembly of the faithful called or gathered out of the world; a communion . . . of those who truly know and rightly worship and serve the true God in Christ the Savior, by the Word and Holy Spirit" (5.125).

In the twentieth century, the definition of the church changed. The Theological Declaration of Barmen (1934) added the assertion that the church "has to testify in the midst of a sinful world, with its faith as with its obedience" (8.17). In the Confession of 1967 the accent shifted almost entirely to action as defining the true church. The preface stated boldly: "Obedience to Jesus Christ alone identifies the one universal church and supplies the continuity of its tradition" (9.03). The stress was no longer on the salvation of the individual but on the mission of the corporate church in the world. Jesus Christ "called the church to be his servant for the reconciliation of the world" (9.19).

The earlier creeds and confessions regarded the church as an ark of salvation. The twentieth-century emphasis was on the church as God's agent of societal change. Both reflected biblical imperatives. But because they were not fully integrated into one, unified view of the nature of the church, both conservative and liberal groups could appeal to *The Book of Confessions* in support of their differing views.

THE *BOOK* OF *ORDER* AND THE MARKS OF THE CHURCH

Conflict between two views of the church was also built into the *Book of Order.* On the one hand, the sixteenth-century marks of the church are articulated in the Scots Confession and implied in the present *Book of Order:* The true preaching of the Word of God, the right administration of the sacraments of Jesus Christ, and ecclesiastical discipline uprightly ministered define and identify the church (*Book of Confessions* 3.18). On the other hand, the *Book of Order* that was adopted at the reunion of the Northern and Southern streams of Presbyterianism in 1983 may be read as adding two additional marks of the church: (1) to be in mission in the name of Jesus Christ is a mark of the true church (G-3.0100–3.0400); and (2) the true church is "a community of diversity" that becomes a "visible sign of the new humanity" by "providing for inclusiveness" (G-3.0401). Thus, conservative congregations can appeal to the sixteenth-century definition for their view of church, while governing body leaders will likely stress the new marks of the church recently added to the *Book of Order.*

The Recent Context of Conflicts over Election as God's Chosen People

The Presbyterian Predicament: A Case Study

Is there one Presbyterian Church, or are there two under one name? Unacknowledged but powerfully different worldviews were operating during the period of Presbyterian reorganization in the mid-1980s. In 1989 Presbyterians celebrated their history—two hundred years as a fully organized denomination in America. At the same time, some experts on religious trends in America predicted Presbyterian demise. One commentator estimated that at the current rates of decline, in the year 2025 the last living Presbyterian would turn off the lights, pull down the shades, and put the "Gone out of business" sign in the window.[17]

Three of the sociological reasons for the loss were clear.[18] First, Presbyterians' own children were leaving the church, mostly going not to other churches but to no formal religious affiliation. Forty-five percent of the young adults who grew up Presbyterian were no longer Presbyterian.[19]

Second, Presbyterians no longer gained members from those who changed churches for reasons of upward economic and social mobility. People less frequently changed churches when they moved up the social and economic ladder. Third, young adults who did remain in the Presbyterian fold tended to have more years of education, thus delaying their establishment of a family, with the result that they had fewer babies than those in some other denominations.

Another aspect of dis-ease was the appearance of continuous and apparently unresolvable conflict in the church. Americans often erroneously thought that Presbyterians were desperately polarized between those on the far left and those on the far right. That was seldom true. Surveys of theological attitudes done through the research arm of the denomination generally showed an almost bell-shaped curve, weighted somewhat to the conservative side.[20]

The eighteenth- and nineteenth-century splits in the denomination had been healed as both sides moved toward the middle to survive. But Presbyterians have been less fortunate in the twentieth century. Denominational schisms of the 1930s, 1970s, and 1980s have not yet been healed. Presbyterians were grateful for the reunion of the major northern and southern branches of Presbyterianism in 1983 that put behind them the shame of divisions of the 1860s occasioned by differences over race and region. But healing the geographical and cultural rifts did not really make Presbyterianism one.

PUBLIC AND PERSONAL POLARITY

Following reunion in 1983 the former Southern and Northern leaders began to dance a delicate minuet together. At times it appeared that some only knew how to waltz while others were used to doing the fox-trot. Far more important was the increasing distance between the leadership involved in the dance and those in the church at large who felt left on the sidelines. While the leaders, both North and South, generally continued to forward the church's public policy agenda, people in the congregations, North and South, wondered where to turn for resources to strengthen personal piety.

In January and February 1985, two major events occurred, each intended to renew and unify the Presbyterian Church following the reunion of 1983: (1) a Congress on Renewal and (2) a Life and Mission Event. Each represented a different vision of the nature of the church and a different concept of its mission. The Congress represented the worldview of those who continued a moderate form of the early American evangelical/mainstream worldview. They carried on the tradition of the New Side/New School of Presbyterianism in its concern for personal piety. The Life and Mission Event represented the worldview of those who had adopted the other concern of the New Side/New School, its desire for social change now put in the context of the liberal/modernist worldview. The two events did not connect with each other. They tended rather to strengthen their respective participants' opposing worldviews and conceptions of the church.

Presbyterians whose agenda was primarily personal piety organized and attended a Congress on Renewal in Dallas in January 1985 and its several regional follow-ups thereafter. All church members were invited, and more Presbyterian laypersons and pastors gathered at these events than at any other comparable events in the history of American Presbyterianism.[21] They worshiped in large plenaries. They attended multitudes of workshops primarily on issues affecting personal piety, individual morality, and the needs of the local congregation. The rhetoric of the major speakers all inclined toward disdain for the governing body polity and enthusiasm for individual and congregational piety.

The result was very positive for those who attended. The people whose agenda was personal piety went home encouraged about the church. Individuals and congregations were nurtured. The organizers hoped that somehow, indirectly, these gatherings would influence the national church. But their efforts remained disengaged from the official structures and systems of the denomination. Therefore, the restructuring of the national church went on largely unrelated to and unaffected by their enthusiasms.

In February 1985, a Life and Mission Event took place at Mo Ranch in Texas. This official event was to renew and refocus the newly reunited church. Seventy carefully selected leaders representing the governing body church and its overseas ecumenical affiliates spent the week going through an elaborate process of committee meetings to prepare a Life and Mission Statement. That statement was amended and adopted in a final plenary session.

The Life and Mission Statement was supposed to be based in large part on the results of a national survey of priorities done throughout the church at the session, presbytery, synod, General Assembly, and General Assembly Entity levels. It was called the Mission Consultation Survey and was taken in the late spring of 1984.[22]

The results of the national survey indicated six largely personal priorities that most people in sessions, presbyteries, synods, and at the 1984 General Assembly wanted the church to adopt: (1) leading others to a saving knowledge of Jesus Christ; (2) promoting peacemaking; (3) equipping and supporting laity in their witness; (4) revitalizing congregations; (5) enriching family life, parenting, and marriages; and (6) emphasizing the primacy of scripture as a standard for our faith and practice.[23] Not incidentally, the results for racial ethnic congregations were roughly the same as those of the majority Anglo ones, the only difference being the legitimate desire for more financial support for the former group's smaller congregations.

This remarkable consensus on primarily personal priorities could be found at all levels in the church except one. The public policy leadership group, composed of elected members of General Assembly agencies and their staff, had a different set of priorities.[24] Only three priorities from the consensus list appeared in the priorities of members of General Assembly Entities (GAE): no. 2, promoting peacemaking, was fifth on the GAE list; no. 3, equipping and supporting laity in their witness, was second on the GAE list; and no. 4, revitalizing congregations, was tied for sixth on the GAE list. The other priorities of the GAE were: (1) developing churchwide strategies for cooperative mission funding; (3) developing skills and strategies for seeking social justice; (4) supporting hunger programs and community and agricultural development; and tied for (6) providing resources and leadership training for racial ethnic constituencies. These four were the public policy priorities with which the leadership had been concerned. There was nothing wrong with the GAE priorities. They were legitimate in the eyes of most Presbyterians. However, some in the leadership appeared fearful that they might not be able to maintain their priorities if those of the church at large were granted.

DECISIONS IN FAVOR OF THE LEADERSHIP AGENDA

During the Life and Mission Event in February 1985, the priorities of the church at large, determined by the survey, were criticized as "unworthy" and largely set aside. The final statement became what one observer called "a treaty among the tribes," with each interest group getting some mention of its concern. No priorities were listed in the Life and Mission Statement. As a result, the Mission Design Team, which was to propose the organizational structure, was able to set its own priorities.

In the church's final structural design of nine Ministry Units, on the one hand four of the six priorities of the church at large were subsumed under one Ministry Unit, Education and Congregational Nurture. On the other hand four of the seven priorities of the General Assembly leadership were embodied in individual Ministry Units, with social justice concerns being serviced by an additional Related Body, the Committee on Social Witness Policy.[25]

The apportioning of the budget appeared even more imbalanced than the structure. An analysis of the 1989 General Assembly mission budget suggested that the public agenda of the church received approximately 70 percent of the money and the agenda for meeting personal needs of its members got about 30 percent.[26] The operating assumption seemed to be that to give money to fund the personal priorities of the church at large would mean taking money away from the public policy concerns of the denominational leadership.

Studies of Presbyterian giving ironically have affirmed that the Presbyterian Church had sufficient money to fund both sets of concerns. What was lacking was a trust in the General Assembly leadership by the membership and by those in the lower governing bodies. Studies in the early 1990s demonstrated that throughout the twentieth century, Presbyterians "steadily and dramatically" increased their donations to the church, even when adjusted for inflation. The dramatic shift, since the 1950s, has been for Presbyterians to give to and disperse funds through the local congregation and to withhold funds from the General Assembly.[27] Funds have simply been shifted from the General Assembly level to lower levels in the church where those giving the money had more confidence in and control over how it was spent.

I believe that if the denomination had been genuinely united in trust, both the personal needs of members and the public policy goals of leaders could have been met.

Paralysis about Priorities

At the 1989 General Assembly, Presbyterians were asked to accept an official set of priorities. An eighty-three-member Churchwide Planning Consultation committee stated the obvious by suggesting that evangelism and social justice were the two basic priorities of the church. However, fifteen other "continuing goals" were presented, each having equal weight. In effect, the problem of two agendas, two churches with multiple sets of values, was recognized, but no attempt was made to integrate, synthesize, or reconcile them into a working whole. Thus the conflict continued that was rooted in the restructuring following reunion in 1983. The leadership and the local congregations generally held different worldviews. They had different visions of the nature and mission of the church. They were each sincere but seemed unable to communicate with each other.

In various public forums in the late 1980s, speakers offered theological metaphors for the continuing Presbyterian decline. At the dedication of the Presbyterian Center in Louisville in the fall of 1988, Professor Walter Brueggemann presented the metaphor of Israel going into exile.[28] At the spring 1989 national staff meeting in San Diego, Jack Stotts, president of Austin Seminary, invoked the metaphor of Israel in the days of the judges when small groups each did what was right in their own eyes and were held together only loosely by the rituals of worship.[29]

It was clear, then, by the late 1980s that American Presbyterians needed but lacked a generally agreed-upon doctrine of the church. The public and personal agendas had not been synthesized in the Presbyterian understanding of the church. There had been some wholesome initiatives dealing with the spiritual welfare of the church through the General Assembly Council, the Theology and Worship Unit, the Evangelism and Church Development Unit, the Global Mission Unit, and others. However, there had not been the will and the leadership to put forth a genuinely new paradigm.

There were some seminal suggestions. The General Assembly in 1988 adopted a paper for study titled "Is Christ Divided?"[30] This study addressed the need for Presbyterians to find unity in the midst of enriching diversity. It spoke strongly to the issue of the need for a clear theological basis for the church, declaring: "The church's preference for 'unity in mission' over 'unity in theology' has led to unity in neither."[31] It concluded with the affirmation that "the church's mission is most faithful and vital when it grows out of carefully articulated theological conviction."[32]

In 1991, the denomination added to its *Book of Confessions* "A Brief Statement of Faith: Presbyterian Church (U.S.A.)." This two-page statement clarified what Presbyterians most deeply believed in the early 1990s. It was crafted over a four-year period by a genuinely diverse group of persons and was affirmed, three years later, after critical scrutiny by revision committees, three General Assemblies, and an overwhelming majority in the presbyteries. It gave clear evidence that there was an agreed theological center in the Presbyterian Church.

It is noteworthy that, with no conscious intent, the drafters of this contemporary statement affirmed the same basic doctrinal concepts listed in chapter two of the present *Book of Order,* "The Church and Its Confessions." There was a continuity of theological commitment between the ancient church of the first through the fifth centuries A.D. and 1990s Presbyterianism in the doctrines of the Trinity and the incarnation of God in the person of Jesus Christ. Twentieth-century Presbyterians joined with their ancestors from the Protestant Reformation in affirming the authority of scripture and the need for justification by grace through faith. The characteristic emphases of the Reformed tradition were also captured in references to the sovereignty of God; the election of God's people for salvation and service; the covenant life of the church; the call for a faithful stewardship of all creation; the recognition of the human temptation to idolatry; and the need for the people of God to seek justice and live in obedience to the Word of God. This constellation of theological emphases in "A Brief Statement of Faith" gave content to the "essential tenets of the Reformed faith" that all office bearers in the church are asked to "sincerely receive and adopt" at their ordination (*Book of Order* G.14.0207 and G.14.0405).

Unfortunately, conflicts between ideological worldviews in the church prevented this theological elaboration of the basic Christian story from playing the unifying role that it could have. It was apparent that when representative theological leaders of the Presbyterian Church had their eye on the issue of identity, they clearly affirmed a continuity with the Christian, Protestant, and Reformed tradition. When the denomination was presented with reports of various kinds representing the concerns of diverse special interests, however, it became apparent that many Presbyterians preferred a pragmatic pluralism of theological options.[33] Once again, ideological worldviews took precedence over a theological elaboration of the Christian story in the 1980s.

Tensions between the Right and the Left about Election as God's Chosen People

Public and Private Church

The mainstream denominations have been deeply divided over the nature and purpose of the church. Wade Clark Roof and William McKinney referred, as did others, to Martin Marty's distinction between "public" and "private" Protestantism. The public, or liberal, view "is concerned with life in this world and the well-being of society." In contrast, the "private" (or perhaps more accurately called "personal") view "emphasizes personal belief, strict standards of morality, and rewards and punishments in the world to come."[34] For all of the oversimplification involved, this characterization seemed to some extent validated in the experience of the researchers.

Something like those two sets of attitudes has persistently marked the history of American Presbyterians. Some described the division as between conservative and liberal factions.[35] Others characterized the division as between the pastors and members in both the congregations and governing bodies versus the cadre of General Assembly leadership composed of staff and lay and ministerial members of General Assembly task forces, committees, ministry units, and councils. These latter persons were selected through complex nominating processes, but were often not elected to their positions by any governing body.[36] However they were named, Presbyterians have experienced tensions between those whose central concerns had to do with personal piety and those whose chief commitments were to matters of public policy. The personal and the public, meaning and mission, the inward journey and involvement with the world, appear always to have been the two unsynthesized sides of the one coin that was stamped Presbyterian.[37]

Presbyterians familiar with this research applied the public-private dichotomy to contemporary Presbyterianism. Louis Weeks and William Fogelman asserted that the PC(USA) "consists in two deeply related, but distinguishable denominations." They designated these two denominations as the Local Congregational Presbyterian Church (LCPC) and the Governing Body Presbyterian Church (GBPC). They noted that in recent years, "competition and distrust have characterized much of the interaction" between the two groups.[38]

The LCPC was historically considered primary. Members served in higher governing bodies as an extension of service to their congregation. In the nineteenth century, another factor was added. Voluntary associations of people formed independent "mission boards" primarily for evangelization and church planting on the Western frontier and overseas. The Presbyterian Church was faced with deciding how to adapt to this new phenomenon. It occasioned a famous debate between a Northern and a Southern theologian. Princetonian Charles Hodge argued that mission boards should be incorporated in the denomination's life and made subject to the jurisdiction of the General Assembly. South Carolinian James Henley Thornwell asserted that mission boards as such were unscriptural and should be rejected since they would inevitably control the governing bodies that sponsored them. The debate was never resolved since the church soon split along North-South lines.

Weeks and Fogelman noted that during the twentieth century the GBPC has gained ascendancy. Board bureaucrats have combined with the cadre of experienced ministers and nearly full-time lay volunteers to provide leadership that has set the agenda for the denomination. That agenda has tended to place high value on the new marks of the church, mission and inclusiveness. Members of the LCPC cling to the earlier definitions of the church and want the denomination to focus on evangelism and on nurturing the personal lives of individual church members.

The Consequences of Polarization

The Presbyterian Church and other mainstream bodies have been wrenched and torn when leaders, holding either conservative or liberal worldviews, have attempted to force their denominations into a stance of supporting a one-sided view of reality. A conservative worldview represents a limiting ideology. So does a liberal worldview. An ideology is a one-sided way of thinking. It oversimplifies reality by looking at it through only one set of lenses.[39] Ideology "binds people together in common opposition to other groupings, creating an 'us-them' dynamic."[40] To identify the church as "liberal" or "conservative" is to acknowledge that it has become the private property of one group of people, pushing their program at the expense of others.

Creating a Contemporary Centrist Worldview of the Church

The Role of the Denomination

A contemporary, creative centrist response would recover the role of the mainstream denomination. Denominations are a peculiarly American invention that grew out of the attempt to find a balance between the contending forces of individualism and community. A denomination is not a sect that overstresses individualism and claims that it alone is the true church. Neither is a denomination an establishment, a state church, which arrogates to itself the right to represent all the people in a nation as the only legitimate religion. A denomination is a voluntary society of Christians that is both an organization and a community.[41] Its members believe that they represent one legitimate expression of the universal body of Christ, but not the only one. They relate to other churches in respect and with the potential of partnership. A mainstream denomination has the twofold task of rooting its members in the biblical and theological tradition and of enabling them to cope with the modern world.

A denomination is both an organization and an organism with a culture of its own. It is designed to provide not only "meaning" but also "belonging."[42] Denominations fit people into the local community while simultaneously giving them access to the larger society."[43] Robert Bellah and his associates noted that mainstream churches "have tried to relate biblical faith and practice to the whole of contemporary life—cultural, social, political, economic—not just to personal and family morality. They have tried to steer a middle course between mystical fusion with the world and sectarian withdrawal from it."[44]

Mainstream denominations are marked by this comprehensiveness of concern and by democratic processes that hold both leaders and members accountable. Because of these characteristics, mainstream denominations have confronted modernity more massively and in a more sustained way than any other religious group.[45] Mainstream denominations have engaged the issues of religious pluralism and privatism more fully and for longer than other American religious bodies.[46] Sects usually are more narrow in their range of concerns, often lack democratic accountability, and attempt to avoid the religious implications of modernity. Many of the difficulties of the mainstream denominations result from their intimate engagement with the culture.[47] That function of enabling people to cope with contemporary culture continues to be needed.

Denominations are a creative centrist response to the need for balance between the claims of individuals and those of the community, of sect and of establishment. Despite sustained criticism from both fundamentalists and liberals, the denomination remains the dominant religious form in America. Among Protestants, when asked in national surveys to state their religious affiliation, 85 percent will use denominational identifications, for example, Presbyterian, Methodist, Lutheran.[48] Especially now that the formerly mainline denominations have moved "beyond establishment," they can play a creative, balancing role.

Denominations have a distinctive role to play betwixt and between other forms of contemporary religious life, according to a recent sociological study, *Beyond Establishment: Protestant Identity in a Post-Protestant Age*.[49] After surveying the criticisms and problems of mainstream denominations, the authors conclude that denominations provide an alternative between the more authoritarian fundamentalist sects and the individualistic, mystical New Age groups.[50] Denominations help people fit into the local community while providing a relationship to the larger society.[51] Denominations can provide "communities of memory" that put people in touch with the ultimate religious worldview and that can provide a contemporary community worldview that enables them to live in continuity with the past and to engage modernity.[52]

A Return to Representative Government

Denominations must model not only a centrist way of believing but also a collaborative way of behaving. For example, Presbyterian polity is certainly not the only way a church can be governed. It may not even be the best way. But it has been the best way for Presbyterians. Presbyterians would do well to try to make it work, just as those in other communions would do well to utilize their own distinctive experience and expertise.

Mainstream Protestants are not interested in self-appointed, authoritarian leaders as sometimes appear in fundamentalism and Pentecostalism. They actually want representative government. Presbyterians do so by having congregations elect elders to a session. These sessions send some elders and all ministers as delegates to presbytery. Some delegates go from presbytery to synod. And every presbytery elects representative elders and ministers as commissioners to the General Assembly.

When Presbyterian-elected leaders are in these representative bodies, they are supposed to vote according to their consciences. But if they have been elected from the people, their consciences will be formed in a different way than if they had been appointed purely to represent some special interest group. That is the way it is supposed to work. Every leader should be elected and responsibly related to some larger community of people.

I believe that if denominational leaders had trusted the people and the process since the mid-1960s instead of managing matters to suit their liberal worldview, we might not be in such a mess now.[53] In their eagerness to accomplish an agenda of inclusivism, the liberal leadership of the Presbyterian and other mainline churches subverted their own rules of representative government. So-called elected leaders fill positions on our national councils and committees and task forces but were never elected. Generally they get these positions by being screened through a national nominating process. That process is built on the liberal worldview that the primary requisite for any church entity is being as inclusive as possible. As a result we get people in places of leadership who have not come up through the ranks. They have never been elected by anyone in a local congregation to any office. They are good people, but they are not a representative of the church but rather of some special interest that someone on a nominating committee thought should be highlighted.[54]

I am not arguing that we should be less inclusive. I am pleading that we be authentically inclusive. Instead of putting our energy and efforts into a cosmetic inclusivism that makes those with a liberal worldview feel better, let us put our money and our creativity, for example, into supporting racial ethnic leaders as leaders in their own congregations as well as in governing bodies. Let us not yank them out of their context and put them on some national committee so they can enter into dialogue with the liberal leadership. We should listen to local leaders and let them set their own agendas. Let us give them financial support and respect their judgment. They can teach us how to build up congregations and reach out to bring people to Jesus Christ and to the Presbyterian Church.[55] We might surprise ourselves and grow to have enough ethnic membership that its leaders would have genuine ecclesiastical power, not just the amount the Anglo leadership is willing to grant them. We need to heed our racial ethnic representatives at all governing body levels and not concentrate our efforts primarily on national advocacy structures.

There can and must be a mainstream church that fulfills the twofold task of rooting its members in the biblical tradition and of enabling them to cope with the modern world. Mainstream denominations can fulfill this role if they will meet the needs for spiritual nurture of their members and then motivate them to engage in service to the world through their collective governing bodies. This will require a worldview that is deeply aware of the centrality of the basic Christian story and that develops an appropriate theological elaboration of it consistent with denominational tradition. That religious and theological worldview can then be applied to create an ideological worldview that enables people to have a sense of belonging to an accepting group as well as an awareness of their distinctive individual identity in the world.

4 | Revivalism: What Is the Role of Experience in Religion?

> The gifts he gave were that some would be apostles, some
> prophets, some evangelists, some pastors and teachers, to
> equip the saints for the work of ministry, for building up
> the body of Christ.
>
> —*Ephesians 4:11–12*

FOCUS: Revivalism is deeply rooted in American church and community life. Many Americans believe that people and institutions can be changed for the good by spontaneous acts of the Spirit. In the 1990s, Presbyterians and other mainstream Protestants have been shaken by the assertion of the validity of personal experience as a theological norm. The experience of one's gender and the experience of one's sexual orientation, for some, vie with scripture and tradition as legitimate authorities in denominational decision making.

To understand how profound is this worldview we must review the defining influence of the colonial revivals that bound most early Americans together. The expectation of a direct intervention of the Spirit of God in our daily lives took newly influential form in America through the Pentecostal movement that emerged in the twentieth century. Evangelical movements, exemplified by the ministry of Billy Graham, have made the revival experience available to millions.

The last three decades have especially shown the power and the problems of experiential religion. A neo-Pentecostal charismatic movement penetrated mainstream Protestantism beginning in the 1960s. The 1970s and 1980s saw immense public attention given to the rise and fall of Pentecostal evangelists, especially Jim Bakker and Jimmy Swaggart. A charismatic leader with an eclectic blend of fundamentalist and Pentecostal theologies emerged on the national political scene in the person of Pat Robertson. All Americans, including those in the mainline churches, are inescapably influenced by these personalities and the movements they personify.

At the same time, more centrist evangelicalism has carried on the revivalist motif without being involved in the excesses associated with Pentecostalism or the reactionary character of fundamentalism. By tracing the diversification and development of evangelicalism since the 1970s, mainstream Christians can find potential allies who are theologically similar to fundamentalists but largely seek a centrist worldview with the majority of mainstream believers. We must certainly understand the power of the revivalist worldview motif if we are to develop a contemporary understanding of the role of religious experience in our lives.

The Contemporary Relevance of the Worldview Motif of Revivalism

A secularized form of the revivalism motif was the desire of Americans to make their personal experience normative. This was illustrated by the behavior of commissioners to the 1993 Presbyterian General Assembly. A former moderator of the General Assembly, Charles Hammond, referred to this phenomenon as the "Quakerization" of the Presbyterian Church.[1] Again and again people in representative committees and on the floor of the Assembly said, "Let's not worry about the *Book of Order* and *Robert's Rules of Order.* Let's just talk informally about this." The appeal was repeatedly to the speaker's individual experience.

Donald McCullough responded to the same phenomenon at the 1993 General Assembly, especially in the activities of the Representative Committee on Human Sexuality. He noted in the *Presbyterian Outlook* in September 1993 that "what 'moved' the committee most were the personal stories shared, the experiences of homosexuals and their families and friends. So when the committee recommended 'study and dialogue,' the emphasis was clearly upon dialogue—learning from one another's experiences." McCullough commented: "Guidance for faith and practice must come from God's Word, not from human experience; it's a one-way street and we ignore the flow of traffic at our own peril."[2] In October, the editor wrote: "Seldom have we received as many responses to an item in the

Outlook as Editor-at-Large Donald W. McCullough's column." Apparently most of the letters took McCullough to task for not giving a greater normative value to experience.[3]

The Historical Setting of Revivalism

The Great Awakening

Personal religious experience has always evoked highly diverse reactions from mainstream Protestants. A series of colonial revivals that took place from the 1720s to 1740s, commonly called the Great Awakening, were like the civil rights demonstrations, the campus disturbances, and the urban riots of the 1960s combined. Together these more recent events may approach, though certainly not surpass, the Great Awakening in its impact on national life.[4] Revivalism was a central worldview motif held in common by colonial Puritans. They did not bring it with them. It was an adaptation to their new environment.

The Awakening produced a revival of the Christian faith and reinforced the notion that America was God's chosen nation.[5] It also brought changes in the organization of society, political commitments, and communication techniques. It was the first truly American event in that it transcended colonial boundaries and denominational affiliations. It also evidenced the negative consequences that often were to accompany religious movements in America. Independent leaders sometimes set people against their pastors, polarized groups within the churches, and in some cases encouraged schism.

For example, a Dutch Reformed minister, Theodore Frelinghuysen, began a revival in Raritan, New Jersey. His Presbyterian neighbor, Gilbert Tennent, reinforced and spread it. Tennent's special and controversial contribution was his published sermon entitled "The Danger of an Unconverted Ministry." In 1740 he attacked some of his ministerial colleagues as "Pharisee-Teachers," "letter-learned," "dead dogs that can't bark."[6] For the most part the objects of his wrath were opponents of his father's Log College, an early Presbyterian apprentice-model ministerial training school.

But revival was not localized in the middle colonies. Jonathan Edwards preached a series of sermons on justification by faith, and revival broke out in New England. Most famous and of greatest effect in this revival was the ministry of the English itinerant evangelist George Whitefield. Whitefield was an Anglican minister closely associated with John Wesley. In 1740,

Whitefield made a tour through New England. He traveled 800 miles on horseback in 73 days. He preached 130 sermons and often addressed crowds of over 8,000 people. His tour has been called the "most sensational event in the history of American religion."[7]

Four consequences of the Great Awakening are important for our understanding of its impact on us. First, theologically, it spelled the end of English Puritanism and the beginning of American evangelical/mainstream Protestantism.[8] The core of this evangelical/mainstream view was not a theological system but a shared concern for personal religious experience and for the renewal of the church. It was not antiorthodox, or at first even anti-Calvinist. It simply stressed the unity of all Christians. Through the revivals four-fifths of all Christians in America now had a common experience and a common understanding of the Christian faith as a personal relationship with God.

Second, the denominational concept of the church blossomed.[9] From the time of Constantine in the fourth century until the American experiment, the state church was assumed—one religion for one nation. Both separatism and revivalism discounted the value of an established state church. Yet the revivals did not yield sects. A sect is exclusive, claiming it is the only true church. The revivals in the American context yielded denominations—particular expressions of the larger body of Christ, the church. The same Gilbert Tennent who was initially so harsh with those he considered nominal believers was later a strong proponent of an ecumenical denominationalism, arguing: "All societies who profess Christianity and retain the foundational principles thereof, notwithstanding their different denominations and diversity of sentiments in smaller things, are in reality but one Church of Christ, but several branches (more or less pure in minuter points) of one visible kingdom of the Messiah."[10]

Third, revivalism fostered what we now call parachurch institutions and movements that enhanced the role of the laity. Colleges were established. Schools and charitable projects for Native Americans, African Americans, and children of indentured servants were founded. Mission societies and Bible distribution societies were begun. Organizations for moral and social reform were created, the most memorable being those dedicated to the abolition of slavery and the emancipation of women.[11]

Fourth and finally, the revivals were "nothing less than the first stage of the American Revolution."[12] The revivals were indigenous mass movements that gave social cohesion to the colonies. They reinforced the notion that God had a special destiny for Americans. The revivals were democratizing. Authority no longer belonged to the elite by birth or by education. Anyone could preach, and if one drew a crowd, then one had authority. The most revolutionary consequence was that ordinary people discovered that they could defy the establishment (first in church and then in government) and get away with it! Revivalism led directly to the American Revolution.

Pentecostalism

Pentecostalism, a profoundly influential twentieth-century religious movement in America, was not at all conditioned by the struggle with modernity in the categories offered by liberalism and fundamentalism. Yet it has had a significant impact on the mainstream churches and evangelical movements. Pentecostalism emerged at the turn of the century. Its adherents were ordinary Christian believers who were not involved in the struggles over the shattered worldview of establishment evangelical/mainstream Protestantism.

These folk did not find their religious expression in intellectual categories derived from either revelation or culture. Rather they knew God in the immediate experience of the Holy Spirit in their lives. During the colonial period Anne Hutchinson and the Quakers had claimed this direct experience of the Spirit and had suffered for it.[13] Many more were to rejoice in and be reviled for this experiential approach to religion. The worldview motif of revivalism was central to their understanding of reality.

The Pentecostal movement has its ecclesiastical roots in the Wesleyan Holiness revival movement of the nineteenth century. Camp meeting evangelism, which began in Methodism, sometimes yielded independent churches and missions. These churches and missions were experience-centered, relying on the guidance of the Holy Spirit and desiring a sanctified, spiritually perfect life.[14]

Pentecostalism was rooted in four theological themes that it inherited from earlier American experiential religion: (1) Christ as Savior; (2) Christ as Baptizer with the Holy Spirit; (3) Christ as Healer; (4) Christ as Coming King. This fourfold gospel was present in the broad stream of American experiential religion in the late nineteenth century.[15]

But something new happened in 1900. The fourfold gospel did not become the "full gospel" for Pentecostals until another distinctive feature was added. "Speaking in tongues" became the "initial evidence" of the baptism of the Holy Spirit. A believer needed a physical demonstration of the indwelling presence of a personal God. From that charismatic experience, a distinctive religious movement was born.[16] From it grew denominations that by the end of the century would be among the fastest growing and most widely known in the world.

Pentecostalism began when Charles Parham, a Methodist revival preacher in the Holiness tradition, started a small Bible school in Topeka, Kansas, in October 1900.[17] At the Bethel Bible School he assigned his students to study what the Bible said regarding healing, conversion, and the second coming of Christ. The students found the concept of the "baptism with the Holy Spirit" the most controversial topic. Parham left to conduct revival meetings in Kansas City in December and encouraged his students independently to carry on their investigations. When Parham returned on December 31, 1900, all forty students had agreed that speaking in tongues was the incontrovertible evidence of baptism with the Holy Spirit.

At a midnight service on New Year's Eve, student Agnes Ozman asked others to lay their hands on her and pray that she be filled with the Holy Spirit. They did, and she began to speak what they took to be Chinese. She could speak no English for three days after the experience. Other students similarly received the "baptism" and spoke in what they believed were foreign languages.[18] This encouraged them to believe that they were on the brink of a missionary explosion. People without formal schooling could be missionaries by going to evangelize in whatever place the Spirit-given language was spoken. Such experience heightened their sense that they were living in the last days when the gospel would be preached everywhere just before Christ returned.[19]

Only in Texas in 1905 was the "full gospel" accepted by people in significant numbers. Parham then established a Bible school in Houston. There an African-American holiness preacher named William Seymour attended and accepted the new doctrine. An African-American woman from Los Angeles, Neely Terry, visited Texas and took the news of Spirit baptism back to her holiness mission. The congregation then invited Seymour to come to Los Angeles as their pastor.[20]

On April 1, 1906, Seymour preached to the group in Los Angeles on Acts 12. He was sent away from the little church because the congregation could not accept his connecting the baptism of the Holy Spirit to the gift of tongues. Seymour then moved to an unpretentious one-story house on Bonnie Brae Street in Los Angeles and continued to preach. There, on April 9, Seymour and others received the gift of tongues. Soon the news spread. Some white folks joined the African-American worshipers.[21] People began to be "overpowered" by the Spirit. They fell off their chairs and gave other manifestations of being possessed by the Spirit.

The group outgrew the Bonnie Brae house and moved to a deserted building that had been the Stevens African Methodist Episcopal Church at 312 Azusa Street in Los Angeles. The revival continued under Seymour's leadership from 1906 to 1913.[22] That series of meetings at the Apostolic Faith Mission (a name Seymour had borrowed from Parham) was of little interest to the white male Protestant establishment. It was remarkable, however, that in a day of racial segregation an African-American man was the pastor, and that in a time before women could vote, church leadership, including exhortation, was also provided by women. The members and officers were both white and black, and Hispanics and Asians also participated in the services.[23]

Pentecostals now refer to Azusa Street as the "American Jerusalem." Eighty percent of the early Pentecostal church founders trace their beginnings to this revival. Twenty Pentecostal denominations owe their origins to the activities at this place soon after the turn of the century.[24]

The Church of God in Christ, now a predominantly African-American denomination and the fastest growing denomination in the United States, was founded in 1907 after three men from Memphis visited the racially mixed Azusa Street meetings. They ordained both white and black pastors. In 1914, a group of white pastors formed the Assemblies of God, now the fastest growing predominantly white denomination in the United States.[25]

Holiness and Pentecostal groups made their witness felt in the larger society in the early twentieth century. Many theologically conservative and experientially oriented churches were involved in social ministry and social reform, although they could not tolerate the social gospel, the mainstream establishment's embrace of a liberal theory about social reform. The Salvation Army and its offshoot, the Volunteers of America, the Church of the Nazarene, the Christian and Missionary Alliance, and the Pentecostal Mission all acted on their theology of perfection in urban slums in defiance of inhumane powers in society. They lived and worked among the poor and people of color. They gave women leadership roles while the establishment churches were thoroughly male dominated.[26]

Despite the generally orthodox theology of Pentecostals and their opposition to the liberal social gospel, early twentieth-century fundamentalists did not want to be associated with Pentecostals.[27] For some fundamentalists, revivalism now entailed primarily a cognitive acceptance of the truths of scripture. They feared the potential for emotional excesses in personal experience.

Neo-Evangelicalism

Revivalism, which stressed a personal experience of God in Christ, had a resurgence of influence in non-Pentecostal conservative religion beginning in the 1940s with neo-evangelicalism. Some young fundamentalists became dissatisfied with the extreme sectarianism and militancy represented by persons like Carl McIntire. At the same time, these young conservatives were unwilling to have anything to do with the burgeoning neo-orthodoxy of the mainline denominations. Men like Harold John Ockenga, Edward John Carnell, Carl F. H. Henry, and Billy Graham exemplified a new generation of leaders who founded a host of new institutions and created a new movement that they dubbed neo-evangelicalism.

In 1941, McIntire and his followers accused the Federal Council of the Churches of Christ (FCCC) of doctrinal heresy and communist sympathy and, in opposition, formed the American Council of Christian Churches (ACCC).[28] One of the younger, less militant fundamentalists, Harold John Ockenga, led the formation of the National Association of Evangelicals (NAE) in 1942. It offered an alternative both to the FCCC and to McIntire's ACCC. Ockenga later described his position: "Doctrinally, the fundamentalists are right, and I wish to be always classified as one. In ecclesiology, I believe they are wrong and I cannot follow them."[29]

In a brilliant strategic move, Ockenga invited Pentecostal groups to join the NAE. McIntire's ACCC, representing the older fundamentalism, had opposed Pentecostal membership. Pentecostals themselves had been reluctant to affiliate with the FCCC because of its roots in liberal theology and the social gospel. After some struggles, several Pentecostal bodies, including the Assemblies of God, did join the NAE.

In 1948, Ockenga officially coined the term "neo-evangelicalism" in a convocation address at Fuller Theological Seminary, where he was president. Ockenga later summarized the distinctive position that he hoped that term would represent:

> Neo-evangelicalism differed from modernism in its acceptance of the supernatural and its emphasis on the fundamental doctrines of Scripture. It differed from Neo-orthodoxy in its emphasis upon the written word as inerrant, over against the Word of God which was above and different from the Scripture, but was manifested in Scripture. It differed from funda-

mentalism in its repudiation of separatism and its determination to engage itself in the theological dialogue of the day. It had a new emphasis upon the application of the gospel to the sociological, political, and economic areas of life.[30]

As defined by Ockenga, neo-evangelicalism was intended to reaffirm the theological viewpoint of fundamentalism but to repudiate fundamentalism's doctrine of the church and its social theory. George Marsden has stressed the struggle that the original Fuller faculty members had in breaking with their fundamentalist past.[31]

A member of Fuller Seminary's board of trustees was the evangelist Billy Graham. The worldview motif of revivalism has been given public prominence from the late 1940s until the present through Graham's evangelistic ministry. Just as the older evangelicalism had been an outgrowth of revivalism, so the neo-evangelical movement of the 1940s was given vitality and visibility by its association with the mass revivals conducted by Graham.

William Franklin Graham, Jr., had been raised in a devout, rural southern atmosphere. His parents were dairy farmers who belonged to the Associate Reformed Presbyterian Church. Graham had memorized the Westminster Shorter Catechism by the time he was twelve. He felt himself to be actually converted under the preaching of an itinerant evangelist named Mordecai F. Ham. After high school, Graham briefly attended Bob Jones College and graduated from Florida Bible Institute in 1940. He was ordained in the Southern Baptist Church. Graham went on to Wheaton College, where he majored in anthropology. He developed a literal interpretation of Genesis 1—11 and was confirmed in his opposition to Darwinism. While at Wheaton, Graham met and married Ruth Bell, whose parents had been Southern Presbyterian missionaries.[32]

Graham first pastored a Baptist church in Illinois. Then in 1945 he took a position as a traveling evangelist with Youth for Christ International (YFC). YFC was at that time a fundamentalist youth organization that had been created in part as a reaction to the liberalism of the YMCA. In 1947, Graham was chosen by William B. Riley, the founder of the World's Christian Fundamentals Association, to succeed Riley as president of his Bible college, Northwestern Schools, in Minneapolis, Minnesota. Graham soon felt too fettered by the demands of administration. In 1947 he also launched into a career as a traveling evangelist.[33]

Graham was not well known until he conducted a revival in Los Angeles in 1949. Just prior to this crusade, Graham had gone through a period of personal struggle regarding his approach to the Bible. A friend and fellow evangelist, Charles Templeton, had chided Graham for his literalistic interpretation of the Bible and predicted that Graham would not be successful unless he abandoned it.[34] One evening during a conference at Forest Home, California, Graham prayed: "O, God, I cannot prove certain things . . . but I accept this Book by faith as the Word of God."[35] He concluded that the Bible did not need to be defended as much as it needed to be proclaimed. Armed with confidence in an infallible Bible, Graham launched his Los Angeles crusade.

Several prominent personalities were converted in Graham's tent in Los Angeles. Then came the national publicity. William Randolph Hearst, head of the Hearst newspaper syndicate, sent out the message to his papers, "Puff Graham."[36] During the crusade, Graham met two evangelical Quakers, the parents of Richard Nixon. Soon thereafter, he met with Nixon in the Senate cafeteria. National attention followed.[37] President Harry Truman invited Graham to the Oval Office in 1949. After returning from a crusade in Seoul, Korea, in 1953, Graham counseled President-elect Eisenhower just prior to his inauguration. Together Graham and Eisenhower planned the establishment of the Annual Presidential Prayer Breakfast.[38]

Graham's personal respectability and national visibility gave neo-evangelicalism a positive public image. The Billy Graham Evangelistic Association (BGEA) that grew up around him provided a strong financial base. All this came together in the mid-1950s as Graham fused his organization and his revivalist ethos into the neo-evangelical movement. With the popularity of Billy Graham in the late 1940s, revivalism reemerged as a central focus of the neo-evangelical version of the evangelical/mainstream worldview.

The Recent Context of Conflicts over Revivalism

Since 1960 the worldview motif of revivalism has been reasserted in a number of influential new forms. The charismatic movement, a form of neo-Pentecostalism, has successfully penetrated the mainstream churches. The mirror image of that movement has been an attempt by traditional Pentecostals to become more culturally mainstream. At the same time, the mainstream churches have been thrown into turmoil by those representing the liberal/modernist worldview who insist on personal experience as a prime theological criterion.

Charismatics within the Mainline

On April 3, 1960, an Episcopal rector brought the Pentecostal experience of 1900 into the Protestant mainline establishment. The Reverend Dennis Bennett put aside his prepared sermon on that Sunday and told his twenty-six-hundred-member congregation at St. Mark's in Van Nuys, California, that he had received the "baptism in the Holy Spirit" and had spoken in tongues. Things went fairly well during the first service. But chaos erupted in the middle of the second service when an assistant pastor tore off his vestments and walked out declaring, "I can no longer work with this man!" Outside on the patio, one man stood on a chair and shouted, "Throw out the damn tongues speaker!" Charismatic members began witnessing to others present. A vestryman demanded that Bennett leave. During the third service, Bennett announced his resignation.

The ruckus at St. Mark's was picked up on the local television news. Then *Time* and *Newsweek* featured it. The media made the expression "charismatic renewal" a public matter. The expression originally came from the magazine *Trinity*, published by Jean Stone, a former parishioner of Dennis Bennett. It was generally preferred to the term "neo-Pentecostal," which was also used. "Charismatic renewal" indicates the occurrence of the distinctively Pentecostal phenomenon of baptism in the Holy Spirit but occurring in a nondenominational or mainstream Christian context.[39]

The majority of mainstream Protestant denominations took a stance of cautious openness toward the charismatic movement. Theological pluralism in mainstream churches did not yet fully extend to Pentecostalism. Many accepted the validity of Pentecostal experience in principle, but rejected the Pentecostal theology of a second baptism subsequent to conversion and the necessity of speaking in tongues. By the mid-1970s, charismatics within the Episcopal, Lutheran, Methodist, and Presbyterian denominations sponsored national conferences. All had organized denominational fellowships and newsletters, beginning with the Presbyterian Charismatic Communion in 1966.[40]

The Rise and Fall of New Right Experiential Religion

Jimmy Swaggart and Jim Bakker

Two Assemblies of God ministers became media celebrities in the mid-1980s. Both believed in the sixteen "fundamental truths" of their denomination, including salvation in Jesus Christ, baptism by immersion, faith healing, speaking in tongues, and the premillennial return of Christ.[41] But their cultural views diverged widely from one another.

When founded in 1914, the Assemblies of God was a countercultural movement. Most of its members came from the lower socioeconomic classes. They were strongly influenced by the Holiness movement, which emphasized separation from the world and personal sanctification. A.G.'s early adherents were convinced that Christ was returning soon and that the charismatic gifts were signs of the end times. Personal evangelism and separation from the world were logical extensions of these eschatological expectations.[42] Jimmy Swaggart represented the worldview of this early, blue-collar Pentecostalism. Martin Marty called Swaggart a "slick version of what the AG *was*" who had built an empire by "dealing with the blue-collar image."[43]

In the 1970s and 1980s, a gradual transformation occurred in the worldview of some in the Assemblies of God. For many, hard work had been rewarded by prosperity, and they had become middle class. After the rise of the charismatic movement in the 1960s, Assemblies of God members discovered fellow believers with similar experiences of the "baptism in the Holy Spirit." Yet these were mostly middle- and upper-class people in the mainline denominations who felt no need to separate from the world.[44]

One wing of the Assemblies of God decided that God had blessings to give people now, in this world. Material prosperity and self-fulfillment became values, and a health- and wealth-theology developed.[45] Jim Bakker represented this new style in the Assemblies of God. Bakker adopted the casual southern California style of dress and a mellow and materialistic ethic. His announced goal was to help the Assemblies of God move beyond "separation" thinking and "legalism." He dropped Jimmy Swaggart's television program from the Praise the Lord (PTL) network because of its "narrowness."[46]

The Assemblies of God denomination officially allowed both Swaggart's and Bakker's approaches to religion and life. As a denomination, precise theological and ethical reflection were deemphasized in favor of individual freedom and denominational unity.[47] The Pentecostal religious experience was primary; all other matters were less important.

Some fundamentalists wanted to distance themselves from other Pentecostal and charismatic conservatives. On September 17, 1986, Jerry Falwell announced that he was withdrawing from active campaigning for candidates for political office. Falwell declared: "I will no longer allow in my pulpit anything but a minuscule amount of politics. We are going back to where we were before [the] Moral Majority."[48] Just prior to Falwell's withdrawal statement, Pat Robertson, founder and president of the Christian Broadcasting Network (CBN), announced that he was poised to run for president of the United States.[49] The reasons that Falwell, a fundamentalist, was not ready to support Robertson, a charismatic, were rooted not only in personalities and struggles for power but in divergent worldviews. Two years into Reagan's second term in office, the media and thus the public suddenly became aware of the potential power of Pentecostal and charismatic Christians.

Pat Robertson

Robertson's theology was an eclectic blend of most of the conservative positions influential in the 1980s. His best-selling 1982 book, *The Secret Kingdom,* could be used as a primer on Reconstructionist thought.[50] (I discuss this influential movement in chapter 7.) Six or seven Reconstructionist books were used as texts in the CBN graduate schools.[51] Robertson's 1986 book, *America's Dates with Destiny,* was an interpretation of American history in the style of Francis Schaeffer.[52]

Robertson accepted fundamentalist theology in its dispensational form. He followed popular dispensational author Hal Lindsey's scenario of the last days; for example, he believed that the biblical book of Ezekiel predicted that Russia would invade Israel. In his view, the European Common Market is the ten-nation confederacy that is a forerunner of the antichrist prophesied in the book of Daniel. The mark of the beast would be inflicted on people by the new generation of "smart card" credit cards used for international bank transfers.[53]

Robertson was also a charismatic who participated in more traditional Pentecostal activities, such as speaking in tongues, having visions, prophesying, and healing the sick. He claimed to have predicted the 1969 stock market crash. He believed that Hurricane Gloria was driven away from the coast of Virginia Beach in October of 1985 because of his prayers.[54] His television prayers were credited with healing bones, reversing cancers, and relieving depressions.[55] Robertson also predicted financial chaos in 1980 and nuclear war in 1982. When neither occurred, he discontinued the newsletter that carried these prophecies.[56]

With all this background, as a political candidate in 1985 Robertson told *Newsweek* that as president his foreign and domestic policies "would be guided by a worldview derived from the Bible."[57] The "biblical" world-view that Robertson espoused sounded much like the early American evangelical/mainstream worldview in its 1980s fundamentalist form, but with a charismatic twist.

THE FALL FROM PROMINENCE OF PENTECOSTAL RELIGION

Early in 1988, newswriters dubbed the drama they had been assiduously covering "Pearly Gate" and "Holy Wars," and nicknamed PTL, "Pass the Loot."[58] Jim Bakker was rated the least trustworthy person in America in a *People* magazine poll, with Jimmy Swaggart coming in second.[59] All the televangelists lost money, public confidence, and followers.[60] The Assemblies of God responsibly disciplined both their ministers through due process. Both Bakker and Swaggart responded by cutting their ties to the denomination. Behind the glitter from the gutter was a serious issue of worldviews that had been shown to conflict with one another and to be inadequate to guide those who held them.

Tensions between the Right and Left Regarding Revivalism

The Resurgence of Religious Experience on the Right

A Pentecostal/charismatic worldview continues to exercise widespread influence through the Pentecostal denominations and within the mainstream churches. Pentecostals and charismatics emphasize a personal experience of God through the Holy Spirit. Many Americans greatly desire that experience. Pentecostal denominations both black (Church of God in Christ) and white (Assemblies of God) are the fastest growing Protestant bodies in the United States. Worldwide, Pentecostalism is the fastest growing form of Protestantism, with 450 million adherents.[61] In 1994, the leaders of the 46-year-old Pentecostal Fellowship of North America, an all-white association of Pentecostal denominations, in repentance voted to disband and urged its members to join a new multiracial Pentecostal association. The new organization, the Pentecostal Churches of North America, encompasses twenty-five denominations and an estimated fifteen million members.[62]

Despite the negative publicity and Bakker's now completed prison term, the Pentecostal and charismatic televangelists continue to have large audiences and wide influence.[63] They preach and promote the possibility of an immediate experience of God in people's lives. The belief that God works through the immediate experience of revival is still deeply embedded in the worldview of many Americans.

Pat Robertson continues to be an important religious and political figure. The Christian Coalition, which grew out of his 1988 presidential campaign, is now the major force on the Religious Right. It has 1.5 million national members in hundreds of local chapters. They used forty thousand churches to distribute election literature to over forty million voters.[64] An estimated 20 percent of the delegates to the Republican Party Convention in 1992 were from the Religious Right.[65] Robertson followers control many state party caucuses.[66] His television program *The 700 Club* on his CBN reaches an estimated one million viewers daily. He is Chancellor of Regent University, with graduate schools of law, business, education, government, counseling, divinity, and communications. Robertson's American Center for Law and Justice (ACLJ) began with a budget of $3 million and eleven full-time attorneys. As a public interest law firm it provides legal counsel for right-wing Christian causes, including arguing before the U.S. Supreme Court.[67] His social service and mission outreach are conducted through Operation Blessing and the Association of Mission Services. Given his past record, it can be assumed that Robertson's fundamentalist/charismatic worldview will not only be promulgated but acted upon in increasingly large areas of the public arena.

Reimagining the Role of Experience on the Left

In the fall of 1993, an appeal to feminist religious experience catapulted many mainline denominations into their worst internal crisis in two decades. The intent of the Re-Imagining Conference in Minneapolis was to bring women theologians together from around the world to re-flect on and re-imagine the import and application of theology in our time. Some 2,000 persons from 32 denominations, 49 states, and 27 countries attended, among whom were 409 Presbyterian women and men.

Reports of the conference created a firestorm in some mainstream churches. Some sources, especially the independent newspaper *Presbyterian Layman,* alleged that the term "Sophia," a Greek Old Testament word for "wisdom," had been used in ways that implied worship of a goddess distinctly different from the one triune God.[68] By contrast, many who attended the conference found it to be wonderfully enriching, spiritually deepening, and profoundly Christian. They could not comprehend the reaction of the critics.

In part, reaction to the Re-Imagining Conference was simply a catalyst that released long-standing and deep-seated concerns from within the Presbyterian Church and other mainstream denominations. Protests were heard in the United Methodist, the Evangelical Lutheran Church in America, and the American Baptist Church.[69] Critics and supporters of the Re-Imagining Conference often had quite opposite views of the role of experience in religion. The conference brought the latent conflict between worldviews to the surface. One feminist commentator described it as "another chapter in this century's battle of the evangelical right vs. the liberal pluralists."[70] Perhaps the deepest cause for the conflict was the appeal of conference speakers to feminist *experience* rather than to scripture, creeds, or church as their authority. A Minneapolis reporter, Martha Sawyer Allen, commented: "They're not just talking about new language that's gender-neutral or new images for experiencing Christianity. They've gone beyond that to find new ways to experience human understanding of the divine. They are talking about women's daily experiences of the divine in every culture as central to theology today. They are reshaping Christian understanding of such elemental issues as suffering and lifting up the voices of ordinary people as foundations of theology."[71] A sympathetic commentator noted that "at the Re-Imagining Conference, the published liturgies certainly did affirm multiple and multicultural dimensions of female experience."[72]

Especially troubling to many was the appeal to women's sexual experience. For some presenters at the conference, sexual experience appeared to be revelatory. Rita Nakashima Brock, author of *Journeys by Heart: A Christology of Erotic Power,* asked those assembled, "What images will open our eyes so clouded by patriarchal ideas and images? . . . What will enable us to touch, to smell, to see and hear the presence of God.?"[73] Roman Catholic feminist Mary Hunt declared: "I picture friends, not families, basking in the pleasures we deserve because our bodies are holy and our sexuality is part of creation's available riches."[74] Presbyterian Jane Spahr told conference attenders that her theology is primarily informed by "making love to Coni," her lesbian partner. She then challenged the church: "Sexuality and spirituality have to come together, and church, we're going to teach you!"[75] A high point of the conference for some, and most offensive to others, was the "milk and honey" ritual, a liturgy that appeared to function as an alternative for the Lord's Supper.[76] In the liturgy women recited, "Our maker, Sophia, we are women in your image, with the hot blood of our wombs we give form to new life . . . with nectar between our thighs we invite a lover . . . with our warm body fluids we remind the world of its pleasures and sensations . . . with the honey of wisdom in our mouths we prophesy a full humanity to all the peoples."[77]

While the liberal Protestant churches of the mainline had successfully insulated themselves from the influence of Pentecostalism and had co-opted and contained the charismatics, they now were torn by the assertion of authority in the nontraditional experiences of the divine by women.

A Response to the Re-Imagining Conference

The PC(USA) and other mainstream denominations did not split in 1994 over the Re-Imagining Conference for several reasons. A principal reason was that the 1994 PC(USA) General Assembly began with an unprecedented "United Call to Prayer" for a full day not only in Wichita but throughout the denomination. Research has demonstrated that if religious people of differing views gather to discuss their differences, they will become more angry with one another. There is one exception to that rule: If you can get them to pray with one another the anger can turn to openness. This kind of shared personal experience of God can be a powerful unifying force.[78]

I experienced the remarkable effects of that pre-Assembly prayer meeting in Wichita. I sat in small groups with people as diverse as one of the chief critics of the Re-Imagining Conference and a General Assembly staff person from Louisville who had attended the conference and felt very criticized. We prayed with and for each other. Then one adversary said to the other: "I need to ask your forgiveness. I have said many harsh things about you behind your back. I still think them, but I need to tell you to your face." And they talked. That prayer meeting set a context of common commitment and willingness to be open to one another that the Spirit used in remarkable ways.

The theme of the 1994 General Assembly was: Theology matters! The church can be unified and at peace only when there is a common commitment to the apostolic rule of faith. So the Assembly indicated that some boundaries must be respected.

The Assembly further recognized that the church can be whole only when it also embraces the diverse experiences of its members. Commissioners to the Wichita General Assembly looked possible fragmentation in the face and opted instead for faithfulness to scripture, confessional standards, and an open, honest, and fair Presbyterian process that included listening to and valuing one another's experiences.

We waited for seven days in Wichita while the committee dealing with the Re-Imagining Conference listened to overture advocates, theological specialists, and 102 other Presbyterians in open hearing. Then they spent a day talking to each other, these sixty randomly selected, representative Presbyterian commissioners from all over the country. They spent another day writing. And on the next to the last day of the Assembly they brought a ten-page report to the floor. It did not call for an investigation or for disciplining staff. Instead it described a "theological crisis" and offered a theological solution.

In addition to making a strong confessional affirmation, the committee called for theological convocations to be held in connection with subsequent General Assemblies and repeated throughout the church. It also honored the experiences of a multitude of diverse Presbyterians. It affirmed the importance of women's voices in doing theology. It recognized God's gift of freedom of conscience and the necessity of exercising that freedom within certain boundaries. And it asked all Presbyterians to "accept apologies offered and to practice forgiveness, acceptance, understanding, and forbearance."

When the report came to the floor of the Assembly no one was sure what would happen. Then speaker after speaker asked that the document be accepted as a whole, without amendment. At the Assembly, commissioners hold up a green card if they want to speak for a motion and a red card if they want to speak against it. For an hour only green cards were raised. Then the vote was taken. It was a dramatic moment. When the electronic tally appeared on the huge television screens it showed a 98.9 percent affirmation of this balanced declaration on the Re-Imagining Conference that avoided none of the issues but sought to begin the process of healing. The presiding officers of the Assembly openly wept with amazement and joy while commissioners embraced and sang hymns. I had attended twenty-one General Assemblies and I have never seen anything to match the depth of relief and reconciliation. It was as close to a Presbyterian revival meeting as I have ever experienced.

When future histories of American Presbyterianism are written, the General Assembly of 1994 may be seen as a bracket closing the period of unrestricted theological pluralism that has existed for over sixty years. We cannot say that anyone may simply follow his or her own experience. We must now regain the balance of the New Side/Old Side Reunion of 1758, which affirmed that we must be able both to testify to our personal experience of religion *and* to be committed to our confessional heritage.

Presbyterians can now make a new beginning in elaborating a contemporary Reformed theology of the center. That is a task for us all. We have helps. We have the Apostles' and the Nicene Creeds, the new Brief Statement of Faith from 1991, and all the documents in our *Book of Confessions*. And we have the rich resources of experience of multitudes of devout Presbyterians. Revivalism as an energizing emphasis on personal experience, within the context of a Reformed confessional structure, has great promise for keeping the church vital and growing.

Religious Experience as Stimulus to Church Growth

Although the Re-Imagining Conference serves as an important illustration, the deeper issue is the reassertion of a liberal/modernist worldview based on experience. Another representation of this worldview is expounded in *Rerouting the Protestant Mainstream: Sources of Growth and Opportunities for Change* by sociologists C. Kirk Hadaway and David A. Roozen. They argue that the source of mainstream renewal lies in the classical liberal commitment to religious *experience*.[79] Their examples of successful, growing churches are those which are "unapologetically liberal and heavily involved in community ministry, with a clear focus on social justice."[80] In addition to justice ministries such churches are noted for deep, meaningful worship experience, which creates a spiritually oriented mainstream church.[81] This is not an appeal to mere pragmatism, giving people what they want. For these authors the answers to questions about reality and definitions of truth are not found in "blind faith, religious tradition, the Word of God, or cold rationality," but are "embedded in experience."[82]

The chief structural flaw in Hadaway and Roozen's argument is the assumption of a false dichotomy. They assume that there are only two ideological worldview choices: a classical liberal/modernist worldview and what they refer to as an evangelical "alternative worldview," for which Rush Limbaugh is treated as an appropriate spokesperson.[83] The 75 percent in the mainstream middle, seeking a balance between the extremes, is ignored.

Creating a Contemporary Centrist Worldview of Revivalism and the Role of Experience in Religion

Creating a Contemporary Evangelical/Mainstream Worldview

When evangelicalism is freed from its bondage to the fundamentalist offshoot of 1940s neo-evangelicalism, it may be possible to discover much commonality among mainstream and nonmainstream evangelical believers. The only definition of evangelicalism that fits all cases is a simple threefold one.

An evangelical is someone who: (1) has a personal relationship to God through Jesus Christ, (2) accepts the authority of the Bible, and (3) wants to share this faith with others. To take away any of those assertions would make it difficult to apply the concept of evangelical to the remainder. To add to these three simple propositions would begin to define fundamentalism or some kind of denomination. This threefold definition would fit most colonial participants in the Great Awakening. It would also fit most contemporary committed mainstream Protestants, including most Presbyterians. When "evangelical" is defined in this simple way the notion of holding to an evangelical revivalism as an aspect of a contemporary worldview could be acceptable to mainstream Protestants.

Evangelicals find themselves in the middle of the spectrum on the worldview motif of revivalism. The appeal to a personal experience of God is now diversely articulated. The general evangelical milieu seems able to hold personal experience and the Christian tradition founded on scripture in some acceptable balance. Evangelicals are found in significant numbers in the congregations of mainstream Protestantism.

As the evangelical movement has become more diverse and thus distanced itself from its fundamentalist roots, its affinities with the mainstream become more apparent. Indeed, Martin Marty contends that social and collective behaviors give impressive evidence concerning the differences between fundamentalists and evangelicals regardless of their nominal doctrinal similarities.[84] He argues that "evangelicals often show more similarities with and affinities to mainstream Protestants, with whom they disagree more openly on the cognitive level but with whom they have more profound similarities so far as world views are concerned."[85]

Reflections on Revivalism and Experience

The revivalist motif in early America was balanced by the creation of denominational bureaucracies. Revivalists tended to behave as if all positive change in persons and society came spontaneously. The denominations, beginning in the late nineteenth century, preferred that all values would proceed from centralized control. In the 1980s the worst excesses of these two views were identified with the fundamentalist televangelists on the one side and the denominational bureaucracies as regulatory agencies on the other. Unfettered individuals and unresponsive structures made caricatures of fundamentalist movements and liberal denominations. In defiance of both the evangelical/mainstream motif of revivalism and its liberal/modernist countermotif of denominational control, the last several decades have seen appeals to experience that are difficult to classify in a Christian context. The question of what a mainstream centrist worldview would look like has become even more urgent.

A contemporary, creative centrist response would be a church that encouraged vital personal religious experience in a communal context that included the experience of people with God recorded in scripture and the accumulated interpretive experience of the church's confessional tradition. Individual conversion must be coupled with nurturing community. Private prayer must be paired with public service. Small groups to share experience are important and small groups to study scripture are vital. The local congregation would be the focus of such activity, but its horizons would be broadened and its piety deepened by interaction with other congregations networked through governing bodies. Scripture would provide normative revelation, and human experience would illumine and provide occasions for reexamining scripture's message.

5 Common Sense: How Do We Interpret Scripture?

We must no longer be children, tossed to and fro and
blown about by every wind of doctrine, by people's
trickery, by their craftiness in deceitful scheming. But
speaking the truth in love, we must grow up in every way
into him who is the head, into Christ, from whom the
whole body, joined and knit together by every ligament
with which it is equipped, as each part is working
properly, promotes the body's growth in building itself up
in love.

—*Ephesians 4:14–16*

FOCUS: Conflicts between conservatives who claim absolute, objective
knowledge based on the Bible and liberals who argue that a relative, subjective perspective is all that is available are all too familiar. We can better understand the persistence and power of these points of view by examining their genesis in American culture.

The claim to know reality objectively is a form of naïve realism that is
solidly entrenched in American religious life. That democratizing and em-
powering worldview appeared as Scottish Common Sense philosophy in
the eighteenth century. It influenced American colleges and universities at
the time they were being formed. It convinced Americans that everyone
could understand the world and that everyone could interpret the Bible.
A majority of Americans shared this view until the mid-nineteenth century when the Civil War and the influence of Darwin broke up this relatively homogeneous way of looking at life.

Liberalism or modernism is an alternative worldview that came out of
that crisis in the 1860s. The extreme extension of it in our day is a critical
relativism that denies the possibility of any objective or certain knowledge.
The conflict between conservative common sense and liberal relativism

focused on how people interpreted the Bible. From the 1890s through the 1920s mainstream Americans were caught up in this debate, known as the fundamentalist-modernist conflict. The heresy case of Charles Briggs illustrates the struggle in ways that enable us to identify the players and define the issues. The assertion of biblical inerrancy, which continues to trouble the mainstream church, developed during this period.

In the 1940s and 1950s mainstream American churches had a respite from conflict, because of the pervasive influence of two new theological forces: neo-orthodoxy, represented by Karl Barth in Europe, and Christian realism, represented by Reinhold Niebuhr in the United States. These movements presented working alternatives to the unresolved conflict of the 1920s. Neither neo-orthodoxy nor Christian realism directly addressed the basic issues of the conflict, however. Therefore, despite neo-orthodoxy's having been institutionalized in the United Presbyterian Confession of 1967, when the leaders of these were no longer active all the old issues surfaced again in neo-fundamentalism and a variety of liberal alternatives.

Mainstream Protestants will have no peace until we come to grips with fundamental issues of how we know the truth and how we interpret the scriptures. Common sense naïve realism is often pitted against critical modernism. A centrist alternative of critical realism must be clarified and utilized if we are to have an adequate mainstream method of knowing. Presbyterians do have a little-known centrist policy regarding the interpretation of the Bible that is rooted in their confessional tradition and that could be fruitful in dealing with contemporary conflicts.

The Contemporary Relevance of the Worldview Motif of Common Sense

Critical Modernism

The Presbyterian Church and most mainstream denominations were dominated by a scholastic fundamentalism based on Common Sense realism from the mid-nineteenth century until the early 1930s or 1940s. Since then, the mainstream denominations, regardless of their academic theological orientation, have held a worldview which theologian Edward Farley calls "critical modernism." Farley defines critical modernism as "an openness to the various discoveries, sciences, and criteria that have arisen with modernity and . . . the task of making positive use of these in the interpretation and understanding of the Christian gospel." He distinguishes this *critical* modernism from *secular* or *cultural* modernism, which tends "to displace the distinctive witness of the gospel with secular or cultural contents."[1]

Farley believes that critical modernism is "the genius of the Presbyterian heritage."[2] It came to full flower after the conclusion of the fundamentalist-modernist conflict in the 1920s. Now its fruits can be described in six questions, all of which he believes the Presbyterian Church, or at least its bureaucratic and theological leaders, would answer in the affirmative. (1) Are the Calvinist theology and theological system modifiable? (2) Are the confessions and creeds that express our corporate faith relative, fallible, and revisable? (3) Is a thorough-going historical approach to the Bible proper, useful, even necessary for its interpretation? (4) Is the gospel, and theological truth, part of and consistent with the larger truth of the world that the sciences, philosophy, and the humanities attempt to discern? (5) Is the Christian church a pluralism of communities that are called to cooperate with and respect each other and even to celebrate each other's differences? (6) Is the Christian gospel social in character?[3]

None of these issues is currently open to debate, according to Farley.[4] Their best official expression is in the Confession of 1967.[5] These convictions are really part of one conviction, according to Farley: "the refusal to make anything human and historical a timeless absolute, dwelling above the flow of contexts and situations."[6]

Farley acknowledges the loss of Presbyterian and mainstream young people to secularity. He also admits that one factor which in part accounts for this loss is the mainstream churches' "critical modernism, and a mood that prevents them from pressing religion on their young in authoritarian ways."[7] For him, however, it is "almost inconceivable" that the youth would be more attracted if the churches became "narrowly denominational, unecumenical, indifferent to systemic social evils, pushing creation science and inerrant scriptures."[8] Farley's characterizations of the alternatives makes clear that for him, as for many mainstream theologians, the only alternatives are a liberal worldview that stresses the early American counterthemes or a fundamentalist worldview that has narrowed and rigidified the themes of the early American evangelical/mainstream worldview, which have already been discussed.

The Historical Setting of Common Sense

Scottish Common Sense Philosophy

An early American adaptation to Enlightenment rationalism was the adoption of Scottish Common Sense philosophy. This approach was an ideal cultural response because it purported to reject skeptical rationalism by demonstrating that the Christian faith supplied a superior form of rationality.

The reigning philosophy in most American colleges for the first century of their existence was Scottish Common Sense, or Scottish realism. It had been popular in Scotland when American educational institutions were being formed and was naturally incorporated into the curriculum. This philosophy enabled Americans to have supreme confidence that they would avoid the intellectual confusion of their European predecessors.

To understand this phenomenon we should review the eighteenth century in Great Britain when the best philosophical minds set themselves to know all things with certainty based on the information received by their five senses alone. According to John Locke, the mind contains ideas caused by sense experiences, which in turn were caused by the material world. George Berkeley, an Irish bishop, was appalled by the notion that all our ideas came ultimately from matter. Berkeley substituted God as the source of our sense experience; thus, in his view, he saved religion while continuing to treat sense experience as valid knowledge. By the end of the century, the Scottish philosopher David Hume acknowledged that all we know for certain, on the basis of sense experience alone, is that we are having sensations. One hundred years of philosophical concentration on the senses resulted in skepticism.[9]

Thomas Reid (1710–1796), a Presbyterian minister in Scotland, was skeptical of Hume's findings. It is said that Reid's sermons were so boring that his uncle had to stand at the foot of the pulpit with a drawn sword to keep Reid's parishioners from dragging him out of the church. Fortunately for Reid, and for the congregation, he was also a brilliant mathematician. So, to the benefit of all, he became professor of mathematics first at King's College, Aberdeen, and thereafter at the University of Glasgow. In those days mathematics and philosophy were in the same department. Reid was soon teaching moral philosophy and devising a way to refute Hume.

Instead of demonstrating that Hume was incorrect, Reid took a more direct approach to solving the problem of knowing. He decided simply to assume that his senses were completely reliable. He further assumed that through his senses he knew objects in the world directly, accurately, essentially. If one asked Reid how he knew that this was so, he would reply that he had an intuition in his heart that his senses brought the essential reality of objects directly into his mind. Why not assume it, since that was the "common sense" of all humanity? Common Sense took Scotland by storm.[10]

Early American Philosophy

Scottish Common Sense was the reigning philosophy in America at the time of the Revolution and for nearly a century thereafter. Thomas Reid and John Locke were the philosophers most important to the country's founders.[11] These two philosophers had differing concepts of the process of knowing. Locke contended that what we knew in our minds were ideas that came from our sense experience of the real world. Reid eliminated these intermediary ideas, arguing that people did not need to worry about whether their ideas corresponded to reality. The mind grasped reality directly, with no intermediary, according to common sense.

This Common Sense doctrine appeared to provide a basis for democracy. As Thomas Jefferson, who read the Scottish philosophers, recognized, this view made everyone equal.[12] It also contributed to the strong American sense of religious individualism. It meant that everyone could read the Bible and know exactly what it meant without needing the interpretation of an authoritative church.[13] Since all persons knew the phenomena of nature and the facts of scripture directly, true science and true religion would always agree.[14]

One notable entry point of Scottish Common Sense philosophy into the American mainstream was through the influence and curricula of two Presbyterian schools in Princeton, New Jersey. John Witherspoon of Edinburgh was enticed by Benjamin Rush and others to accept the presidency of the College of New Jersey (later Princeton University) in 1768. Witherspoon became crucial to the spread of Scottish Common Sense realism in the new nation. He trained dozens of thinkers who would be influential for the new nation, including James Madison and Aaron Burr. Invariably, the Scottish philosophy, including its moral precepts, dominated Witherspoon's "capstone" course, which all seniors had to take.[15]

One of Witherspoon's students, William Graham, became the tutor of Archibald Alexander. Alexander, in turn, was appointed in 1812 by the Presbyterian General Assembly to found a theological seminary distinct from the college at Princeton. With Samuel Miller, a scholarly pastor from New York, Alexander fashioned the curriculum at the new Princeton Theological Seminary around the confessional theology of the post-Reformation era. The Swiss scholastic Francis Turretin's works were among the earliest textbooks. This theological tradition was supported with the insights and methods of Scottish Common Sense realism.

Miller called Scottish Common Sense the "tribunal paramount to all the subtleties of philosophy."[16] In his popular work *The Evidence of the Christian Religion,* Alexander sought to demonstrate that Christianity was eminently rational and readily systematic. Alexander hoped to beat the Deists, skeptics, and unbelievers at their own game, and Scottish Common Sense philosophy was his handiest weapon. By midcentury Alexander had trained more than eleven hundred students, and the famed *Princeton Review* spread this "Princeton Theology."

Alexander added experiential emphases through Sunday evening worship services, first in his home and later on the campus. For Alexander, learning and piety were complementary and equally valid. They were never in conflict nor were they fully integrated. In the epilogue to *Facing the Enlightenment and Pietism: Archibald Alexander and the Founding of Princeton Theological Seminary,* Lefferts Loetscher, the Princeton Seminary historian of Presbyterianism, commented: "These two great forces of the era [Enlightenment and Pietism], antithetical in so many ways, yet had strange parallels. Both had a tendency to weaken the authority of the group and to strengthen the authority of the individual."[17] According to Loetscher, the Enlightenment contributed to individualism by its appeal to the individual's critical reason. Pietism enhanced individualism by its emphasis on the individual's experience of conversion and of divinely illuminated conscience. Loetscher observed that these twin forces were both present in the Reformed faith, especially in its expression in seventeenth-century Puritanism.

Thus the melding of the perspectives of Puritanism with those of the Enlightenment should not surprise us. Perhaps they had much in common from the start. It would be difficult to separate the Puritan commitment to religious certainty from the Enlightenment confidence in rational certainty either in Alexander or in the early-nineteenth-century evangelical/mainstream generally. Alexander and his contemporaries would probably have been surprised had the issue been raised.

During the first half of the nineteenth century, American intellectuals were so influenced by the Scottish school that Common Sense philosophy became virtually the common language of philosophical discourse in the young republic. Scottish Common Sense philosophy was often linked with what was popularly called the "Baconian Method." Francis Bacon's name and the notion of induction from facts obvious to the senses was attached to every area of life and added authority to it. Bacon, the early empirical scientist, was also viewed as the exemplar of Protestant piety. Between 1800 and 1860 the majority of scientists were Christians and eager to demonstrate that Newtonian/Baconian science supported religious belief. James Dwight Dana, editor of the *American Journal of Science,* wrote that "almost all works on science in our language, endeavor to uphold the Sacred Word."[18]

Just as the scientists were concerned to show their commitment to religion, the theologians were equally concerned to demonstrate their use of scientific method. In his *Systematic Theology,* published in 1871 but embodying his lectures prior to 1860, Charles Hodge of Princeton Seminary declared: "The Bible is to the theologian what nature is to the man of science. It is his store-house of facts; and his method of ascertaining what the Bible teaches, is the same as that which the natural philosopher adopts to ascertain what nature teaches."[19] Pre–Civil War scientists and theologians were engaged in a quest for certainty and order. They thought certainty could be derived from a Common Sense harmonization of all "facts." After midcentury, some of the "facts" appeared to be very different from what they had been. The publication of Darwin's *On the Origin of Species* in 1859 caused most scientists to abandon a static, Newtonian model of the world for a dynamic, developmental model. Some leading theologians clung to Scottish Common Sense and could not understand the new science. They then turned against the scientists and accused them of being not truly scientific—in a Scottish realist sense.

Darwin's theory of evolution was a catalyst that hastened the breakdown of the intellectual consensus in the United States predicated on the evangelical/mainstream worldview. In this period of disruption, some people turned to the countermotifs of the early American worldview and developed a new perspective on reality called liberalism.

Liberalism

Liberalism began as an attitude, an outlook, a mode of thinking.[20] When fully articulated, it became a worldview in competition with and attempting to supplant the main themes of the evangelical/mainstream worldview. American liberalism was first identified and consciously held as a theological position early in the nineteenth century. The Unitarians fused its main premises into expression as a denomination. By the late nineteenth century, however, when some Unitarians were moving "beyond Christianity," the basic ideas of liberalism had taken firm root in the mainstream establishment Protestant denominations.[21]

Liberal ideas constituted a theological perspective sharply at odds with traditional or orthodox Protestantism. Nineteenth-century liberalism was built around at least four persistent ideas. Each was a contrast to traditional, orthodox Christianity. First was immanence. God was not transcendent, above and outside the world. God was known *within* nature and human nature.[22] Second was optimism. Humans were not corrupt and incapable of doing good. Humans could join with God in improving themselves and the world.[23] Third was incarnation. The most important doctrine of traditional Christianity was that the word of God had become flesh in Jesus Christ. For liberalism, however, the incarnation meant that God entered all human personality and the natural world itself. All creation was precious and of ultimate value. Liberalism also centered on human experience rather than the biblical word.[24] Fourth was good works. More important than the traditional emphasis on doctrines were deeds, individual and collective, which contributed to improving persons, their institutions, and their environment.[25] All four ideas were expressions of the liberal rejection of dualism. Liberals wished to overcome what they viewed as artificial distinctions between revelation and reason, religion and culture, the sacred and the secular. God was in, and could be known in, all of life.[26]

"Modernists" became a term applied to people who were liberal or progressive in the religious realm. Liberals conceived of themselves as agents of change who wanted to modernize religion so that it would be acceptable to modern, highly educated people in the contemporary culture.[27] The new sciences, which developed a distinctly modern conception of the world and our human place in it, compelled some theologians to reshape the Christian faith. At this point "liberalism" and "modernism" became roughly equivalent terms.[28]

The evangelical/mainstream worldview was repudiated by liberals or modernists, who rejected a worldview predicated on particularities. They no longer believed that God appeared only in one person or spoke only through one book. They looked rather to universals. God was immanent in nature and in all persons and spoke through all cultures. There was a unity, or at least a continuity, between God and humankind. The vocation for all Christians, therefore, was to work ecumenically for a united church in a united world. Changing the competitive structures of society so that the reign of God could be realized here and now was the goal.

Liberals expanded and adapted what had been the muted counterthemes that gave balance to the evangelical/mainstream worldview prior to 1860. Liberals understood themselves to be not separatists but leaders of the Protestant religious establishment. They gradually moved away from a narrow nationalism that saw America as God's chosen nation. Liberals brought a global, ecumenical perspective to their life and work. They did not trust revivals to bring reform, but developed denominational and ecumenical structures to manage all aspects of Christian witness and service. Liberals rejected what they perceived to be the outmoded moralistic stances of the fundamentalists. They affirmed, at least in principle, a pluralism of values that could be achieved through a variety of lifestyles. The otherworldly end-times orientation of fundamentalists seemed to liberals to stifle the critical call to bring God's kingdom to earth in the here and now. What had been common sense, and remained so for fundamentalists, seemed quite unreasonable to modern people. The modernists assumed that all assertions needed interpretation and that truth in the modern world was relative at best. Thus, a form of the earlier counterthemes of the evangelical/mainstream worldview became the recognizable perspective on reality of early twentieth-century liberals.

Fundamentalist-Modernist Conflict over Scripture

The terms for religious discussion in the late nineteenth and early twentieth century were largely set by conflict between the two most extreme worldviews that emerged after the mid-nineteenth century, fundamentalism and modernism. The dynamics of the fundamentalist-modernist conflict in the late nineteenth and early twentieth century can be illustrated by examining the manner in which differing views regarding the authority and interpretation of scripture were debated.

BIBLICAL CRITICISM

A deeply divisive controversy regarding biblical interpretation developed in the mainline churches in the late nineteenth century. In the Presbyterian and Baptist churches, a number of formerly evangelical/mainstream seminary professors were forced out of their teaching positions and their denominations because of their use of higher-critical methods of interpreting the Bible.

The Reformers of the sixteenth century used scholarly methods of textual study developed during the Renaissance. In the seventeenth century "lower criticism" developed. It involved the examination of manuscripts and the dating of them in an attempt to establish the oldest and most reliable text. Francis Turretin, a seventeenth-century Swiss theologian whose theology was standard at Princeton Seminary from 1812 until the 1920s, had resisted this endeavor. By the late nineteenth century, however, most scholars had accepted "lower criticism" as necessary and useful.[29]

Higher criticism, as it was often called, was another matter. It was the attempt to take fully into account the human character of the biblical writings. It sought to establish the author's identity, the historical setting, the cultural context, and in some cases to read between the lines to establish the author's intentions. At best, higher criticism clarified the divine message given in scripture. At worst, in the minds of some, it reduced the Bible to a purely human book with no divine message.[30]

THE BRIGGS CASE

One of the most famous American ecclesiastical controversies over higher criticism involved Charles A. Briggs, a professor of Old Testament at Union Theological Seminary in New York.[31] Union was then a Presbyterian seminary and Briggs was a Presbyterian minister. Union represented New School Presbyterianism with its roots in revivalism and social progress. Briggs saw it as his mission to introduce the scholarly methods of higher criticism to evangelicals so that the liberals would not have a monopoly on those methods. He was also in favor of confessional revision and movements toward church union.

Briggs was opposed by Benjamin Breckinridge Warfield and the faculty of Princeton Theological Seminary. Warfield stoutly defended the older evangelical/mainstream worldview with its Scottish Common Sense approach to scripture. Such an approach to the Bible, in his mind, excluded the findings of the higher critics. Warfield also opposed changes in the denomination's confessional standards and its organizational structure.

Briggs broadcast to the Presbyterian Church that Warfield's approach was not true to the Westminster Confession or to Calvin, but was rather the imposition on Presbyterians of the scholastic theology of Turretin and old-fashioned Scottish Common Sense philosophy. Historically, Briggs was correct. Denominationally, he was doomed. Most of the ministers, and through them the voting elders in Presbyterian churches, had been trained in the Princeton tradition. Briggs was charged with heresy in the Presbytery of New York for his views on the Bible.

The heresy trial lasted two years, twice going from presbytery to synod to General Assembly. Chairman Birch of the committee prosecuting Briggs in 1892 exemplified the attitude toward scripture of the fundamentalists who were pushing the case. In his opening statement to the Presbytery of New York, Birch said of the Bible: "God is the arranger of its clauses, the chooser of its terms, and the speller of its words so that the text in its letters, words, or clauses is just as divine as the thought."[32] Briggs assured the presbytery that he accepted the Holy Scriptures as the only infallible rule of faith and practice as directed in the Westminster Confession. But that was not enough. In 1893, the General Assembly voted to remove Briggs from the Presbyterian ministry.

Union Seminary was threatened with expulsion from the Presbyterian fold unless it removed Briggs from his professorship. The seminary stood by its faculty member and Union became independent of General Assembly control. Briggs resigned from the Presbyterian ministry rather than be removed. He became an Episcopalian and spent the rest of his life working for church unity.[33]

The Recent Context of Conflicts over Common Sense

Neo-fundamentalism and Inerrancy

As evangelicals in the 1970s were becoming conscious of how diverse and dynamic they were, a neo-fundamentalism arose from within the neo-evangelical establishment founded in the 1940s. It attempted to press all evangelicals back into the constricting theological configurations of the Old Princeton theology of the early twentieth century.

Harold Lindsell, who had succeeded Carl Henry as editor of *Christianity Today*, published a book titled *The Battle for the Bible* in 1976.[34] Lindsell, a Southern Baptist, reiterated the Old Princeton position of Hodge and Warfield that the Bible is inerrant, by current standards, on all matters that it mentions, including "chemistry, astronomy, philosophy, or medicine."[35] Lindsell further asserted that this had been the central Christian tradition, held by the church for two thousand years. He attempted to demonstrate his thesis by quoting theologians throughout history who said that they believed in the inspiration and authority of the Bible. He assumed that their statements dovetailed with the Old Princeton view of inerrancy; he did not demonstrate such an identity. Lindsell coupled the Common Sense literalism of the older evangelical/mainstream worldview with the militant separatism of 1930s fundamentalism.

Lindsell clearly identified himself with the fundamentalist doctrinal concerns and the fundamentalist militant strategies of the 1930s.

The battle being fought today is the same battle that was fought and lost by those who held to inerrancy decades ago. The Presbyterians, the Methodists, some of the Lutheran denominations, the United Church of Christ, and the Episcopal Church capitulated during the earlier struggle. Now the same war rages over the same issue and the same question remains: Which side will win? This time around, the battle involves the few large denominations that did not surrender in the earlier struggle, as well as smaller and generally more evangelical denominations, many of which are to be found in the membership of the National Association of Evangelicals.[36]

In 1979, as a sequel to his controversial *Battle for the Bible*, Lindsell wrote *The Bible in the Balance*.[37] He now admitted that a significant portion of those calling themselves evangelicals did not regard inerrancy as the historical position of the church. This situation led him to conclude that those holding his theory of inerrancy "should abandon the use of the term *evangelical* as a label."[38] His decision as to an appropriate designation for inerrantists affirmed his identification with the fundamentalists of the 1930s: "Maybe it would be better to accept the term *fundamentalist* with all of the pejoratives attached to it by its detractors."[39]

The diverse evangelical community was further confused in 1978 when a group formed under the name "The International Council on Biblical Inerrancy" (ICBI). This group announced a ten-year drive "to win back that portion of the church which has drifted away from this historical position"[40] of inerrancy. While tacitly distancing themselves from some of Lindsell's attitudes and tactics, this group appeared to share his view that the Old Princeton definition of inerrancy, including its tendency toward literalistic interpretation, was the historical position of the Christian church.

The choice of "inerrancy" as the symbol of evangelical unity masked significant differences among persons in the leadership of the ICBI. Some militant separatists were using that group to foster a neo-fundamentalism in the style of Lindsell. They rejected standard scholarly approaches to scripture in favor of literal interpretation. Moreover, they asserted as absolutes some ideological positions of the earlier fundamentalism such as antievolutionism and the necessary subordination of women to men.

Others who cooperated in forming the ICBI were there because their churches, schools, or subcultures had traditionally employed the word "inerrancy" as a symbol for biblical authority. They managed to write many qualifications into the "Chicago Statement" of the group in order to give themselves some freedom from all the implications that the neo-fundamentalists attached to inerrancy.[41] But these moderates declined to challenge the neo-fundamentalists, at least in part, to avoid having suspicion cast on the moderates' own evangelical credentials. The resulting impression was, however, that the fundamentalist form of the evangelical/mainstream worldview motif of common sense was standard among conservative Protestants.

Neo-Orthodoxy

By the 1930s most American church people had wearied of extremists of both the liberal and conservative varieties. Just at that time, a new theological movement appeared from Europe that, for many, broke the deadlock of the fundamentalist-modernist controversy. Variously called "new Reformation theology," "neo-Calvinism," and "Theology of Crisis," the name "neo-orthodoxy" became most general to describe not a well-defined school of thought but a new movement in theology. The Swiss theologians Karl Barth and Emil Brunner were the most prominent figures.[42]

Neo-orthodoxy reacted as sharply to the doctrinal content of liberalism as had fundamentalism. Neo-orthodoxy and fundamentalism shared a deep skepticism toward the liberal belief that human beings were essentially rational and good and as partners with God would bring the kingdom of God into being on earth. Liberalism had viewed the Bible as a merely human book reflecting the evolutionary development of human religions from primitive ritualism to a religion of love and peace exemplified by Jesus. To liberals in the latter half of the nineteenth century, human progress seemed unlimited and inevitable. It appeared that science would alleviate all human problems.[43]

A young Swiss pastor, Karl Barth, became disillusioned when many of his liberal theology professors publicly supported the German Kaiser in World War I. After the global conflict in which twenty million people died, Barth and other young European theologians lost their confidence in human goodness and rationality and in the inevitability of scientific progress.[44] A decade later that disillusionment took root in the United States. In 1929, the year that Machen withdrew from Princeton Seminary, the stock market crashed. Depression spread like a pall over the country. One-half of the nation was ill-housed, ill-clothed, and ill-fed. The insight that salvation came from God and not from mankind, which was developed by the neo-orthodox in Europe, became attractive. Then came World War II, the murder of six million Jews by the Nazis, and the use of science to create atomic holocausts at Hiroshima and Nagasaki.

Neo-orthodoxy dared to look to the Bible and orthodox doctrine for a response to these catastrophes. Neo-orthodoxy became a viable doctrinal center for mainstream Protestantism. But neo-orthodoxy differed from fundamentalism because the neo-orthodox would not abandon the critical scholarly study of scripture often developed by liberal scholars.[45] The defining insight of early neo-orthodoxy was that God was not revealed in facts in a book that could be subject to criticism. Rather, God was revealed in a person, Jesus Christ. The Bible might be fallible as a literary document, but it was an adequate witness to the one revelation of God, Jesus Christ.[46]

For modern persons, used to living with partial knowledge, biased authorities, and agonizing ethical dilemmas, the inerrancy of long-lost manuscripts had little relevance. For many, the world between 1930 and 1950 no longer seemed explainable by common sense and simple moralisms. Millennial schemes offered unrealistic and even fantastic scenarios of hope. Amid the cluttered remnants of past certainties the neo-orthodox voice seemed to speak with both realism and hope.

Christian Realism

On the American scene, a chastened liberalism arose. Known as "Christian realism," it used many of the same biblical categories as European neo-orthodoxy and was often identified with it. These two schools of thought performed similar functions in attacking the naïve optimism of liberalism, although they relied on quite different sources of authority.

The spokesperson for this new "Christian realism" was Reinhold Niebuhr, the most influential theologian and ethicist in mid-twentieth-century America. His renewed use of the central Christian symbols established him in the eyes of many as the greatest American theologian since Jonathan Edwards.[47] His ability insightfully to apply those symbols to the social and political realm opened the way for him to consult with American political leaders and to develop a new genre of political theology. Independent of Barth's work and often in sharp opposition to it, Niebuhr devised his own reformulation of the liberalism in which he had been schooled.[48]

In 1941, *Time* called Niebuhr "the high priest of Protestantism's young intellectuals." The American secular press hailed Niebuhr's *The Nature and Destiny of Man* as an epochal work. *Time* called it the religious book-of-the-year and announced that "it puts sin right back in the spotlight."[49] Niebuhr's firm support of the American role in World War II and his stern Cold War anticommunism put him in tune with the times.[50]

After the war, *Time* featured him two or three times a year in its religion section, and in 1948 carried his picture on the cover of its twenty-fifth anniversary edition. Niebuhr had become the official establishment theologian.[51] Even the U.S. State Department used him, bringing him into membership in the elite Council on Foreign Relations.[52]

A Mainstream Consensus

For the majority of ministers in most mainline American denominations during the 1940s and 1950s, the emphases on biblical concepts in Niebuhr's Christian realism and in Barth's and Brunner's neo-orthodoxy made the Christian faith seem freshly available and vital. For example, after John A. Mackay became president of Princeton Seminary in 1936, that seminary ceased to be a bastion of the theology of the Hodges and Warfield and instead became a leading American center for the new theology represented by Brunner and Barth. Neither Mackay nor others at Princeton wished to be called "Barthians," but they praised Barth for introducing them to the insight that revelation came in Jesus Christ, to whom the Bible bears witness.[53]

Now mainstream Americans had a new model for doing theology. Preaching, teaching, and church school curriculum in most mainline denominations were informed by biblical insights but avoided the conflicts between revelation and reason that had marked the earlier fundamentalist-modernist conflict. In the PCUSA, for example, the Faith and Life Curriculum was a product of neo-orthodox consensus among theologians in the seminaries, curriculum writers at denominational headquarters, and editors in the publishing house. Its books and magazines gave solidity to the post–World War II expansion of suburban Sunday schools. The use of it by congregations became an informal test of Presbyterian orthodoxy. By the end of the 1950s, it seemed that mainline American Protestantism once again had a well-established, working theological consensus for the first time since the Civil War.[54]

Despite this comfortable fit with postwar culture, neo-orthodoxy understood its role as that of a critic—of liberalism, of fundamentalism and evangelicalism, but just as much of mainstream denominationalism. Its leaders were skeptical not only of Billy Graham's revivalism but of the general postwar boom in religiosity and suburban church growth. This critique was tolerable and stimulating as long as it came from within the Protestant establishment, and as long as most mainstream leaders were committed to a relative consensus on moral and social values.

Ironically, and largely unintentionally, neo-orthodoxy contributed to the undermining of mainstream Protestant institutions.[55] When new challenges to establishment religion arose in the 1960s, the leaders of neo-orthodoxy and the new realism were gone or no longer functioning, and their legacy did not prove adequate to stem a new tide of criticism. Church historian Sydney Ahlstrom charged that the neo-orthodox theologians had merely laid down "a very thin sheet of dogmatic asphalt over the problems created by modern critical thought."[56]

Tensions between Right and Left Regarding Common Sense

Naïve Realism

In its original setting, Scottish Common Sense philosophy was a scholarly and creative response to the skepticism of David Hume and the dominance of Deism. After a change in the general cultural worldview to a developmental approach to reality, Scottish realism no longer dealt seriously with reality as it was understood by the expanding sciences.

Scottish realism could not accommodate the growing complexity and logic of science. The Scots' notion of the identity of all people everywhere and at all times was considered naïve by modern historians, anthropologists, and sociologists. The Scots' assumption that all people held to the same basic ethical verities was brutalized by the American realities of slavery, racism, and nationalistic wars. Yet fundamentalists insisted that Common Sense realism was operative and viable for modern thought.

Fundamentalism assumed Common Sense and proclaimed that no scholarly interpretation of scripture was necessary. It treated the Bible as if each sentence had been written directly to the contemporary American individual. Indeed, in one of his less fortunate statements, B. B. Warfield argued that one proof of the divinity of scripture was that it accurately anticipated the results of nineteenth-century science.[57]

Perhaps the most distinctive feature of contemporary fundamentalism has been its continued commitment to Scottish Common Sense philosophy. That commitment more than any other tied it to the early American evangelical/mainstream worldview and separated it from the perceived subjectivism and irrationality of neo-orthodoxy and Christian realism. Contemporary fundamentalist teachers no longer identified their methodology as Common Sense realism, but they had internalized as essential its basic principles of objective, factual rationality.

Critical Modernism in the Confession of 1967

The United Presbyterian Confession of 1967 would appear to have been an effective application of the liberal/modernist worldview. Its overall theme was reconciliation. It explicitly called the church to oppose war, poverty, racism, and anarchy in sexual relations. Its authors asserted that it was the first Reformed confession to speak directly to contemporary social problems. The authors of the Confession of 1967 also believed that it was the first and only confession successfully to deal with the problem of biblical criticism.[58] By shifting the locus of authority away from a book to the person of Jesus Christ they believed that the problem was solved. The Bible pointed away from itself to Christ. Therefore, critical scholarship could be free to analyze the Bible as a human book. No amount of biblical criticism could, however, negate the function of the Bible as a witness to Christ.

Jesus Christ was the one revelation of God. Not the inspiration of scripture but the revelation of God in Jesus Christ was the source of true knowledge. This knowledge was the result of the Holy Spirit working in and through the words of scripture to bring people into a vital relationship with the living Word of God, Jesus Christ. By the work of the Holy Spirit the Bible would become the Word of God to a person as that person encountered Jesus Christ usually in preaching from scripture. After much debate in the denomination, the drafting committee of the Confession of 1967 succeeded in retaining a small *w* for the "word" of God when referring to scripture and a capital *W* when referring to Jesus Christ.[59]

It was this perceived "existentialist" approach of neo-orthodoxy, an emphasis on revelation in a person rather than in verbal propositions, that made the rationalistic fundamentalists so deeply opposed to it. They had been convinced by Common Sense realism that the truth could be objectively known by the mind. The truth had to be there, objectively and authoritatively, in the words of scripture. The work of the Spirit was only to warm the heart to accept what the mind clearly knew.

In the mainstream, neo-orthodoxy lost its theological power soon after the Confession of 1967 was adopted. Among church leaders, concerns for the liberation of non-Western people arose which had not been addressed by the founders of neo-Orthodoxy. Neo-orthodox theology had not penetrated the worldview of the average Presbyterian church member. Many still unreflectively thought as naïve realists. Neo-orthodoxy had bypassed the issues raised by this worldview rather than having shown its problems

103

and posed a clear alternative. The Confession of 1967 was further weakened by the fact that the neo-orthodox era was over in academic theology, which turned to analysis of language and science-oriented process thought. Few creative voices were left to invoke neo-Orthodoxy's usefulness. It was a creed for the pastor, but not for the parishioner. It was seldom taught in the classroom, nor was it positively invoked in the public media.[60]

Neo-Orthodoxy in the South

Among Presbyterians in the South, the theology of the "spirituality of the church" from the Civil War until the 1930s and beyond had an intimate, but not necessary, relationship to a worldview that held African Americans to be unequal partners in society. As that worldview changed, it became essential for some in the leadership of the PCUS to reject the doctrine of the church's "spirituality."

Neo-orthodoxy thus had a different flavor and function in the South than it did in northern Presbyterianism. Theologians in the PCUS embraced neo-orthodoxy as an alternative to the theology of Thornwell and Dabney.[61] These nineteenth-century theologians had taught a doctrine of the "spirituality of the church," which allowed them to avoid societal issues. Neo-orthodoxy allowed theological moderates to retain basic orthodox doctrine while distancing themselves from an outmoded, racist worldview.

The PCUS adopted "A Brief Statement of Belief" in 1962 that presented the theology of the Westminster Confession of Faith in contemporary language and opened the door for neo-orthodoxy and biblical theology to enter the official life of the church.[62] Some of the authors of this document could nonetheless oppose the Confession of 1967, the Northern Presbyterian means of making neo-orthodoxy confessional, because it was connected for them with different worldview concerns.

THEOLOGICAL SHIFTS IN THE LATE 1960s

The Confession of 1967 made neo-orthodoxy confessional in the northern stream of the Presbyterian Church by the late 1960s. The bureaucracies of the Protestant establishment by this time were committed to the social vision of the Confession of 1967 even as its theological influence was declining. Commitment to direct involvement in civil rights and later in antiwar protest had given mainline church leadership new energy and a fresh vision of the function of the church.

Theological energies and assumptions for American mainstream academic theologians went through a parallel realignment. Theology turned away from system and became issue oriented. A younger breed of theologians contextualized theological discourse in issue-oriented efforts known as black theology, political theology, the theology of revolution, ecological theology, and feminist theology. Liberation theologians, process theologians, and story theologians began to fill academic posts formerly held by their liberal and neo-orthodox predecessors. The issues of authority and truth returned in new forms.

Creating a Contemporary Centrist Worldview of How We Interpret Scripture

Critical Realism

A contemporary, creative, centrist worldview could offer the philosophical alternative of *critical realism*.[63] Critical realism believes, with naïve or Common Sense realism, that there is a real world outside us and that we can know it. With critical modernism, however, critical realism also believes that human beings never have absolute knowledge. Our knowledge is limited, partial, but adequate for our human needs. As Paul says in 1 Corinthians 13:12: "We see in a mirror dimly." Only when we come into the presence of God will we see face to face.

Common Sense realism assumes that the human mind can know reality exactly as it is, without error. Sense experience, for this naïve realism, is like a photograph of reality. Critical realism affirms that the human mind can know reality in a limited but adequate way. Science, for critical realism, offers a map or a model of the world. It points us in the right direction, but is not infallible or exhaustive in what it tells us. Progress in knowing comes as we compare many maps or models and together we come to approximate ever more closely the reality they are all attempting to describe.

The danger for critical modernism is always the possibility of slipping over into secular modernism. For example, Farley is critical of Presbyterianism for being slow to acknowledge "that God might be salvifically working through the communities of other religious faiths, that Buddhism and Hinduism and Judaism and Native American religions are genuine faiths, and that if they are, we can learn from them even as they might learn from us."[64] That comes very close to his definition of secular modernism in that it displaces "the distinctive witness of the gospel with . . . cultural contents."[65]

The distinction here between critical realism and critical modernism is subtle but important. Both reject a naïve or Common Sense realism that identifies American culture with the gospel, and thus both reject other religions because they are not like Christianity. Both critical realists and critical modernists are cultural relativists. They would argue that the gospel could be understood in non-Western forms of thought and expressed in non-Western forms of worship.

The issue is joined, however, at the level of ultimate, religious worldviews. Do Buddhism, Hinduism, and Native American religions tell the same story about God and reality as the Christian story? At root, do they have the same religious worldview? A critical modernist could apparently say yes, they do. A critical realist would be more cautious and would want carefully to compare the actual, definitive elements of the worldviews and acknowledge that all religions do not say or mean the same thing. Modernism tends idealistically to lump all differences together and claim they really mean the same thing. Or it becomes relativistic and claims that we cannot know the truth, and therefore every different worldview is equally valid for those who hold it.

ADEQUATE RELATIONAL KNOWLEDGE

The Christian creeds and confessions all claim that we can truly know God and that the Bible gives us true insight into God's will for our lives. Our knowledge of God is not perfect, but it is adequate for coming into a right relationship to God and our neighbor. The biblical witness to God's will for our lives needs to be interpreted, but it can enable us to function as Christians in this world.

The creeds summarize the biblical story, which is our ultimate religious worldview. And the various denominational confessions elaborate various historically—and culturally—conditioned theological worldviews by which people reflect on their relationship to God and work out their relationships to their neighbors in this world. This is the way we will constructively redefine the word "mainstream": by being critical of our own limited cultural perspective, but being committed to the essentials of the Christian faith.

Guidelines for Interpreting Scripture

It will come as a surprise to many Presbyterians to discover that their church has a policy regarding biblical interpretation. When Presbyterians say "policy" they usually mean "social policy." Any position that a General Assembly adopts, however, is a policy of the church unless and until a subsequent Assembly changes it. The last two General Assemblies of the UPCUSA and the PCUS before reunion adopted policies regarding the interpretation of the Bible. They remain the official policy of the PC(USA) at the present. These two policy statements, which are self-consciously coordinated and harmonious, represent a contemporary centrist worldview regarding the interpretation of scripture.

In 1978, at the same UPCUSA General Assembly that forbade homosexual ordination, a Committee on Pluralism reported on its two-year study. "Pluralism" was a euphemism for "conflict." For two years, the group had been trying to find out why Presbyterians fought with each other so much. They noted their finding: "Widely different views on the way the Old and New Testaments are accepted, interpreted, and applied were repeatedly cited to us by lay people, clergy, and theologians as the most prevalent cause of conflict within our denomination today." They concluded that "it is our opinion that until our church examines this problem, our denomination will continue to be impeded in its mission and ministry, or we will spiral into a destructive schism."[66]

Accordingly, the General Assembly established a Task Force on Biblical Authority and Interpretation. While the Task Force was meeting, the Pluralism Committee's prophecy came true. In 1981, some sixty congregations left the denomination. Their reasons were varied, but most cited a perceived difference in understanding of the authority and interpretation of the Bible as a central factor in their dissatisfaction.

In 1982, the Task Force on Biblical Authority and Interpretation presented a report showing that Presbyterians had held to at least three different understandings of the Bible during their American history.[67] The three principal models of biblical interpretation are as follows:

Model A. The Bible as a Book of Inerrant Facts. This is the model of Old Princeton scholasticism that prevailed in the denomination from 1812 until 1927. Its leading exponents were Alexander, the Hodges, Warfield, and Machen. Its philosophical resource was Scottish Common Sense. Scripture's function is to provide inerrant facts concerning all matters including science and history. This model utilized a strict grammatical-historical approach to interpretation.

Model B. The Bible as a Witness to Christ, the Word of God. The leading exponents of this model were the Swiss theologians Barth and Brunner. They drew on Kierkegaard as a philosophical resource. Scripture's function is to provide a normative witness to Christ. The interpretive approach was therefore christological.

Model C. The Divine Message in Human Forms of Thought. A leading exponent of this model is the Dutch theologian G. C. Berkouwer. He drew on Augustine as a philosophical resource. The function of scripture is to provide a message that is infallible, completely reliable, in leading people to salvation and guiding them in living the Christian life. The Bible is to be interpreted contextually, utilizing the tools of scholarship and in light of its saving function.

These models correspond closely to the three ways of knowing discussed above. Model A is a form of naïve realism. Model B represents critical modernism. And Model C is a form of critical realism.

The Task Force, which reported in 1982, had as its main function to propose guidelines for a "positive and nonrestrictive use of Scripture in matters of controversy."[68] Six guidelines were developed based on a study of what the Reformed confessions in the UPCUSA *Book of Confessions* said about biblical interpretation. The Task Force commented: "Within the *Book of Confessions,* one finds a general harmony, a broad consensus, and a functional unity to which one can appeal. Even though the creeds and confessions do not display one voice in all matters, one can find coherence in the following general areas of agreement in all the confessions from the sixteenth century to the Confession of 1967."[69] The standing committee of the 1982 General Assembly added a seventh, summary guideline.

The Task Force prefaced the guidelines with a practical admonition: "One cannot expect to use the Bible in a positive way for guidance and direction in the midst of controversy if one is not accustomed to using it for guidance and direction in daily lives, both individually and corporately. In fact, a more faithful and constant reading of Scripture might provoke more and not less controversy. Nor should this be something to be afraid of. Controversy is a part of life and growth; it may give us the experience of struggling together with Scripture in an authentic and helpful way."[70]

In that spirit, the guidelines for the interpretation of scripture in times of controversy were offered to and adopted by the UPCUSA General Assembly in 1982. They are as follows:

1. Recognize that Jesus Christ, the Redeemer, is the center of scripture.
2. Let the focus be on the plain text of scripture, on the grammatical and historical context, rather than on allegory or subjective fantasy.

3. Depend upon the guidance of the Holy Spirit in interpreting and applying God's message.
4. Be guided by the doctrinal consensus of the church, which is the rule of faith.
5. Let all interpretations be in accord with the rule of love, the twofold commandment to love God and to love our neighbor.
6. Remember that interpretation of the Bible requires earnest study in order to establish the best text and to interpret the influence of the historical and cultural context in which the divine message has come.
7. Seek to interpret a particular passage of the Bible in light of the whole Bible.

These guidelines derived from a study of the Reformed confessions held by the denomination. In 1983, the year of reunion between Northern and Southern Presbyterians, the PCUS (Southern) adopted a parallel set of Reformed guidelines for interpreting scripture.[71] They had reworked the seven guidelines into nine and offered detailed citations of the places from which they were drawn in the confessions and the manner in which they were to be applied.

Presbyterians should be comforted to know that there is a centrist position on the interpretation of scripture that is rooted in the Reformed confessional tradition and is alert to the concerns of the modern world. The lesson seems to be that when Presbyterians focus on the issue of whether there are norms to which all can appeal, they find them in their tradition and embrace them. There are useful normative guidelines that could help greatly if they were consistently invoked. This is true despite the fact that when Presbyterians deal with particular issues to which such guidelines might apply, they often ignore the guidelines and behave pragmatically and appeal to pluralism. There is, however, an implicit critical-realist worldview containing norms of biblical interpretation that can be operative for the centrist majority in the church.

6 | Moralism: What Are Our Moral Standards?

> But each of us was given grace according to the measure of Christ's gift.
>
> —*Ephesians 4:7*

FOCUS: The United States is a nation of moralists. We believe that what we do is more important than what we say or think or feel. No matter how often some may deny it in practice, a majority of Americans insist that there are moral rules that everyone ought to know and obey. That is a heritage from our colonial history. From that conviction have come intense conflicts in our communities and major movements of social reform.

Our recent history, especially since the 1950s, was dominated by the moral issue of the equality of persons. The first overriding issue was civil rights for African Americans. The leadership of Dr. Martin Luther King Jr. provides an instructive case study of how this battle was fought and won. Then came the fight for equal rights for women. Most recently, and still hotly debated, is the matter of the role of homosexuals in the church and in society. To gain perspective on this most recent conflict we must understand the way in which the preceding moral issues of equality were handled for good and for ill.

Mainline churches, once dominant in American culture, experienced three disestablishments. The first, in 1833, ended governmental subsidies. The second, in the 1950s, ended Protestant hegemony by demonstrating that Roman Catholics and Jews were as good Americans as Protestants. These two disestablishments did not greatly trouble mainstream Protestants as long as all religious people recognized common moral norms. That informal establishment of a common set of moral norms ended in the 1960s. Presently, mainstream Protestants have experienced an unsettling shift by their leaders from indirect moral persuasion to direct confrontational action on moral issues.

Great movements within the churches have coalesced around the moral issues I identified above. Liberalism made racial equality its foremost agenda in the 1960s and the equality of women its focus in the 1970s. In the late 1970s we experienced an unprecedented awakening of religious conservatives, who reversed their earlier aversion to politics and entered the public arena in large numbers. The Moral Majority was so named because the New Religious/Political Right proclaimed that it was fighting to save the moral fabric of the nation. In opposition to the liberal emphasis on individual rights, these conservatives asserted "family values." Mainstream church members will be unable to face the continuing conservative challenge unless they understand the deeply ingrained worldview that informs and motivates the New Right.

Presbyterian and mainstream Christians are stymied over the issue of the rights and role of gay and lesbian persons in the church. We must examine our history to discover how we have successfully dealt with such difficult moral issues in the past, for there is a mainstream approach that maintains the standards of the community while protecting the rights of individuals.

An Example of the Contemporary Relevance of Moralism: Abortion

The issue of abortion illustrates the deep conflict of moralistic worldview motifs. Fundamentalists insist that no one should have an abortion and would make laws to prevent it. Liberals appear to allow freedom of choice to mean abortion on demand for any woman.

This worldview conflict is illustrated by the 1992 PC(USA) report of the Special Committee on Problem Pregnancies and Abortion, "Do Justice, Love Mercy, Walk Humbly (Micah 6:8)." For example, the majority centrist report took the position that there were legitimate community standards and equally legitimate exceptions to protect the rights of the individual. Therefore, the sacredness of life is the norm. Birth is preferable to abortion. But many circumstances demand exceptions to that norm. These need to be dealt with on a case-by-case basis, with pregnant women making the final choice in consultation with their doctors and their religious community.

This centrist majority report was opposed from both the right and the left, not because of the details of the report but because of differing worldviews. The right-wing minority report insisted, "for the sake of purity," that abortion is "unjustified and a sin before God," although it went on to say, "except in cases of rape and incest, of serious fetal deformity, and of threat to the mother's life."[1] On the other side, a liberal paper, circulated by the official Women's Ministry Unit of the denomination, sought to uphold a pure pro-choice position that nonetheless was described as "anti-abortion." The three sides were very close to agreement on actual cases. All affirmed that they were against abortion in principle but all would allow it only in certain cases. They remained far divided in worldview theory. A creative centrist worldview could have provided cognitive categories that would have heightened the possibility of clear communication and agreement.

The Historical Setting of American Moralism

Moralism assumes that there is one and only one right answer to any moral question. It further assumes that one can know the answer and that one can and should take simple, direct action on that knowledge.[2] Historian of American religion Catherine Albanese has asserted:

> If any one characteristic gave its overall shape to the Protestant code, that characteristic was *moralism*. The activism of Protestant Americans and their wish to simplify life led to a concern for the rules of action. Morality became the uppermost test of Christian witness and the key reality in Christian life.[3]

Moralism led to the creation of independent, voluntary societies for spreading the gospel and perfecting the culture. Historians call this network of societies in the nineteenth century America's "Benevolent Empire." America's modern foreign missionary movement resulted in part from a prayer meeting at Williams College in 1806. The American Board of Commissioners for Foreign Missions, formed in 1810, sent out some of the early, famous, pioneer missionaries, like Adoniram Judson and Luther

Rice. Other voluntary societies formed to make America more moral, including the American Bible Society (1816), the American Tract Society (1825), and the American Society for the Promotion of Temperance (1826). This last group had 1.25 million members in the 1830s.

One of the most important of these offshoots of moralism was the American Antislavery Society. By 1838 it claimed 250,000 members. Theodore Weld, a Presbyterian, and others representing this society held revival meetings that had a dual purpose: to save souls, and to abolish slavery from the American scene.

The ultimate test of American evangelical/mainstream religion became what a person did or did not do. Both the Puritan/evangelical stream and the developing Enlightenment/liberal stream advocated the two great moral causes of pre–Civil War America: temperance (versus intemperance or drunkenness), and abolitionism (versus slavery).

In the 1920s the number of mainstream Protestants began to decline relative to the general population. Not until the 1960s, however, did a dramatic membership decline begin in "real numbers," not just relative to the population as a whole.[4] But far more disconcerting than membership decline was the cultural disestablishment of the mainstream churches.

In the early nineteenth century, New England Congregationalism had been legally disestablished. After 1833 no official government subsidy was given to any denomination. At first church leaders despaired, but later they decided it was the best thing ever to happen to them.[5] All churches had to depend on voluntary support from the people. The churches soon discovered that this was a blessing, and volunteerism became a principal aspect of American church life. Although the mainstream churches were no longer a legal establishment, they basked in a cultural acceptance that constituted an informal, national establishment as the mainstream in American religion. As long as such a consensus in the majority culture prevailed, things worked fairly smoothly.

From 1830 to the 1950s, a second, almost unnoticed disestablishment of religion was taking place. Prior to World War II, most Americans uncritically accepted the white, Anglo-Saxon Protestant denominations as the mainstream in American religion. In 1955, sociologist Will Herberg published *Protestant—Catholic—Jew,* in which he indicated that a broader religious pluralism had become culturally acceptable. Herberg's thesis, which few disputed, was: "To be a Protestant, a Catholic, or a Jew are today the alternative ways of being an American."[6] To be a Buddhist or a Muslim in the 1950s was to be somehow "foreign." And to be an atheist, agnostic, or even a "humanist" was to be obscurely "un-American." Herberg noted another phenomenon of the 1950s that later developed far beyond what he then perceived: "Protestantism in America today presents the anomaly of a strong majority group with a growing minority consciousness."[7]

By the end of the 1950s, professing Protestantism was no longer the only acceptable way of being American. Yet the mainstream churches hardly noticed. What remained was what seemingly mattered most in American religion: there was still a moral consensus in America. Whether Protestant, Catholic, or Jew, religious Americans knew and generally agreed on what was right and wrong. Sociologist of religion Robert Wuthnow wrote of this period, "Common to all sides was also the conviction that religious values were universally valid."[8]

The task of the churches—and of all American religious institutions—was to preach and teach commonly held and universally valid moral principles. The task of legislators was to implement those values in domestic and foreign policy. Furthermore, fundamentalists could safely say that Christians did not need to be involved in politics because their basic moral values were embodied in American culture. It was, seemingly, a winning combination.

Direct political action by the churches was rejected by establishment leaders. John C. Bennett, a liberal social ethicist at Union Theological Seminary in New York, wrote that churches were better off concentrating on the political education of their own constituencies. It was generally agreed that the churches should focus on the moral and political education of their members and let the laity decide how to put their ideals into political action.[9]

Throughout the 1950s, the mainline denominations understood their role to be one of influencing society by inculcating moral principles in individuals.[10] For example, an official of the Federal Council of Churches in 1946 could assume "general agreement" that "evangelism is of the essence of the Christian task as Protestants conceive it." Wuthnow noted that "at the close of World War II, only a handful of religious organizations had political influence as their primary goal."[11] Then came the Civil Rights movement.

The Recent Context of Conflicts over Moralism

Race, Religion, and Martin Luther King Jr.

In the 1950s and early 1960s, the preoccupying moral issue in the United States was the question of racial equality. In May 1954, the U.S. Supreme Court decided, in *Brown v. the Board of Education*, that racial segregation in the public schools was illegal. It thus reversed the doctrine of "separate but equal" that had been sanctioned in *Plessy v. Ferguson* in 1896.[12]

A lawyer for the victorious side in *Brown v. the Board of Education* was Charles Sheldon Scott. He argued from the premise laid down in a brief for the losing side in *Plessy v. Ferguson.* In that decision, Albion W. Tourgee, an African-American leader in the social gospel movement, had repeatedly argued that "justice is pictured blind, and her daughter, the Law, ought at least to be color-blind."[13] In 1954, the social gospel movement, which came late to the issue of racial justice, finally prevailed.

Also in May 1954, Martin Luther King Jr., preached his first sermon as pastor of the Dexter Avenue Baptist Church in Montgomery, Alabama. He was twenty-five years old and had agreed to come on the stipulation that the church grant him time and expenses to finish his Ph.D. thesis for Boston University. The intellectual and emotional journey that King had made from his childhood home in Atlanta to Montgomery, where he would be thrust into the national spotlight, was one of a radically evolving worldview made possible within the formative context of the African-American Protestant church.

On Thursday, December 1, 1955, Rosa Parks, an African-American seamstress, finished her shopping after work and boarded a bus for home. She sat in between the white section in the front and the black section in the back. As the bus filled up, the driver ordered her and three other African Americans to give up their seats to whites. Rosa Parks's feet hurt, and she was too tired to move. When she refused, the driver stopped the bus and got the Montgomery police to arrest her.[14] It was the first time an African American had been formally charged for violating the city segregation code.[15]

After day-long meetings, the African-American leaders decided to boycott the city buses. King was the compromise choice to be president of the Montgomery Improvement Association, an organization to manage the boycott. Leaflets were distributed, the African-American churches gave notice on Sunday, and on Monday morning, December 5, not one of the forty thousand African Americans in Montgomery rode a bus. That night, King spoke to a packed rally at the Holt Street Baptist Church. Although in one sense he had twenty minutes to prepare, in another sense he had been preparing all his life for that speech.[16]

King preached to people who knew that they were oppressed. They heard a sermon in plain speech with a biblical admonition from Amos to let justice run down like water. But imbedded in that sermon was a Niebuhrian nuance. It was not enough merely to talk about love. To provide for the well-being of a people, justice must be added to love. Justice must challenge that which would defeat love. Drawing on both Niebuhr and Gandhi, King asserted that persuasion was not enough. To change an unjust society called for coercion.[17] Nonviolent protest that countered unjust power with just power was biblically justified. King proclaimed that if his hearers could combine love of their enemies with the courage to oppose injustice, they would inject new meaning into the history of civilization.[18] What is known as the Civil Rights Movement of the 1960s had begun in 1955 in an African-American church.

King made creative use of the central categories of the early American evangelical/mainstream worldview. The African-American community was *separated*, through no choice of its own, from the Protestant mainstream in church and community. King was able to rally a people who knew themselves to be an oppressed minority in much the same way that early American religious and political leaders had solidified opposition to an oppressive English church and government. Rather than attacking the notion of the United States as *God's chosen nation*, King called his white opponents, as well as his African-American audience, back to the highest ideals of an elect nation whose Constitution provided the promise of liberty and justice for all. King used the techniques of *revivalism* as in the early American setting, where the appeal was not only to change lives but to change the structures of society. The Montgomery bus boycott was effective, in part, because of the weekly "revival meetings" at which King preached, using biblical imagery to strengthen people in their resolve to pursue a just cause. King constantly reiterated some basic principles of justice and personhood as *common sense* that no person, black or white, could deny as valid. He constantly held a *millennial* hope before his people, using images of the promised land to encourage their belief that "we shall overcome." King denied the validity of many white southern moralisms. But in their place he offered an alternative set of moral precepts that appealed to a higher morality in the Bible and the Constitution that took precedence over the Jim Crow laws of the land.

The Liberal Social Witness Agenda

In January 1963, a National Conference on Religion and Race was sponsored by more than seventy religious groups, including the Department of Racial and Cultural Relations of the National Council of Churches, the Social Action Commission of the Synagogue Council of America, and the

Social Action Department of the National Catholic Welfare Conference. Six hundred and fifty-seven delegates came for four days of speeches and workshops marking the one hundredth anniversary of Lincoln's Emancipation Proclamation. For the first time in American history, representative bodies of the religious establishment—Protestant, Catholic, and Jewish—had come together for the purpose of launching a nationwide social reform. Their intent was "to increase the leadership of religion in ending racial discrimination in the United States."[19] They wished to make common cause with other forces for reform in American society. The consequence was to increase the involvement of the leadership of American establishment religion with the racial issue. A commitment to civil rights soon became the identifying mark of the liberal religious establishment.

For many white liberal religious leaders in the North, Birmingham became the turning point that moved them from contemplation to action. On April 2, 1963, King had opened a major desegregation campaign in Birmingham.[20] When he was arrested for violating a state court injunction against demonstrating, eight white Christian and Jewish clergymen from Alabama published a statement calling the protests "unwise and untimely."[21] They urged local African Americans to forsake the demonstrations and press their case in the courts.[22] King responded with his epochal "Letter from a Birmingham Jail," the most eloquent statement of the philosophy of nonviolence in all of protest literature.[23]

Northern white liberal clergy responded positively to King's persuasive statement of why African Americans could no longer wait. The nationally televised pictures of Public Safety Commissioner Bull Conner's police dogs and fire hoses attacking African Americans was repulsive. It was time to move from moral support to direct action. "I decided that I just couldn't stand for such behavior any longer," Eugene Carson Blake, stated clerk of the PC(USA) General Assembly, recalled. "I was angry and I went to the Des Moines General Assembly in that mood." At the urging of Blake and others, the 1963 Presbyterian General Assembly established the Commission on Religion and Race (CORAR), with three staff persons and an unprecedented $500,000 program budget.[24]

Blake was the first mainline Protestant executive officer personally to put into practice what the denominations had been proclaiming.[25] Blake's personal involvement then further committed the denomination. On July 4, 1963, Blake, along with a noteworthy group of African-American and white Protestant, Catholic, and Jewish leaders, was arrested for attempting to integrate an amusement park in Baltimore, Maryland. Blake marched to the gate beside Furman Templeton, an African-American Presbyterian elder, vice-chairman of CORAR, and the executive of Baltimore's Urban League. NBC television photographed their arrest. Both *Time* and the *New York Times* noted that this symbolized a new escalation of racial protest.

The summer of 1963 saw a massive assault on segregation in the United States. Thousands of swimming pools, parks, schools, restaurants, and hotels were desegregated in 261 cities.[26] Then came the August 28, 1963, March on Washington with 250,000 people of every color facing the Lincoln Memorial. King closed the long afternoon of speeches and songs with his now immortal "I Have a Dream" speech.[27]

The Church as an Agent of Direct Social Action

The March on Washington in 1963 and King's leadership became critical in turning large numbers of mainstream church leaders from indirect to direct social action. According to Wuthnow, "After this date, white church leaders found it increasingly difficult to stand by while their black counterparts were staging demonstrations, engaging in active civil disobedience, and increasingly becoming the targets of racial violence."[28]

Civil disobedience, noncooperation with the government, and confrontational action were traditional behaviors for those raised in an Anabaptist model of Christian faith. It was the appropriate and available strategy for persons in the lower socioeconomic classes who lacked access to governmental power. Mainstream middle-class Protestants, such as Presbyterians, however, had been brought up to believe in a Reformed, transformative model of social change. They assumed that they had access to power. By working cooperatively with their peers in government, they were confident that they could right wrongs and effect the general welfare. Indirection was always preferable to confrontation.

At first, direct action by mainstream Protestants was "limited to a small elite, often officials of denominational bureaucracies."[29] These people were shielded from congregational reactions and were highly visible nationally. Then came official endorsements by denominations. This public support encouraged campus ministers, young people, and parish clergy to take active roles.[30]

The growing involvement of clergy in civil rights activism evoked cries of "foul play" both from some of their peers and from many in the pews.[31] King's leadership came from within an African-American community that was ready for change. They knew that they were children of God equal to white people and they knew that they were being unfairly oppressed. King reinforced this view of reality through preaching at revival-like meetings in which he insisted that the Bible and the U.S. Constitution were on their side. King as leader and the community as support shared a common worldview. No such consensus existed in the white mainstream churches, and there was little preparation for this major change in perspective. Mainstream Protestant church members were asked to alter their worldview almost overnight. They were called upon to adopt a worldview nearly opposite to their own in which the enemy was now the government, their own race, and values of gradual change that they had always embraced.[32] Despite the rightness of the cause, the strategy of direct confrontational action was anathema to most mainstream Protestants.

Political scientist Anne Motley Hallum published an article titled "Presbyterians as Political Amateurs" that illustrated the problem of the mainline leadership worldview. She examined the "attitude of church leadership that sometimes seems bent on self-destruction."[33] She characterized the "*style* of the political amateur" as one of "uncompromising statements of principle even at risk of losing a broad base of support or long-term participation."[34] When denominational leaders could not get their members to ratify their positions, they switched to the stance of speaking "to" the church and not "for" the church. In Hallum's view, this shift led to political ineffectiveness. What resulted were "two visions" of America and where it should be heading, and two visions of the church's role and responsibility in the culture.[35] Evangelism and social justice came to oppose one another.[36] Denominational leaders and members became alienated from one another. If the purpose of denominational leadership was to rally their members against racial injustice, their strategy was ineffective.

Beginning in the late 1960s, mainstream Protestant church leaders became increasingly committed to King's call for racial equality and equal justice for all. Whereas King was able effectively to appeal to the roots of the early American evangelical/mainstream worldview, mainstream church leaders no longer had a grasp on those categories or a confident appeal to biblical or constitutional norms of authority. Their critique of established authorities had been too effective; no constructive theological program endured. Their appeals for participation in the Civil Rights movement therefore fell on mostly deaf ears of mainstream church members who had not been prepared to reinterpret the evangelical/mainstream worldview that they still held as supportive of traditional racial and cultural realities.

In the civil rights struggle, church leaders at least could appeal to the common humanity of African Americans and white Americans. They could increasingly point to acts of violence against even women and children by die-hard segregationists. When denominational leaders added to their concerns opposition to the American government's involvement in the war in Vietnam, this was beyond the comprehension of those who still held to the rudiments of the early American evangelical/mainstream worldview. An American church and nation elect as God's chosen people could surely not be wrong in opposing a Communist regime in non-Christian Asia.

To leaders whose liberal/modernist worldview provided an internationalist perspective, the insular American viewpoint of many church members was simply incomprehensible. Rather than engaging in mutual education and understanding, church leaders and members tended to doubt each other's sincerity and Christian commitment.

By the late 1960s it appeared that the era of mutually recognized norms in theology and morality had ended. Until the 1960s, mainstream religious bodies and their conservative counterparts had assumed a common biblically based framework of values and moral ideals. In the 1960s liberals and conservatives had different sets of moral issues and offered different styles of moral decision making. Sociologists of religion Wade Clark Roof and William McKinney referred to it as "moral denominationalism" and a "moral marketplace."[37] The Protestant community as a whole could not even find a common way of framing the moral question in many disputed issues.

When the moral consensus was finally lost in Protestantism in the 1960s, the decline of the mainline churches accelerated decisively. Fundamentalists, who had stayed out of politics, entered the political arena when they feared that the moral fabric of the nation was threatened.

The United States has always been a nation of moralists. And it is at the point of moral issues that the worldview conflicts become the most difficult and divisive for people who feel that their personal and societal well-being is most at risk.

Tensions between the Right and Left

Christians in Politics: Role Reversals on the Right

Fundamentalists who composed the core of the New Religious Right had opposed the involvement of Christians in politics until the late 1970s. At that time they rejected as illegitimate liberal mainline religionists' participation in the Civil Rights movement and protests against the Vietnam War. On March 21, 1965, Jerry Falwell had preached a sermon, "Ministers and Marchers," in which he condemned the clergy who were then gathering with other civil rights advocates to resume a march from Selma to Montgomery, Alabama. "Believing the Bible as I do," Falwell declared, "I would find it impossible to stop preaching the pure saving gospel of Jesus Christ, and begin doing anything else—including fighting communism, or participating in civil rights reforms." According to Falwell, "preachers are not called to be politicians but to be soul winners." The clergy activists were fomenting hatred and unrest, Falwell believed, and their methods of protest were contrary to the minister's calling. "Nowhere are we commissioned to reform the externals," Falwell argued. "The gospel does not clean up the outside but rather regenerates the inside."[38] By 1979, Falwell had dramatically changed his view regarding the involvement of ministers in politics.

The Moral Majority was founded not by church groups but by a coalition of direct-mail fundraisers for right-wing political causes.[39] In 1979, after months of debating who the right leader might be, Richard Vigurie and Paul Weyrich of the National Conservative Political Action Committee, Howard Phillips of the Conservative Caucus, and Robert Billings and Ed McAteer, political fundraisers who established organizations with religious titles, decided to approach Falwell. Their insight was that the new conservative religious leadership was being provided by the television preachers of what was being called "the Electronic Church." Falwell, as one of the leading television preachers, claimed immediate access to twenty million religiously and presumably politically conservative American citizens. After first declining, Falwell reconsidered and accepted the offer. This preacher, known primarily in fundamentalist circles, then was propelled into national prominence.

The fundraisers perceived that their most effective means of reaching people were direct mail and the electronic media. Their plan was to create one umbrella under which to unite many diverse groups, each of which was upset about some specific thing, for example, abortion, the Equal Rights Amendment, gun control, the United States' military posture, the Panama Canal, and so on. By exchanging mailing lists and fusing these individual concerns into one great moral crusade, the conservative fundraisers believed they could unleash a potent and previously untapped political force.[40] And so they did.

Falwell was on the cover of *Newsweek* on September 15, 1980. *U.S.*

News and World Report's lead feature that same week was "Preachers and Politics." The *Christian Century* declared the most important news story of 1980 to be the ascendance of the New Religious Right to prominence as a political force.[41] The claim that this movement had significantly influenced the election of Ronald Reagan as president in 1980 brought it to public prominence. In the popular mind, the term "evangelical" was now widely associated with what Jim Wallis, editor of the radical evangelical magazine *Sojourners,* termed "Evangelical nationalists."[42]

The secular organizational form of this fundamentalist bid for power was the Moral Majority, and its manifesto was Falwell's 1980 book, *Listen America!*[43] The explicit connection between religious fundamentalism and Erling Jorstad's *The Politics of Moralism* was confirmed in Falwell's later book, *The Fundamentalist Phenomenon.*[44]

Why did Falwell have power? Why did people follow him? Because what he said somehow sounded right to them. In his speaking and writing he appealed to all six motifs of the earlier evangelical/mainstream worldview. He was so proudly a separatist that he would not allow Billy Graham into his pulpit at Thomas Road Baptist Church because Graham associated with people Falwell considered liberals. Falwell believed that the United States was an elect nation and that its citizens were God's chosen people because its founding fathers had established its laws on the laws of the Bible. According to Falwell God had raised up the United States for the evangelism of the world, a revivalist calling. Falwell frequently appealed to "common sense" and liked to say his assertions were "obvious." He was a supreme moralist, asserting always the one right and unambiguous answer to any question. Falwell's church has published a doctrinal statement that commits members not only to premillennialism but to a dispensational derivative of it, the pretribulation rapture. For many Americans the motifs of the early American evangelical/mainstream worldview were still deeply embedded in their psyches. Falwell embodied this worldview in a particular fundamentalist form. Those six motifs remained meaningful to many, perhaps the majority, of American Christians in the late twentieth century.

To conservatives, saving "one nation under God" meant redressing moral decline in the nation during the presidential terms of two previous "born-again" Protestants, Gerald Ford and Jimmy Carter. Conservatives had discovered that articulating a Christian commitment did not guarantee what they considered appropriate political action. A constellation of concerns, all declared to be moral in nature, now formed the 1980s manifestation of the evangelical/mainstream worldview. That worldview became more important in judging candidates for office than their Christian commitment. It was to this worldview that politicized fundamentalists were committed.

In the 1980s, conservatives were openly encouraging political involvement, an about-face that, for the most part, they willingly acknowledged.[45] Their attitudes were different because, for them, the issues were different. The very existence of the United States as a moral nation under God now seemed imperiled. A chief task of fundamentalist preachers became the registration and political education of their followers. They were determined to "get out the Christian vote" in the November 1980 election.[46]

A Crusade for Family Values

Even though New Right fundamentalists of the 1980s continued to affirm the need for individual conversion, their new focus was a moral crusade to return America to traditional family values. Historian Erling Jorstad summarized:

> Being "saved" in the 1980 parlance meant (1) accepting Christ as one's Lord and Savior—that was familiar enough, but it also meant (2) taking secular political power and using it for moral crusading to save by revival the nation from total collapse. Revival became politics, politics was the road to revival.[47]

This revival saw any emphasis on individual human rights as potentially destructive to the individual and the nation. What individuals needed was the security of a well-ordered family.

What the American people needed, it was argued, was the security of a government that enforced civil laws which mirrored natural and divine laws. For the New Religious/Political Right, the primary task of the state was to defend against enemies. The state should identify evil and defend the existing order. Its military function was paramount. It was not an appropriate function of the state to provide social services or to initiate social change.

The New Right was clear that the United States was *not* a democracy. It was, in their view, a *republic.* A democracy derives its authority from the majority opinion of the people. That can be threatening to people who, even though they call themselves the Moral Majority, still understand themselves to be a religious and ideological minority in a country dominated by a secular, humanistic, elite leadership.

124

A republic receives its authority from a code of law and order. For the New Right, authority in the United States resided in the Constitution, which in turn was based on God's law in the Bible. Fundamentalist Christians who interpreted the Bible literally were therefore the naturally right readers of the intent and meaning of the Constitution. Thus, in a republic only moral people should rule, whether in the majority or minority, because they alone lived according to the law.[48] The extremist theory of the Reconstructionists, who believe that the law of God in the Bible should be applied in minute detail in civil law, thus was given a central place in the practical application of the New Religious/Political Right.

Ironically, with the exception of issues of war and peace, the New Religious Right appeared to reverse the list of what had previously been considered public and private matters. For example, the place and form of prayer, what one read and viewed, and how one's sexuality was expressed were no longer private matters but issues of public and political moment to religious conservatives. Conversely, those issues that had exercised mainline Protestants in the 1960s and 1970s as matters of public debate were now relegated to the province of the "private sector" and the individual conscience as objects of potential charity: poverty, hunger, homelessness, the environment, and civil rights for minorities and women.

Christians in Politics: Regrets on the Left

The most important sociological study of community in the early 1980s was *Habits of the Heart: Individualism and Commitment in American Life,* written by a team of Berkeley sociologists led by Robert N. Bellah.[49] The authors took their cue from the French social philosopher Alexis de Tocqueville, whose 1830 study of American society provided their title.[50]

Tocqueville perceived the American commitment to individual freedom as a threat to the preservation of a coherent moral community. James Wall, editor of the *Christian Century,* echoed that concern, wishing "that mainline church leaders had read Tocqueville before they took us into the great social battles of the 1960s and '70s."[51] Wall's point was that the campaign waged by religious liberals for individual freedoms such as women's rights and gay rights had the side effect of undermining commitment to protective societal structures. He argued that excesses in the fight for individual freedoms "led to the current religious New Right's takeover of Tocqueville's three categories: family, religious tradition and politics."[52] Wall declared self-critically: "In our battles alongside secular allies for individual freedoms in the '60s and '70s, mainliners spent too much time in the streets and in the halls of Congress, and not enough in worship or in strengthening the family unit."[53] Sociologically it seemed apparent to some liberals that the wholeness of an earlier evangelical/mainstream community had been bifurcated as communities polarized around issues of individual freedom.

The most trenchant criticism by the sociologists of religion was that, for liberal Protestantism, the personal and public realms "have come so uncoupled that the tradition has lost much of its ability to mobilize personal energies on behalf of public causes."[54] In public affairs, the liberal was activist and absolutist. But these absolute standards were not applied to private matters. "The result is a disjointed ethic."[55] It is no wonder that liberal Protestantism lost influence with the general populace.

The Ordination of Women

Ironically, the left's focus on diversity and desire to be sensitive to the needs of individuals brought back the necessity for community norms. Again, the Presbyterians can illustrate. The authors of the Confession of 1967 thought they had ended once and for all the Old Princeton insistence on "essential and necessary articles" of belief. But a new issue, beyond their 1960s purview, brought the matter of essentials again to the fore. The issue was the equality of women.

The PC(USA) had ordained women as elders in 1930 and opened the door to women as ministers in 1956. Until the mid-1970s, however, few had walked though that open door—less than 3 percent of the ministers in the denomination were women. The attitude that the ministry was a man's profession prevailed.

In 1974, a young man named Walter Wynn Kenyon graduated from Pittsburgh Theological Seminary. He applied for ordination to serve as stated supply of a small congregation while he pursued graduate study in medieval philosophy. He made clear to the Candidates and Credentials Committee of the Presbytery of Pittsburgh that he did not believe that the Bible permitted the ordination of women. He also recognized the legal right of women to be ordained in the Presbyterian Church. He was, however, willing to be ordained in this denomination since the error of ordaining women was a detail of Presbyterian government and constituted a "nonessential" matter that did not destroy the Presbyterian system.

Formal complaint was made against the presbytery's decision to ordain Kenyon. It became a judicial case that was appealed to the synod and finally to the Permanent Judicial Commission of the General Assembly.

The Judicial Commission in its ruling invoked not just Presbyterian polity but the essential beliefs of the church's confessional standards. "The question of the importance of our belief in the equality of all people before God is thus essential to the disposition in this case. . . . It is evident from our Church's confessional standards that the Church believes the Spirit of God has led us into new understandings of this equality before God."[56] The Confession of 1967 was cited to the effect that those who "exclude, dominate, or patronize their fellowmen [sic], however subtly, resist the Spirit of God." Kenyon's ordination was denied on the grounds that he could not affirm an "essential" belief of Presbyterianism.

To get away from the Old Princeton five "essential and necessary articles," the General Assembly in 1927 had said, in effect: Let the presbyteries decide on matters of doctrine. Now it was not the conservatives but the liberals, with support from the centrists, who turned from the right of the presbytery to ordain to the overruling norm of the church's belief system in the constitution. Apparently, to protect the rights of individuals, there had to be some universal norms.

Creating a Contemporary Centrist Worldview of Moral Standards: Issues of Sexuality

Moralism was a motif developed during the eighteenth-century Enlightenment, and its countermotif of a pluralism of values was a product of late-nineteenth- and early-twentieth-century modernity. Moralism, which fundamentalism co-opted as its own, contends that there is always only one right way. Liberalism, to fundamentalists, gives the impression of sanctioning an attitude of "anything goes." Fundamentalism tends to act as if everyone is basically alike and that all should be compelled to think alike and behave alike. Liberalism argues that everyone is different and varied opinions and diverse lifestyles are to be celebrated. In the 1990s issues of sexual morality severely tested whether a middle ground could be found.

Ordination of Homosexuals

In the Presbyterian Church, the central moral question of the early 1990s was the issue of the rights and appropriate roles of gay and lesbian persons in the church and in society. The issue had been near the surface in the church for almost two decades. In 1976, the Presbytery of New York City asked the General Assembly of the United Presbyterian Church for "definitive guidance" as to whether a candidate who was in every other respect qualified for ministry could be ordained if he or she was a self-affirming, practicing homosexual. A two-year study was called for and the Task Force reported to the denomination in 1978.

A majority of the Task Force favored removing any impediment to the ordination of gay and lesbian persons. The General Assembly, however, set aside the majority report and declared that homosexual behavior was a sin that, if continued, prohibited one's ordination. While defending the civil rights of homosexuals and decrying the sin of homophobia, the General Assembly nonetheless refused to permit practicing homosexuals to occupy the role model of Presbyterian ministers.

Those who believed that Presbyterians in the 1970s were living in an era of pluralism that permitted a variety of lifestyles were disappointed. The sense, widely held before the 1960s, that all religious people shared some universal moral norms was still deeply ingrained in the worldview of most Presbyterians. They might be willing to make exceptions, especially for themselves, but they insisted that some moral laws could not be abrogated.

Norms and Exceptions

A contemporary, creative, centrist worldview would articulate that there are both norms and exceptions to them. There must be norms for the good of the community and its majority, and there must be exceptions to protect the rights and freedoms of individuals who constitute a minority.

This issue is currently challenging the concept of a mainline, mainstream, or centrist church in our culture. The function that centrist churches have traditionally performed has been to enable persons to be rooted in a biblical and ecclesiastical tradition and yet to cope with modernity. A fundamentalist church can hold only to the tradition: The Bible says homosexuality is wrong and that decides it. A liberal church can embrace modernity: Science has shown us a great variety of sexual expressions each having their own validity, and we will include all. A genuinely mainstream church cannot settle the matter so easily. A variety of complex and controversial issues must be resolved together if people are to be able to live as biblically faithful persons in the midst of the modern world.

Early in 1741, the Presbyterian Synod, organized in 1716, split apart. The issue was individual experience versus community norms. Which was more important: experiencing a revivalist conversion, or subscribing intellectually to the Westminster Confession?

The solution was a compromise that recognized the validity and values of both factors. The reunion of 1758 turned to the Adopting Act of 1729 and insisted that all candidates for the ministry had to subscribe to the Westminster Confession. But the formula for subscription was to "all the essential and necessary articles," which meant not every jot and tittle, but the main principles. Dialogue between the candidate and the presbytery would interpret which items were essential and about which there could be latitude. But most important, a new factor was added. All candidates for the ministry had to be examined on their "experiential acquaintance with religion." From the beginning, American Presbyterianism has always had to have a balance between the validity of individual experience and conformity to community norms.

Today, some gay and lesbian leaders are asking the church to affirm that their homosexual orientation is a gift from God. That can be done only if the community can be convinced that this experience is not in conflict with its confessional and scriptural norms. In Presbyterianism the discussion cannot move forward if some assume that their experience is self-validating and unquestionable, while others want to claim a priori that scripture and the confessional tradition eliminate that possibility. There needs to be a context in which personal experience is tested and the norms of the community are interpreted such that these two complementary factors are evaluated and brought into relationship with one another.

For that interaction to be possible several steps are necessary. First, both sides must express and acknowledge their ultimate commitment to the God who is revealed in Jesus Christ. Religious dialogue becomes only more divisive unless both sides agree that they are members of the same body. We must stop un-Christianizing each other. The present rhetoric on both sides is potentially unhelpful. Some liberal rhetoric asserts that the church as a community is in sin by refusing ordination to homosexuals. Some conservative rhetoric can easily imply that individuals are sinful simply by having a homosexual orientation, which they have not willed nor could have prevented. The prerequisite to any negotiation regarding such a volatile subject is to recognize that those to the left, right, and center actually, at root, share a common ultimate commitment. That would make everything else easier. We would still have a lot of hard arguing to do, but we could, hopefully, do it in a more tolerant and respectful mode. We could do it as those who belong to the same family. If we would spend the time and make the effort to share our basic ultimate religious commitments with each other, that absolute could relativize the emotional impact of other levels of dialogue. There can be no real unity unless we genuinely believe that we share something more important than all our differences.

The second step is to agree on the process by which decisions regarding ordination will be made. Some gay and lesbian persons assume that their experience is so obviously good and right that experience itself is sufficient to decide the matter. They hope that if "straight" Christians get to know them, the problems between them will dissolve.

We all need to know gay and lesbian persons and hear their testimony. It took the church a long time to deal with the issue of the ordination of women to church office. Yet all of us knew women and had opportunity to hear their testimony. Until recently, most heterosexual Christians were unaware that they knew gay and lesbian persons since most of the latter had felt it necessary to conceal their sexual preference.

Personal experience is not enough. Presbyterians have too keen an awareness of human limitations and too strong a sense of human sin to allow individual testimony to seal an argument. We need to agree together to study scripture, regarding not just homosexuality but the function of sexuality in God's intention for humankind.

Gay and lesbian persons are sometimes understandably impatient with the call to study scripture, because their opponents often simply use scripture in a literalistic manner to bludgeon them. But just because scripture can be misused does not mean that it should not be used at all. A study done of seventeen attempts to deal with human sexuality in the mainstream Presbyterian churches in the past fifty years demonstrated that the church could accept only conclusions that were based on biblical warrants.[57] The eighteenth attempt, by the Special Committee on Human Sexuality that reported in 1991, reinforced that point. By declaring that they accepted only those scriptures that agreed with their definition of justice and love, and rejected others that seemed to disagree, the Task Force majority assured the massive rejection that its proposal received.

Most mainstream Protestants are not literalists. Complex and controversial matters are rarely settled at the level of particular biblical texts. Biblical texts must finally be dealt with in terms of what overall set of interpretive premises we will allow as best expressing a Christian mind-set. That is, they are interpreted in the context of a worldview.

Many biblical scholars now argue that the texts which speak against homosexuality are not directed toward faithful, enduring relationships between persons with a homosexual orientation. Rather they are directed toward sexual practices in the Near Eastern fertility cults and in Greek culture that allowed the systematic exploitation of boys by adult men. Such practices, which identified sex with religion and which allowed one group of people to exploit another group for their sexual gratification, were idolatrous, making the desires of humans ultimate rather than the worship of their creator. The intention of the biblical texts is to speak against such idolatry.[58] The texts, when understood in context, may apply to the misuse of God-given sexuality in ways that were particularly blatant in ancient society but may not describe all homosexual practice as we now know it. Christians, for whom the Bible is the final authority in matters of morality, must take special care to interpret the text correctly and not simply cling to tradition. The experience of our previous misreading of scripture regarding race and women must make us cautious and open to a careful reexamination of God's written Word.

The debate over the proper understanding of the biblical texts regarding homosexuality and their ancient contexts is relatively recent and still ongoing. If it should be demonstrated that the Bible does not assert a blanket condemnation of all homosexual conduct, many pastors would become more openly supportive of faithful, monogamous homosexual relationships. My observation is that many evangelical pastors, including those of large churches, counsel gay and lesbian parishioners to live in faithful, long-term unions. These same pastors would be reluctant publicly to support such unions for two reasons. First, they do not wish to appear to be ignoring biblical prohibitions regarding same-sex activity. Second, they do not wish to appear to be supportive of the "homosexual lifestyle," which the public mind equates with promiscuity and the spread of AIDS. A contextual understanding of scripture could enable them to have a theory that supported their pastoral practice. The pastoral support of faithful, monogamous, same-sex unions would strengthen those in the gay and lesbian community who wish to distance themselves from a promiscuous lifestyle.

A contemporary centrist interpretation of the Bible would surely emphasize strongly the overarching biblical mandate of faithful, committed sexual relationships. There is no question that God's primary intent is for sexual relations to be between one man and one woman, thereby establishing a bond from which family life can develop. It is also clear that there are exceptions in the biblical record that are approved by the contemporary church. Old Testament heroes of faith often had multiple wives and concubines. Their cultural practices did not prohibit them from serving God effectively and with divine approval. Despite the general prohibition of divorce in the New Testament, most mainstream Christians now understand that prohibition as an ideal rather than an absolute one that bars divorced persons from further ministry.[59]

131

The issue is, finally, what kind of moral worldview can a mainstream Protestant church accept? Some persons on both the left and the right can give quick and unequivocal answers to these questions. The mainstream church, however, cannot move forward until the majority in the middle share a common perspective.

Clergy Sexual Misconduct

The recent publicity surrounding the epidemic of clergy sexual misconduct has belatedly forced American churches to recognize this idolatry and misuse of sexuality. The Roman Catholic Church and many Protestant denominations have had to take official action. They are involved in legal cases that are costing hundreds of millions of dollars. Statistics suggest that 10 to 23 percent of clergy of all faiths nationwide have engaged in inappropriate sexual behavior or contact with parishioners, clients, or employees.[60] Most sexual misconduct is by male heterosexual clergy with female church members. There are also instances of female heterosexual and homosexual misconduct, and the victims include children and youth.[61] A report to the PC(USA) in 1993 states: "We face a crisis terrible in its proportions and devastating in its implications."[62]

The misuse of office and the wrongful use of power is a form of idolatry in which the clergyman sets himself or herself above the laws of God, church, and society. We are finally realizing and beginning slowly to come to terms with this. I agree with Marie Fortune, founder of the Center for the Prevention of Sexual Abuse and Domestic Violence in Seattle. Conservatives treat sexual misconduct as a sin and want the perpetrators to repent. While that view is true, it is not enough. Liberals treat it as a psychological problem that needs therapy. That view is also true and equally inadequate. Sexual misconduct is fundamentally a breach of professional ethics. The perpetrator is disqualified to practice the profession of ministry.[63] Anecdotal evidence suggests that persons who have violated their professional ethics more than once are likely to do it again.[64] They should not be allowed to practice a helping profession in which others are vulnerable to them.

The context of a church just beginning to deal with heterosexual clergy sexual misconduct is significant for the church's attempts to evaluate the status of homosexuality. Attitudes toward sexuality vary widely. Mainstream Protestant churches have not developed generally acknowledged standards for homosexual conduct. The conventional view has been that all homosexual activity is morally wrong, so no moral discriminations have

132

been made. Now some gay and lesbian persons are asking the mainstream churches to accept their homosexual behavior as a gift from God. That would be a worldview shift that most members of mainstream churches would not be prepared to make. Many Christian homosexuals assert that they participate only in loving, long-term relationships. Other gay and lesbian people, including some mainstream Protestant leaders, regard sex as ultimately valuable and dismiss both celibacy and monogamy as unrealistic and impossible to practice.[65] These differing attitudes are true for heterosexuals as well.

Crafting a Moral Consensus

Presbyterians have always struggled with the tension between freedom of individual conscience and the integrity of the community's standards. There is always the judgment call between what seems necessary and right here and now for the individual and the implications of that decision for the future of the community. The resolution historically has been to maintain the norms but to allow exceptions.

The way in which mainstream Protestants deal with divorce offers an example of the principle of maintaining the norm while allowing exceptions for good cause. The church does not bless divorce or say that it is a good gift from God. But when divorce tragically, and often inexplicably, occurs between people, we offer forgiveness, understanding, and the opportunity to begin again. Sometimes that leads to another marriage. We have learned to interpret the explicit biblical prohibition against divorce as serving to maintain the norm of marriage. When divorce does occur we are able to view it in the larger context of biblical admonitions for forgiveness and new beginnings. We are also aware that God understands the complexity of life in ways that we do not. We therefore pastorally allow the possibility of exceptions on biblical grounds. The same contextual exegesis that even some quite conservative Christians use to allow divorce and remarriage could offer a model of biblical interpretation that would allow acceptance of faithful, long-term commitments between persons of homosexual orientation.

What would a centrist worldview regarding human sexuality look like? The center is a place where commitment and civility, law and grace, are joined. God's creation is not only good but also inexplicably flawed and continually marred by human sin. Sex, more mysterious than almost any other human activity, is marked by a mixture of the good gift of God and the misuse of God's gifts by sinful humans. We are not forced to choose between rigid laws shorn of compassion for those who do not fit them, and acceptance of any experience that a person or group claims to be sanctioned by God because it is natural to them.

The centrist view would distinguish between God's preference for humanity and God's willingnesss to accept less than perfect people in a broken world.[66] It would acknowledge not only that we are all sinners but that our human understanding is limited. It would, at the same time, affirm that we can and must make scripturally based faith commitments that are adequate guides for living in a complex world.

Centrist Protestants need to maintain that there are clear norms of human behavior that apply to all persons. God's intention for sexual expression is the marriage of one man to one woman in lifelong fidelity. We do not live in Eden, however, but in a world after the Fall. Humans sin and can be forgiven. And there are exceptions to the norm that we simply do not understand. Some people are apparently born or conditioned to feel sexual desire for those of the same rather than the opposite sex. That is an exception to the rule, but an exception that does not invalidate the rule. A centrist view could acknowledge and accept such exceptions without making them normative.

There is little possibility that a liberal worldview on human sexuality will be accepted in the near term by the Presbyterian or by most of the other mainstream churches. Research conducted among representative Presbyterians, for example, show that over 80 percent in all categories of members, officers, and ministers reject extramarital sex, premarital sex, and homosexual sex as behaviors inappropriate for Presbyterian believers.[67]

The nuanced and balanced character of official Presbyterian statements on sexual matters indicate that the majority of Presbyterians are not comfortable with a rigid fundamentalist view of sexuality either. Presbyterian pronouncements defend the civil rights of gays and lesbians and accept them as persons and church members.[68]

As Christians and church people we appear to be dealing with issues regarding homosexuality in the wrong sequence. Pastorally, the primary moral question is surely how to provide gay and lesbian persons with supports and sanctions for their sexual relationships equivalent to those prevailing in the heterosexual community. Intimate human relationships are complex and demanding. The church needs to provide all its members with better education and pastoral care regarding sexual relationships.

Only after dealing with the moral question of appropriate sexual relationships can we deal with the issue of ordination of homosexuals. Then we would have to deal with gay and lesbian persons not as a class of people but individually according to the same standards of knowledge, competence, and personal morality by which we judge other candidates for ordination.

A centrist view of human sexuality will not please the most radical leaders of the struggle for gay and lesbian ordination. Nor will it be acceptable, presumably, to the approximately 15 percent in the church who will insist on a "purist" stance in opposition to gay and lesbian ordination. But a centrist view could enable the majority in the middle to fashion a compromise that would keep the church together in a way consistent with its character. We can handle this matter in a manner faithful to our twofold mainstream tasks. We can remain faithful to the biblical and confessional tradition and we can enable people to cope with the modern world. We have done it before by adopting a balanced, biblical, centrist position.

7 Millennialism: What Is Our Future Hope?

Until all of us come to the unity of the faith and of the knowledge of the Son of God, to maturity, to the measure of the full stature of Christ.

—*Ephesians 4:13*

FOCUS: We are approaching the third millennium of the Christian era. The closer we get to the year 2000 the greater will be the speculation as to our true hope for the future. Christians have pondered the future and constructed three different theories of a future kingdom lasting a thousand years (millennium). There have been pessimistic visions (premillennial), optimistic speculations (postmillennial), and grimly realistic expectations (amillennial).

These differing worldviews embody different understandings of history that influence our daily conduct. Dispensationalism, a nineteenth-century theory of biblical interpretation, has influenced a broad spectrum of conservative Christian movements with a pessimism about this world and a fervent activity of evangelism to save individuals from a tragic fate. The ecumenical movement in mainstream Protestantism is founded on an optimistic vision of our ability to form communities and to transform society to make it conform more nearly to the realm of God.

Religious worldviews were closely identified with presidential politics from John Kennedy to Ronald Reagan. Liberals attempted to unite all mainstream Protestants to gain political strength in the 1960s. Conserva-

137

tives coalesced around the candidacy of Ronald Reagan in the 1980s. In each case a vision of future hope was projected that engaged religious people.

In direct opposition to the pessimism of dispensationalism, conservative Reformed Christians have now developed a utopian Reconstructionism that insists that this world can be governed by the minute application of the principles of Old Testament law. Unlikely as it may sound, this theory is at work currently in many of the programs of the New Religious Right and especially in the political programs of Pat Robertson.

Mainstream Protestants need to know what they believe about the future. A realistic appraisal of traditional Augustinian millennialism may provide an alternative to the extremes by giving hope for the future and motivation for seeking justice in the present.

The Contemporary Relevance of Millennialism

The creedal statement of the PC(USA), "A Brief Statement of Faith," has an eschatological (end-times) section. It utters the fervent prayer found at the end of the biblical book of Revelation, "Come, Lord Jesus!" During the word-by-word and line-by-line debates in the drafting committee, one member said forthrightly: "I've never prayed that prayer myself, and I'm not sure that I'm likely to do so." On grounds of contemporary relevance, that person wondered if the phrase should be retained. A Hispanic member of the committee, who had grown up in the barrio of East Los Angeles, reacted strongly: "Some of us need to know that Christ is coming back to straighten things out. Besides, it's in the Bible." The drafting committee left it in and it remained through a lengthy and complex process of revision.

Surveys have indicated that 61 percent of Americans believe that Jesus is coming to earth again. Six out of ten Americans also think that the world will come to an end, although there is no consensus on the exact relationship between Christ's return and the end of the world. About one-third of those who expect the end of the world think it will happen within a few decades. Over one thousand groups (both Christian and non-Christian) attach cosmic significance to the coming of a new millennium in the year 2000. The closer we approach that date the more attention will be given to end-time predictions.[1] A contemporary worldview needs the perspective offered by knowing that the future is in God's loving hands, and that in the future justice will be done.

138

The Historical Setting of Millennialism

The final motif of the evangelical/mainstream worldview is millennialism. The term "millennium" refers to the notion derived from the biblical book of Revelation that Jesus Christ will return to reign on earth for a millennium—one thousand years—of perfect peace. Christians have long affirmed that end-time hope but have disagreed strongly about two aspects of the notion: (1) whether the thousand-year period is meant to be symbolic or literal; and (2) the timing and manner of Christ's return.

Amillennialists (traditional Augustinians and Calvinists fit here) have treated the thousand years mentioned in Revelation as symbolic of the Holy Spirit's presence now in the church rather than referring to a literal future event. For amillennialists, human history has ups and downs and will continue to have them until the final consummation with a new heaven and a new earth.

Premillennialists expect a literal thousand-year reign of Christ on this earth. They generally believe that this world is growing progressively worse and will continue to do so until it becomes so bad that Christ will break into history and institute his messianic reign. Dispensationalism adds a mass of detail to this scheme that goes beyond premillennialism as such. Premillennialism gained public notice in the nineteenth century through the efforts of Baptist preacher William Miller, who collected a large following by 1839. Miller predicted confidently that Christ would return to earth on October 22, 1844. The failure of this prophecy caused Millerites to be ridiculed. They reinterpreted the prophecy, formed the Seventh Day Adventist Church, and ignored the critique of the rest of Protestantism.

By the early nineteenth century most evangelical/mainstream Americans were *postmillennialists,* though they may not have used the term.[2] Their assimilated Enlightenment cultural confidence in human capability fitted well with the notion that the world was getting better and better. They believed that the Holy Spirit working through Christians would so Christianize culture that Christ could come finally to provide the capstone to a thousand-year reign of perfect peace. Christian moral effort was both instrumental and necessary.

The early nineteenth century provided a setting in which a combination of cultural optimism and biblical faith came to full fruition. Revivalism and its accompanying social reform seemed ready to usher in the millennium. Two large-scale religious awakenings had seemed to sweep America clean religiously and behaviorally. By the mid-1830s, postmillennial religious leaders were confident in their predictions. Charles Finney asserted: "If the church will do her duty, the millennium may come in this country in three years."[3] Presbyterian Charles Hodge, a noted conservative, supported postmillennialism in his systematic theology.[4]

Dispensational Pessimism

After the breakup of the evangelical/mainstream worldview in the 1860s, people looked for new interpretations of the future and its hope. One of these, a pessimistic vision, was provided by dispensationalism. Its founder was John Nelson Darby (1800–1882), who left the Church of Ireland and became a leader in the separatist Plymouth Brethren movement.[5] Darby taught that the institutional churches were growing worldly and apostate, denying fundamental theological beliefs. The true church was the faithful remnant of people who remained "separate and holy" from the world.[6] Darby visited America several times in the 1870s and persuaded some prominent evangelical pastors to adopt his theology.[7]

Dispensationalists founded independent congregations rather than denominations. People were trained in Bible conferences and Bible schools such as the famous Moody Bible Institute in Chicago.[8] Beginning in 1924, Dallas Theological Seminary (originally called the Evangelical Theological College) set a model for seminaries with a dispensational commitment. Dispensationalists majored in a literalistic, futuristic interpretation of biblical prophecy that promised the premillennial return of Christ and a specific and complicated timetable of attendant events.[9]

Especially important in propagating this viewpoint was the publication in 1909 of the Scofield Reference Bible with notes that interpreted all of scripture according to the dispensational system.[10] C. I. Scofield, a self-taught lawyer and pastor, defined a dispensation as "a period of time during which man is tested in respect of obedience to some specific revelation of the will of God."[11] According to the dispensational system, God dealt differently with people in each of the six dispensations, or economies, that have thus far occurred.[12]

We are now in the dispensation of grace, or the church age, the period between Pentecost and the second coming of Christ. The final dispensation, for which there is much expectation, is the millennial kingdom. This thousand-year reign of peace will occur after Christ returns. Before the thousand years of peace can occur there will be the turbulent happenings of the "last days." Christ will "rapture," or take up to heaven, all true believers, the church. Then on earth there will be a series of apocalyptic events: the great tribulation, the rise of the antichrist, the battle of Armageddon, then Christ's second coming, the binding of Satan, and the final establishment of the millennial kingdom.[13]

Dispensationalism fit well with the rigidified form of the evangelical/ mainstream worldview developed by the fundamentalists. Dispensationalism gave definitive shape to the worldview of some large segments of fundamentalism. Separatism was justified by the dispensational view of the organized church as apostate. Separated believers were certainly God's elect. Revival was the only hope by which individuals could be saved from the awful fate of hell or from the tribulation of the last days. Dispensationalism followed common sense in interpreting the Bible literally. They preferred strict individual morality. And their premillennial view provided an overarching interpretive scheme.

Ecumenical Optimism

The liberal/modernist worldview held to an interpretation of reality and the future radically different from that of the dispensationalists. It had great confidence that organizational unity in the church would hasten bringing the kingdom of God to the world. After the triumph of the forces of democracy in World War II, this optimism was unleashed and put to work.

Organizationally, American establishment church leaders gave themselves to the practical tasks of mobilizing public support for two world organizations: the United Nations on the secular side and the World Council of Churches on the religious side.[14] The United Nations was founded in 1945, the World Council of Churches in 1948. Both were dedicated to a new worldwide interdependence for peace after the chaos of a world war.

Establishment Protestants in the late 1940s and 1950s were not embarrassed to identify their values with American values. When the National Council of Churches was formed in 1950, its first assembly met in an auditorium decorated with United States, United Nations, and Christian flags. The theme of the convention was "This Nation Under God." Its first president, Episcopal bishop Henry Knox Sherrill, announced that "the Council marks a new and great determination that the American way will be increasingly the Christian way, for such is our heritage. . . . Together the Churches can move forward to the goal—a Christian America in a Christian world."[15]

Most liberal Protestant leaders who claimed to be prophetic in this period were not actually speaking against the dominant culture but were successful precisely because they were so attuned to the general morality of the times.[16] John Foster Dulles, who held diplomatic posts under three Democratic presidents and was the Secretary of State, was a prominent leader in the Federal Council of Churches. He helped turn the attention of the Council away from the problems of American capitalism to the "evil faiths," the secular and totalitarian ideologies that were expanding in the world and were inimical to American values. Other establishment Protestant leaders took up the theme that only a renewed commitment to Christian social ideals could save Western and world civilization. Communism became the chief among the rival faiths to combat.

The American Protestant establishment's optimistic worldview was influential in the general culture in the 1950s. Nearly one-half of all the religious news covered by *Time* and *Newsweek* referred directly or indirectly to mainline Protestant denominations. Between 1951 and 1961, six establishment Protestant leaders were featured on the cover of *Time:* Henry Knox Sherrill, Henry Pitney Van Dusen, Theodore Adams, Eugene Carson Blake, Paul Tillich, and Franklin Clark Fry. During this period, the American media were partial, almost deferential, to the mainline Protestant establishment. That was soon to change.[17]

The Recent Context of Conflicts over Millennialism

The Liberal Worldview and Presidential Politics

On September 12, 1960, in the ballroom of the Rice Hotel in Houston, Texas, John F. Kennedy stood to address the city's ministerial association. "I believe," the presidential candidate announced, "in an America where the separation of church and state is absolute—where no Catholic prelate would tell the President (should he be Catholic) how to act, and no Protestant minister would tell his parishioners for whom to vote." He followed that declaration with a pledge: "If the time should ever come—and I do not concede any conflict to be remotely possible—when my office would require me to either violate my conscience, or violate the national interest, then I would resign the office, and I hope any other conscientious public servant would do likewise."[18]

Kennedy was not addressing just the ministers in Houston. He was seeking to persuade, or at least to neutralize, two groups of national religious leaders who had raised objections to his candidacy. In May, Methodist bishop G. Bromley Oxnam and Eugene Carson Blake, a Presbyterian, both former presidents of the National Council of Churches, in an article in *Look* magazine had expressed their reservations about having a Roman Catholic in the White House. On the day of Kennedy's Houston speech, however, one hundred Protestant, Catholic, and Jewish leaders had issued a "Statement on Religious Liberty in Relation to the 1960 Campaign." It proposed the following test for religious integrity in office: "If he cannot reconcile the responsibilities entailed by his oath with his conscience, then he must resign, lest he fail his nation and his God."

Kennedy's Houston pledge explicitly met that test. Establishment Protestantism thereafter joined in interfaith union with Catholics and Jews in insisting on the right, in principle, of citizens of all faiths to run for the presidency.[19] Mainstream liberal Protestants put their hopes for reforming the nation on the possibility of electing a liberal president.

Another Protestant group remained largely unpersuaded. On September 8, 1960, the National Conference of Citizens for Religious Freedom was founded to oppose Kennedy's candidacy. While the nominal head was Norman Vincent Peale, and retired *Christian Century* editor Charles Clayton Morrison was listed as a member, it was predominantly a neo-evangelical movement sponsored by the founder of the National Association of Evangelicals (NAE), Harold John Ockenga. He was supported by the NAE's public affairs secretary Clyde W. Taylor, Daniel Poling of the conservative *Christian Herald,* and L. Nelson Bell, Billy Graham's father-in-law and an editor of *Christianity Today.*

The liberal Protestant establishment replied a few days after Kennedy's Houston speech in an article by John Bennett:

> Those who take the leadership in this Protestant attack on the Roman Church as a campaign issue are also persons who would not support a liberal Democrat no matter what his religion. . . . The opposition on the religious issue centers in that part of the country where the opposition is equally strong on the issue of civil rights and on the economic philosophy of Senator Kennedy and his platform.[20]

THE LIBERAL PROTESTANT AGENDA

In a manner that would become increasingly divisive during the 1960s, 1970s, and 1980s, the contrasts between liberal and conservative persons, churches, and movements were defined by issues, especially political issues, rather than by theology. Liberalism in the late nineteenth century had been one movement among others within the establishment churches. Now the mainstream Protestant establishment became identified as *liberal* Protestantism. What had been the muted counterthemes of the earlier evangelical/ mainstream worldview were now asserted as the only legitimate agenda for the church. Liberals proclaimed: not separatism, but ecumenical inclusivity; not nationalism, but a global perspective; not revivalism, but the need to change structures of society; not an old-fashioned common sense, but a new openness to the relativities of racial and cultural pluralism; not rigid moralism, but situational ethics; not pie-in-the-sky-by-and-by, but justice here and now.

On December 6, 1960, the inclusivist ecumenical agenda of mainstream Protestantism was dramatically asserted. In the 11:00 A.M. service in the Episcopal Grace Cathedral in San Francisco, Eugene Carson Blake, stated clerk of the United Presbyterian Church, was the guest preacher. Episcopal bishop James Pike had invited his friend Blake to preach just prior to the opening of the fifth triennial General Assembly of the National Council of Churches, of which Blake had been president from 1954 to 1957.

Blake felt that the Kennedy-Nixon election campaign had illustrated the point that "the Christian churches, divided as they are, cannot be trusted to bring to the American people an objective and authentic word of God on a political issue."[21] To a packed church, including over one hundred members of the press, Blake proposed the merger of four mainline Protestant denominations—Episcopal, United Presbyterian, Methodist, and United Church of Christ—as the first step toward reuniting America's separated Christian churches.[22] Immediately following the sermon, Bishop Pike enthusiastically endorsed the proposal, calling it a "prophetic proclamation [that] is the most sound and inspiring proposal for unity of the church in this country which has ever been made in its history."[23]

What came to be called the Blake-Pike proposal set the ecumenical agenda for American mainstream Protestantism for several decades.[24] *Time* termed it "a landmark in Protestant history." *Newsweek* gave an extended analysis of the proposal. *Life* devoted a rare religious editorial to Blake's "fresh idea" for the ecumenical future.[25] Blake appeared on the cover of *Time* on May 26, 1961, and that same year he was voted the "religious newsmaker of the year" by the Religious Newswriters Association.[26]

Not everyone was impressed. Some leaders in the denominations that were called upon to merge expressed skepticism. L. Nelson Bell, representing the neo-evangelical movement, expressed concern about a possible step toward "the eventual creation of a super-Church." What was needed, according to Bell, was rather a "spiritual unity of believers which transcends denominational, racial, and national borders."[27] In April 1962, representatives of the four denominations Blake had named met in Washington, D.C., and constituted the ongoing Consultation on Church Union (COCU).[28]

The Conservative Worldview and Presidential Politics

On August 21, 1980, Ronald Reagan addressed a massive rally of conservative Christians in Dallas, Texas: "Over the last two or three decades, the federal government seems to have forgotten both that old-time religion and that old-time Constitution. We have God's promise that if we turn to him and ask his help we shall have it. With his help we can still become that shining city upon a hill."[29] Then he brought the delegates to their feet in elation by declaring: "I know you can't endorse me, but I want you to know that I endorse you and what you are doing."[30]

The group Reagan excited had been assembled under the sponsorship of a politically conservative umbrella organization, The Religious Roundtable. Twenty thousand conservative Christian ministers and lay people were invited to Dallas for instructions in voter registration, fund-raising, and use of the media. Falwell and other leading electronic preachers were present along with conservative political fundraisers, leaders of single-issue political groups, senators, congressional representatives, and military leaders. Reagan's appeal to these fundamentalists was as effective in securing their support as Kennedy's 1960 pledge in Houston had been in ensuring the backing of the liberal Protestant establishment. The marriage of the New Religious/Political Right and Reagan Republicanism was consummated.

All three presidential candidates had been invited. Only Reagan came. The other two, Jimmy Carter and John Anderson, had impeccable credentials as evangelical believers. Reagan had many liabilities. He was divorced and a movie actor, both previously unacceptable behaviors to conservative evangelicals and fundamentalists. That Reagan was overwhelmingly accepted evidenced that a commitment to the evangelical/mainstream worldview, in its more recent fundamentalist form, was more important to American religious conservatives than either correct doctrine or properly pious behavior.

After Reagan's election, Martin Marty wrote: "The morning after the November 4, 1980 national elections in the U.S., a cluster of forces codenamed the Moral Majority took credit for having helped turn America to a more conservative course."[31] What the media and the public conveniently labeled the Moral Majority was actually a loose coalition of sometimes co-operating and often competing religious groups. Some, like the Religious Roundtable and the Christian Voice, had been organized with overtly political goals. Others, such as Campus Crusade for Christ, had long been in existence as evangelistic agencies, but had lent their support to this religious-political crusade. Most visible were the television evangelists like Jerry Falwell and James Robison. Analysts of the election speculated that the religious groups were perhaps less politically powerful than they claimed to be. They were, however, far more significant in their influence than many in the general public had expected them to be.[32]

On January 20, 1981, Reagan, at age 69, became the oldest person ever to ascend to the U.S. presidency. In contrast to his age, he seemed to many to exude vigor, confident expectations, and new beginnings. Religious and political conservatives, who felt that Reagan truly was their candidate, looked forward to a second American revolution in which the early American evangelical/mainstream worldview would become a guide to twentieth-century political action.

Tensions between Right and Left Regarding Millennialism

Reconstructionism on the Right

In the early 1960s, a small cadre of extreme Calvinist fundamentalists organized the Chalcedon Foundation. It called for a new reformation or reconstruction of American society. It and its several offshoots provided much of the intellectual underpinnings for the social policy of the New Religious/Political Right of the 1980s. Falwell endorsed a series of Reconstructionist books as a "tool Christians need." Francis Schaeffer's *Christian Manifesto,* much praised by the Reagan administration, was built on Reconstructionist social analysis. Pat Robertson invited Reconstructionist leaders to appear on his *700 Club* television show. And Reconstructionist disciples Joseph Kickosola and Herbert Titus taught in Robertson's CBN University Graduate Schools of Law and Public Policy.[33]

The founder of Reconstructionism was Rousas John Rushdoony. Born in 1916, he was the son of recent emigrants from Soviet Armenia. Rushdoony later pointed with pride to the fact that in A.D. 300 Armenia was the first country to make Christianity its state religion. This Armenian state church had split from both the Roman Catholic and the Eastern Orthodox Church because it refused to adopt the Chalcedonian Creed, which asserted that Christ had two natures, one human and the other divine. The Rushdoonys belonged to a tiny Protestant minority that viewed the Chalcedonian Creed as the foundation of Western liberty. Since for them Christ alone was true God and true humanity, a unique link between heaven and earth, then all human institutions were to be under the direct mandate of explicit Christian revelation.[34] Rushdoony's 900-page *Institutes of Biblical Law,* published in 1973, expounded the implications of the Bible for every sphere of life.[35]

The philosophical foundation of Reconstructionist theory was the presuppositional apologetics of Cornelius Van Til of Westminster Seminary (although Van Til denied that he was a Reconstructionist). Reconstructionists compared Van Til to Einstein and spoke of the "Copernican dimensions" of his thought. They adopted Van Til's view that one must presuppose the Christian system of thought found in the Bible in order to make sense of anything. The direct antithesis of this view was "secular humanism." By Reconstructionist definition, a humanist was "someone who thinks that man, and only man, can solve the problems men face—and solve them without any reference to God or to the Bible."[36]

The Reconstructionist response to secular humanism was sometimes called "theonomy." This concept meant that a blueprint for every area of life was to be found in God's law in the Bible, primarily in the Old Testament. Reconstructionists claimed to take their cues from New England Puritanism. Like them, the Reconstructionists viewed ancient Israel's theocracy as the model for how all nations should be governed. By following the Old Testament law, the United States could yet become "a city on a hill" that the Puritans had envisioned.[37]

In *Theonomy in Christian Ethics,* Greg Bahnsen argued that the Old Testament law applied to the contemporary United States in "exhaustive" and "minutial" detail. Christ's coming had abrogated only the ceremonial law. All the other laws should be kept. For example, capital punishment should be applied to fifteen crimes, including murder, rape, homosexuality, sabbath breaking, apostasy, witchcraft, blasphemy, and incorrigibility in children. There would be no prisons in Reconstructionist society. Criminals would be executed or rehabilitated while serving as slaves.[38]

Reconstructionists assume that it will take two hundred to two thousand years to bring about a completed Christian state. They disavow violent revolution, believing that their radical reforms will be gradually accepted as most people are persuaded of the correctness of Reconstructionism. They hold to the postmillennialism popular in the nineteenth century. They believe that the church will slowly but ultimately triumph and bring in a period of one thousand years of perfect peace. Christ will come at the end of this period to crown the church's achievement.[39]

Little attention was paid to Reconstructionism in the 1960s and 1970s outside close Calvinist fundamentalist circles. In the new atmosphere of the 1980s, leaders of the New Religious Right used Reconstructionism to buttress a host of conservative causes. It claimed to have provided the intellectual underpinnings that made possible the rise of the New Religious/Political Right.[40]

THE CREATION OF SECULAR HUMANISM

One example of Reconstructionism's conceptual power was the elevation of the concept of secular humanism to the status of archenemy of the New Religious Right.[41] Francis Schaeffer's *Christian Manifesto,* built on Reconstructionist social theory, became widely influential in fundamentalist circles and through them into Washington political circles in identifying a humanist worldview as the enemy of American values.[42] Schaeffer popularized the use of the term "secular humanism" in his films and books, *How Should We Then Live?* and *Whatever Happened to the Human Race?* In them, Christians confront two exclusive and opposite philosophies or worldviews—Christianity and secular humanism.[43]

Schaeffer's political message is predicated on his interpretation of American history. According to Schaeffer, the United States was founded on the social principles of the Protestant Reformation with the Bible as their base. After 1848, America's Protestant consensus was broken up by waves of immigrants—especially Roman Catholics—who "did not have the Reformation base." By the turn of the century, God-denying humanists began to gain control of the splintered public consensus.[44] According to Schaeffer, "the things which have come into our country which have troubled us are the inevitable results of this humanist world view."[45]

Tim LaHaye, a Baptist pastor in San Diego, California, and founding member of the Moral Majority, picked up the Reconstructionist critique of secular humanism and gave it specific political application. In 1980, LaHaye published *The Battle for the Mind,* in which he used Reconstructionist analysis and added to it a worldwide conspiracy theory. According to LaHaye, "a hard-core group of committed humanists . . . set out over 100 years ago to control the masses." He alleged that "there are only

275,000 of them, but they control everything—the mass media, government, and even the Supreme Court."[46]

One of the avowed purposes of the secular humanists, according to the conspiracy theory, "is to reduce the standard of living in our country so that someday the citizens of America will voluntarily merge with the Soviet Union."[47] LaHaye's challenge to Christian fundamentalists is: "We must remove all humanists from public office and replace them with pro-moral political leaders."[48]

In the mid-1970s, many fundamentalists had never thought of secular humanism as an identifiable, organized movement. It was not mentioned in sermons. By the early 1980s, nearly all fundamentalists had adopted secular humanism as the identifiable enemy. It made a convenient category in political debate as well by lumping many attitudes to which they objected under one rubric.

In 1980, a small group of fifty-eight humanist scholars played right into the fundamentalists' hands by attacking fundamentalism in "A Secular Humanist Declaration."[49] In 1982, representatives of seven groups created the North American Committee for Humanism. Its hope was to correct the institutional and ideological weakness of humanism on the American continent.[50] However, Paul Kurtz, identified as the leading humanist scholar in America, lamented that humanism was "failing as a mass movement." According to him, it had "collapsed and does not exist in North America."[51] For adherents to the New Religious/Political Right, it nonetheless made a convenient catchall concept for everything they opposed.

LaHaye next founded the American Coalition for Traditional Values (ACTV). Its thirty-three-member founding board included televangelists Jerry Falwell, Jimmy Swaggart, Jim Bakker, James Robison, Rex Humbard, Kenneth Copeland, and Pat Robertson. Other members were Campus Crusade founder Bill Bright and then-president of the Southern Baptist Convention, Charles Stanley. Its purposes were voter registration and education, and especially getting "born again" candidates to run for office.[52] LaHaye estimated that 40 percent of all Americans were born again. Therefore, he concluded, 40 percent of all officeholders should be born again. By his calculations, there were 97,000 elected offices above the community level and 110,000 Bible-believing churches. If every Bible-believing church had one born-again member elected to office, then Christians could take over the country.[53]

In 1985, LaHaye moved his office to Washington, D.C., to lobby full time. The reversal of fundamentalist theory regarding the role of

Christians in politics was complete with LaHaye's assertion: "Politics is the key to moral revival."[54] Pat Robertson's Christian Coalition, similarly informed by Reconstructionist theory, is actively implementing LaHaye's slogan.

The Influence of Dispensational Date Setting

In the 1970s dispensationalism reached out to a more general audience with Hal Lindsey's *Late Great Planet Earth,* the best-selling book of the decade. President Reagan liked to discuss its theses with his pastor and others. He speculated that the prophecies foretelling the final battle of Armageddon were being fulfilled that could make this the last generation of people on earth.[55] John Walvoord, a former president and professor of systematic theology at Dallas Theological Seminary, had written a dispensational treatise in 1974, *Armageddon, Oil, and the Middle East Crisis,*[56] which he updated in 1990 to include current events. On the night that President George Bush launched the Gulf War against Iraq, Bush invited Billy Graham to stay with the first family. Graham apparently recommended Walvoord's book, and the White House ordered six copies for the president and his staff.[57] Falwell's brand of fundamentalism was strongly dispensational. He asserted that his children would not live out their lives before Christ returned.[58] At the farthest extreme, David Koresh exploited this kind of thinking in a twisted and tragic manner with the Branch Davidian sect members under his influence.[59]

Pat Robertson's role as the strongest political figure of the New Religious/Political Right makes his millennial views especially important. They are also very confusing. He often draws on postmillennial Reconstructionist thinking. Simultaneously, in *The New Millennium: 10 Trends That Will Impact You and Your Family by the Year 2000,* Robertson outlines an ideological worldview that imbibes deeply of premillennial dispensational date setting. Although Robertson had set dates that later had to be revised, he is willing to speculate that Christ's return to establish his millennial government may occur in the year 2007.[60] Robertson's desire is that the new millennium may be "the Millennium of the rule and reign of Jesus Christ."[61]

In the meantime, while waiting for his premillennial expectations to be fulfilled, Robertson pragmatically follows the sociopolitical program of the postmillennial Reconstructionists. In the 1970s many Pentecostals and charismatics such as Robertson discovered Reconstructionism as an ally and extension of their beliefs. The more extreme charismatics' "name it and claim it" theology asserted dominion over their personal lives, expecting health and wealth. Reconstructionism taught charismatics to extend their dominion over the political and social realm as well.[62]

Despite their differences regarding the timetable for Christ's return, dispensationalists, Pentecostals/charismatics, and Reformed Reconstructionists shared many other fundamentalist distinctives. They all claimed to interpret the Bible literally. They have low regard for the institutional church. They value common moral commitments more than precise theological formulations. They share a utopian hope of bringing the kingdom of God to earth.[63] The combination creates a powerfully motivating ideological worldview. More than anyone else, Robertson has been able to direct those holding this worldview into concrete political action by asserting that God supports—indeed requires—their commitment to reforming the nation.

The Rise of "Secular" Theology on the Left

In 1965, a small group of formerly neo-orthodox academics enjoyed brief notoriety by announcing that it was no longer possible to speak about God. The *New York Times* published an article, " 'New' Theologians See Christianity without God." And on April 8, 1966, *Time*'s cover asked: "IS GOD DEAD?" Harvey Cox authored a 1965 best-seller, *The Secular City*, and blessed secularization as "an authentic consequence of biblical faith." He too declared a moratorium on "God talk." According to Cox, in the secular city "the political was replacing the metaphysical as the characteristic mode of grasping reality." These academic theologians provided theoretical justification for the move to direct political involvement by denominational leaders. The church, for Cox, was to be "God's Avant-Garde." The "real ecumenical crisis," Cox warned, was not between Catholics and Protestants, but between "traditional and experimental forms of church life."[64]

No Compelling Vision for the Center

By the late 1960s, academic theologians had generally abandoned the neo-orthodox theological consensus. Issues of social relativism, religious pluralism, and the place of metaphysics occupied teachers of religion. The neo-orthodox giants of theology, who were no longer active, had not specifically addressed these issues. By the 1990s still no systems of theology had won the allegiance of large numbers in the mainstream churches.

Tragically, those on both the right and the left had put their hopes in political activity to accomplish their worldview goals. The moderate middle, as usual, had difficulty articulating a vision of future hope for the church and the nation.

According to sociologists and historians of religion, mainstream Protestantism was preoccupied with and polarized by a division between liberals and conservatives reminiscent of the fundamentalist-modernist split of the 1920s.[65] That theological cleavage sundered every mainstream denomination. It also corresponded, in part, to a cleavage between clergy and laity, or more accurately, between some clergy and a cadre of highly educated laity involved at higher governing body levels on the one hand, and the majority of clergy and laity in the congregations on the other.[66] Another evidence of this polarization was the proliferation of special interest groups that tended to cluster in what Robert Wuthnow called "humanistic" and "evangelical" groupings, corresponding roughly to the liberal-conservative theological divisions.[67]

Mainstream Protestants have long memories and are more self-conscious regarding their heritage than fundamentalists. Many were still reacting to their more than half-century of conflict with the fundamentalists. Mainstream Protestant leaders remained committed to Reinhold Niebuhr's 1930s scathing critique of cultural and social sin. Many mainstream leaders thus appeared to oppose orthodox theology, capitalism, and middle-class values. Unfortunately, such apparent opposition alienated them from the majority of members of most mainstream congregations.[68]

By the late twentieth century nothing seemed to go smoothly for the six former mainstream denominations. In size and media attention they had been replaced by conservative denominations, such as the Southern Baptists, and by independent and Pentecostal/Holiness churches.[69] Martin Marty suggested that present members of the former establishment churches could now only define themselves as NEFOPEGS (Not Evangelical, Fundamentalist Or Pentecostal, Generally Speaking).[70]

Here, according to the researchers in mainstream Protestantism, was Protestant liberalism's degenerative weakness. Sociologist Benton Johnson asserted: "The only weakness for which a recovery course cannot now be charted is the churches' theological predicament."[71] Wade Clark Roof and William McKinney thought it "unlikely" that religious groups as "communities of memory" would have "the requisite resources—the symbols, the language, the conviction—to restore a broadly based public faith."[72]

According to Glenn T. Miller, Southern Baptist church historian, in his study of the last fifty years in American theological education, what hurt the old establishment churches even more was that the problem lay right on the doorstep of their theological institutions. The one distinctive area of teaching that seminaries offer, according to Miller, is how to think theologically. Yet, in their desire to imitate other professions, that is what they had not been doing.[73] Miller suggested that "Christianity must be studied on its own terms and from its own classic documents" in the larger religious and cultural context.[74]

John Mulder, president of Louisville Presbyterian Seminary, and Lee Wyatt, a pastor of Harvey Browne Presbyterian Church in Louisville, came to a similar conclusion in their article, "The Predicament of Pluralism: The Study of Theology in Presbyterian Seminaries Since the 1920s." Noting that Presbyterian seminaries had played an important role in encouraging the rise of pluralism, they concluded: "Yet the unintended consequence of the enrichment of theological discourse within these educational institutions has been the impoverishment of a distinct theological vision, informed by the Presbyterian and Reformed traditions." Such a "blurred and inchoate identity" taught to and promulgated by seminary graduates proved insufficiently compelling to warrant the faith and obedience of many church members.[75]

What people have always needed and apparently continued to need was a system of beliefs that give meaning to life.[76] It is answers to the why questions that provide hope for the future for individuals and a people.[77] A system of meaning is another way to speak of a worldview. Conservatives had seemed to do better than liberals in giving people a coherent worldview by which to live as individuals and to guide their vision for the church and the nation.[78]

Creating a Centrist Worldview of Hope

Millennialism was one of the themes of the early American evangelical/mainstream worldview. The balancing countertheme was the concern to Christianize the world here and now. When the fundamentalists and the liberals divided these themes and counterthemes among them, the fundamentalists became increasingly otherworldly, looking to a future end-time, and the liberals increasingly focused on improving human welfare in this world at this time.

Calvinistic and intellectually oriented fundamentalists often responded to general cultural trends by holding a *postmillennial* view in times of cultural optimism. Postmillennialism teaches that things are getting better and that by cooperating with the Spirit of God, Christians can bring the world to a state of peace that Christ will return to bless. Both Old Princeton and twentieth-century Reconstructionist leaders held that view.

The less scholastic fundamentalists and Pentecostals were usually *premillennial.* They were culturally pessimistic, holding that things were getting worse and worse and that nothing could change society's descent into degradation until Christ returned again to create the millennium of peace. Dispensational fundamentalists provided complicated schemes (frequently revised) detailing the events leading to and following Christ's premillennial return.[79]

An Amillennial Alternative

A contemporary, creative centrist worldview would offer theological middle ground. Another classical millennial position, the Augustinian and Reformed theological tradition, has been amillennial. Culturally, the Augustinian/Reformed tradition is neither pessimistic nor optimistic. It describes history as having ups and downs that we cannot predict. There will be both progress and human failure as long as human history lasts.

The Augustinian tradition believes that the Spirit of God is at work in the world through the church now. We live in the millennium because the Spirit is here bringing God's will to bear through those who obey God's Word. For example, great acts of healing through doctors and hospitals and the dramatic growth of the church over the whole world can be offered as evidences of the presence of the Spirit of Christ in the world now.

The amillennial position thus provides what the liberals seek in a focus on human welfare in the present. It also has a future orientation that is the concern of the fundamentalists. Amillennialists in the Augustinian/Reformed tradition firmly believe that Jesus Christ will return bodily to earth. Christ's return will signal the end of human history, a time of final judgment, and the inauguration of a new heaven and a new earth.

The chief value of an amillennial position for a contemporary centrist worldview is to put all our present activity in the context of God's ultimate just consummation of human history. A contemporary psychologist, Rex Julian Beaber of Los Angeles, noted that humans have been fascinated with the end of time since the beginning of human time. "It is the end that somehow infuses life with meaning," he asserted. That end-time perspective prods people to deal with ultimate questions they otherwise might avoid.[80] As we approach the year 2000 and a new millennium, we can expect human interest in millennial questions to grow. The perspective that God's Spirit is at work for good in the world in the present and that God's future is one in which justice will be done should be a powerful incentive for religious people to seek personal wholeness and justice in our human communities now.

8 | Worldview: A Resource for Reconciliation

> The holy Christian Church, whose only Head is Christ, is
> born of the Word of God, abides in the same, and hears not
> the voice of a stranger.
>
> —*The Ten Conclusions of Berne, A.D. 1528, number 1*

FOCUS: What role is there for the mainstream churches? Can they provide their members with both roots in the biblical tradition and an ability to cope with the modern world? They can if they understand the central role that worldviews play in guiding people's thought and behavior. Worldviews are rooted in a religious story. They are elaborated in denominational theologies. They are applied to social issues through transdenominational ideological movements. And they are colored by individual experience. An early American evangelical/mainstream worldview continues to have power. If mainstream churches will come to grips with the power of this worldview and develop a constructive, contemporary alternative, they can claim the center, ecclesiastically, intellectually, and morally.

An Attempt at Application

Now I wish to speak personally. I run the risk of being viewed as having "quit preaching and started meddling." Having presented a lengthy and sometimes complex narrative, I need to take responsibility and ask what we can learn from all of this that is relevant to our present situation as

Protestant Christians, as formerly mainstream churchpersons, and, for me, as a Presbyterian.

We Need the Mainstream

My thesis is simple. There is a necessary role in our culture for mainstream denominations if they will claim the center, ecclesiastically, intellectually, and morally. Most people are struggling to find the center. They want to be rooted in a stable tradition, but they need support in coping with modernity. They are neither fundamentalists nor liberals. They are somewhere in the middle. And that is where a mainstream church should be.[1]

The issues of our day are complex and difficult. We need a place where they can be addressed with attention to the nuances from every side. We also need a place where people can be sure that conviction will finally form and action will result. Mainstream churches need to pair urgent priorities in a way that balances them instead of letting them become conflicting concerns.

We need, for example, to balance:

Biblical authority and contemporary interpretation.
Redemption of individuals and transformation of society.
Essential beliefs of the community and integrity of individual
    conscience.
The call to leadership and the recognition of human limitations.
The teaching role of the church and its legislative role.
Congregational vitality and a connectional system.
Denominational identity and ecumenical cooperation.

If mainstream denominations will return to playing their appropriate centrist role, they can provide a needed balance betwixt and between those more one-sided groups to the left and the right.[2] Mainstream churches can help people find a secure center between authoritarian fundamentalist sects on the one side and extreme liberalism to mystical New Age groups on the other side. Mainstream churches can help provide people with a vital local community while enabling them to relate to the larger society. Mainstream churches can provide "communities of memory" that put people in touch with the ultimate religious worldview, as translated through their theological tradition, and also provide a contemporary ideological worldview that enables people to cope constructively with modernity.[3]

If we did not have mainstream denominations, we would have to invent them! Indeed, conservative independent congregations continually do create denominations by planting many new congregations that are clones of themselves. The difficulty is that these "denominations" rarely have the safeguards of democratic procedure and group decision making. Too often one person continues to have all the policy-making authority. And their ideology does not perform the balancing functions that are needed by the majority of people who occupy the moderate middle.

The Predicament of Pluralism

From the 1960s onward we, the formerly mainstream denominations, lost touch with the center in our attempt to cope with the complexities of modern culture. Mainstream leaders rightly realized that the Christian faith was not the exclusive property of white, Anglo-Saxon Protestants. Thus we correctly sought to become more diverse in our membership and leadership.

But we lost sight of the goal. Instead of working to broaden our base to include all who desired to share in our ultimate and theological worldview, we became enamored with diversity itself as a goal. From diversity around shared goals we moved to inclusivism as *the* goal, and our diversity became pluralism, which makes diversity in itself an ultimate value.

We began from a right and necessary desire for racial, ethnic, gender, and cultural diversity within our denominations. Our legitimate goal was unity with everyone who believed and wanted to act out the same values that we shared. Soon we began to welcome such a diversity in ecclesiology, theology, and moral values that there was no longer any discernible unity. We now have many different goals and values. We have different conceptions of the church, different visions of truth, and different understandings of morality.

By emphasizing diversity as a goal in itself, we have lost the sense of a shared center. Mainstream denominations are no longer unified communities, but collections of diverse interest groups under a common umbrella.[4] This book is about reclaiming a sense of a genuinely shared center. This center is not just a passive midpoint between extremes to the right and left. It is a substantive core of conviction.[5] We begin that process of centering by rekindling our commitment to Jesus Christ and a common ultimate Christian worldview.

Re-Creation of a Responsible Worldview

An Ultimate Christian Worldview

Our ultimate worldview is rooted in the simple narrative story that distinguishes the way a Christian relates to reality from that of, for example, a

Buddhist or a Hindu. The narrative thread that runs through the scriptures can be stated quite simply. God made a good world. We sinned against God and damaged the world. God came in Jesus Christ to restore us and the world to a right relationship with God and wholeness of life. Those three sentences work as a summary of the faith for me. The Apostles' Creed does it better using a few more phrases.

Different stories explain reality. For Christians the biblical story is the most compelling one. It makes sense of everything for us better than any of the others. We need to keep reminding ourselves how important, how fundamental, how life-giving this story is. Only then can we begin to build on the story.

A Theological Elaboration of a Presbyterian Worldview

As we elaborate the story, we must be careful to acknowledge that we come with different building blocks and different tools. Each of these is helpful, but none is absolute. Each mainstream denomination needs to reconstruct a theological worldview that is consistent with the theological worldview which brought that communion into being, and which at the same time will enable its members to cope with the modern world.

For example, Presbyterians have a framework that we call Reformed theology. We love to say the Latin phrase *Ecclesia reformata, semper reformanda*, "Reformed and always willing to be reformed." Some of my Presbyterian friends think that means that the more often you change your mind the better Presbyterian you are. That is not quite it. It means that we have a content-filled tradition coming from our northern European Reformation ancestors. It also means that we are not locked into the centuries-old form of that tradition but can adapt and expand it to cope with the modern world.

For example, a diverse group of twenty-one Presbyterians was able to compose a two-page doctrinal statement, "A Brief Statement of Faith: Presbyterian Church (U.S.A.)," which was officially adopted and widely accepted by the denomination in 1991. At a time when many questioned whether any common identity could be found, this succinct statement of a contemporary Presbyterian theological worldview was produced, based solidly in the biblical story.

That theological achievement did not prevent struggles within the denomination at the ideological and experiential levels over issues such as abortion and human sexuality. It did, however, demonstrate that there was a core of common commitment at the ultimate religious level and in its theological elaboration that could provide cohesion in the church. A recognition of commonality at the level of religious commitment and a basic belief system are potentially the most powerful resources available to encourage reconciliation among conflicting groups in the mainstream churches. This provides a baseline on which to build toward further understanding in the application of this ultimate and theological worldview to issues of ideological application and individual experience.

We are open to being reformed "according to the Word of God and the call of the Spirit."[6] We listen to our equally Reformed partners from the two-thirds world and gain insight and motivation from their understandings of our common heritage. And we listen to other Christian and religious traditions and to the secular world.

We can learn something from every quarter. But we cannot tack on other religions and tuck in conflicting worldviews. We need to be relatively consistent in developing our own theological elaboration of the ultimate religious worldview. It will only confuse us and makes us less useful as dialogue partners if we do not work within our own theological framework and develop the values that are there for the good of the ecumenical whole.

A Contemporary Ideology

A theological framework formerly played a large part in defining what it meant to be a Presbyterian, or a Methodist, or a Baptist. That is much less true today. We must recognize that the ideological worldviews of liberal, fundamentalist, charismatic, and so forth cut across every denominational line. Conservative Presbyterians and Episcopalians often feel they have more in common than do liberal and conservative members of the same denomination.

We all have, and as human beings must have, an ideological worldview that enables us to relate our Christian faith and theology to the general culture of which we are a part. It helps us to place ourselves in relation to others and gives us a sense of belonging. Persons who hold the same ultimate Christian worldview can differ dramatically in the way they understand the implications of that ultimate worldview as it applies to the culture in which they live.

I have given so much attention in this book to the views of those on the extremes to the right and left because they tend to identify the Christian faith with their ideological worldview in a way that causes conflict within the Christian community. They will not go away, and we ignore them at

161

our peril. We need, rather, to learn how to cope with them by acknowledging and affirming their core Christian beliefs while declining to adopt their ideological worldview applications. We need to develop our own centrist ideological position between the extremes of the right and the left.

A FUNDAMENTALIST WORLDVIEW

Fundamentalists will continue to hold and defend an ideological worldview that is a rigidified form of the earlier evangelical/mainstream worldview. In the fundamentalist worldview, life is structured according to unchangeable laws. Commitment to obey these laws is the highest good. The United States should be returned to its (mythical) former ideal condition as a Christian nation. Christians should rule, and all people should be required to conform to Christian laws.

Reconstructionism is the most elaborate form of this view, and it continues to exert a strong and, to mainliners, largely invisible influence, since mainliners tend to ignore fundamentalist literature. Pat Robertson is committed to the ideals of Reconstructionism, and he will be back as a political candidate seeking to put them into effect legislatively. His followers are already doing a highly effective job of controlling regional party caucuses and winning local elections.[7]

In terms of national influence, we have not heard the last of fundamentalists like Robertson and Falwell and a whole host of others with similar ideas and aspirations. We had better realize that they have power and can produce votes because they appeal to the residual early American worldview that is buried deep in most American psyches. Unless we old-line folks can get in touch with those worldview themes and show a way of bringing them into creative engagement with modernity, then we may be talking only to ourselves. And our circle is getting smaller all the time.

A LIBERAL WORLDVIEW

Liberals will continue to try to commend the church to the world by being like the world. For them, life is infinitely open and reality is boundlessly varied. The job of the church is to keep a civil discussion going in a pluralistic and inclusive society. In this worldview, the church should model the new humanity by exhibiting an attitude of openness and inclusivity that is hopefully possible and in the liberal view preferable for all people.

A Centrist Worldview

The center is the place where conviction and civility should be joined. A centrist worldview holds that reality was ordered according to God's intention. Now some of the great variety in reality is the expression of God's good creation, and other aspects are the result of profound mystery, inexplicable evil, and human sin. We need both to respect God's laws and to be civil in carrying on careful and open discussion with others leading to appropriate interpretation of God's guidance regarding all aspects of reality.

Ecclesiastically, we are not forced to choose between only a private expression of the church or a public one. Many congregations and governing bodies have evidenced a deep commitment to evangelism and to meeting the personal needs of members, while at the same time being active in the public arena, developing programs and taking actions to provide a more abundant life for all people on this earth. Intellectually we are not forced to be either naïve Common Sense realists nor cynical critical modernists. We can be critical realists, believing that reality is knowable, but in a limited, human way. Morally, we are not forced to choose between rigid laws shorn of compassion for those to whom they are applied on the one hand, and, on the other hand, an acceptance of any avowedly moral action that a person or group claims to be sanctioned by God. A worldview of the center can uphold an ordered moral law and at the same time allow appropriate exceptions given our limited knowledge and our need for grace.

We must remember that an ideological worldview is *not* synonymous with the ultimate Christian worldview. An ideological worldview is essential and it is dangerous. We cannot live without a worldview that makes sense of our experience as members of a culture. But often, and usually unintentionally, our ideological worldview takes precedence over our religious commitment. How else can you explain the enthusiasm of fundamentalists in 1980 for a divorced, seldom churchgoing, former movie actor as their temporal savior when they had a Sunday-school-teaching Southern Baptist already in the White House?

Our Experience

The coloring that personal experience gives to our worldview is determinative for our outlook and difficult to integrate with the theological and ideological worldview levels. Each of us sees from our own unique perspective.

The earliest question the ancient Greek philosophers pondered was: Is reality many or is it one? They struggled to discern the principles that made for change and those that produced continuity.[8] Experience is the principle of change. Coming uniquely from each individual, it keeps our unity from being uniformity and introduces new elements for us to consider. The principles of continuity, however, must be ones outside ourselves to which we all have common reference. In the Reformed Presbyterian tradition, the principles of unity are scripture, the creeds and confessions that interpret scripture, and Presbyterian rules of procedure.

I once was asked by another theologian: "What is the matter with my experience being normative for my theology?" My response was that it would make it difficult for us to find common ground. Each of us has unique and valuable personal experiences. We will understand each other and ourselves, and communicate with each other helpfully, when we all bring our unique perspectives to a common touchstone, the scriptures. Then we have a common frame of reference and common concepts by which to clarify and hopefully to coalesce our individual viewpoints.

Renewing the Evangelical/Mainstream Worldview

The early American evangelical/mainstream worldview was called into question in the mid-nineteenth century, but since then nothing generally acceptable to American Protestant Christians has taken its place. In a pluralistic society, with a rich diversity of cultures, it is essential that the center, the mainstream, of the Protestant church be defined by an ideological worldview that grounds people in the biblical tradition and at the same time enables them to cope with the modern world. We need to renew, refurbish, and make relevant a contemporary form of the evangelical/mainstream worldview.

Claiming the Ecclesiastical, Intellectual, and Moral Center

Claiming the Ecclesiastical Center

In the early 1990s, two popular books called people back to a centrist view of the church. Leander E. Keck, retired dean of Yale Divinity School, published his Lyman Beecher lectures as *The Church Confident.*[9] Keck notes that for every person from a nonreligious background who joins a mainline church, three leave it for no church at all.[10] Demographically, the future growth of the mainline churches depends on attracting and keeping eighteen- to thirty-four-year-olds. Yet statistics show that the more liberal the church is, the less attractive it is to this age group.[11] Keck's answer is that the church should return to: authentic worship of God; theological substance; pastors who are coaches, developing the talent of lay leaders; and communicating the gospel competently and confidently.

The most quoted book about the church in the early 1990s was probably Loren Mead's *The Once and Future Church*.[12] According to Mead, we are at the end of the era of Christendom when the United States could be considered a Christian nation and mission was something we did out there, far away. Mission is now on the doorstep of every congregation. The congregation is the frontline of mission. Congregations do not exist to fund the mission agendas of national denominational bureaucracies, but those bureaucracies should exist only to support the mission agendas of local congregations.

MOVEMENT TOWARD THE CENTER IN THE MAINLINE

There has been a discernible movement toward the center in the leadership of the former mainline churches. As early as 1985, James Wall, editor of the *Christian Century,* declared self-critically that mainliners had in the 1960s and 1970s focused too exclusively on the public policy aspect of the church and not given enough attention to worship or to the needs of families.[13]

A wake-up call to the mainstream churches was sounded by the *Christian Century* in 1989. The November 8 issue was devoted to the theme "Where Is the 'Mainline' Headed?" The writers were well-known liberal sociologists and historians, but none of them supported the one-sided, liberal, social policy emphasis of the church during the previous twenty-five years. Instead, the writers repeatedly expressed appreciation for what could be learned from the emphases of more evangelical Christians.

The viewpoint of the contributors was summed up by Martin Marty. He began his article by asserting: "No one—well, almost no one—in America belongs to a church or synagogue *in order* to get political signals and find denomination-wide company for expressing them."[14] Reviewing a book by Robert Booth Fowler, *Unconventional Partners: Religion and Liberal Culture in the United States,* Marty noted political scientist Fowler's contention that effective churches seek the sacred and the transcendent, meaning and truth. Marty averred that this was not a call for an "introverted, self-enclosed worshiping community," but concluded: "Unless religious leaders understand the hungers of the heart expressed by Americans who inhabit and enjoy but are not finally satisfied by liberal culture, there will be no followers with which to work."[15] Marty, who coined the much-used category "public and private church," was clearly opting for a centrist church that evidenced the values of both.

Mainline denominations are recognizing that they must shift from emphasizing the national and public policy role of the church to stressing the congregational and nurturing role. That shift is not to deny the legitimacy of a public policy role. It is a necessary redress of emphases that have too long been ignored: openness to growth, especially in new church development and redevelopment; evangelism, especially among youth, young adults, and racial ethnic persons; support for marriages, parenting, and family life; and revitalizing of Christian education and congregational nurture.[16]

All of this will only make a difference if the people occupying posts of national leadership recognize that they, by and large, have a liberal worldview and that they must now become open to affirming the values of a renewed centrist evangelical/mainstream worldview. If budget and programmatic activity at the national level do not follow the verbal professions of emphasis on congregational ministry, then further alienation and financial loss will result.[17]

TRUSTING PEOPLE TO REPRESENT US

I need to repeat one more modest proposal. The awful gulf between church leadership and membership can be solved. We simply need to return to the principle of representative government. In its inception that principle meant that everyone in leadership needed to represent a community that elected them as leaders. All representatives should be elected and thus be responsibly related to a governing body in the church. For Presbyterians that means that everyone serving in leadership must be elected to that position by a congregation, a presbytery, a synod, or a General Assembly.

We Presbyterians have become at best two churches with differing worldviews and at worst a conglomeration of competing special interest lobbies. That divisiveness occurs, in part, because we have moved so far away from representative government. Commitment to the whole church and communication within it will more likely occur when leaders are responsible to an electorate and not to some invisible national nominating process or some special interest advocacy group. We need to listen to everyone. We must consult widely. But only people elected through governing bodies should make decisions. That is Presbyterian representative government. Working through a representative electoral process will tie us to-gether so that the issues of worldview will have to be revealed and resolved.

A CREATIVE SYNTHESIS

The polarities can be synthesized. It requires only a willingness to set priori-ties and get things in the proper order. The primary commitment of the church must be to the sovereign God revealed in Jesus Christ. If that message is not proclaimed and accepted then there will be no church in the future.

Evangelism is the first priority of the church. If we do not keep evan-gelizing there will be no church. The unified witness of the creeds and con-fessions from the first to the twentieth century that the church is an ark of salvation is valid. The message of Ephesians 4:4–6 and the message of the Presbyterian General Assembly in 1994 are the same: Theology matters! The church is unified by common beliefs. The center of that belief system is that there is one body and one Spirit, one Lord Jesus Christ, one God and Father of us all. The basic Christian story is elaborated in the creeds and confessions of the ancient, Reformation, and modern church.

Confessional, theological clarity frees the church to see the implications of its belief system. The radical claim that there is just one sovereign God relativizes every attempt to absolutize aspects of the created order and ex-poses such attempts as idolatrous. Barriers of race, gender, sexual orienta-tion, language, culture, social class, and economic stratum are all irrelevant to church membership.

Justice is the second priority of the church. If we do not act for the good of all we will cease to behave as the church. The church is a covenant com-munity created by God that has a responsibility to work for the renewal of the whole human community. The insight of twentieth-century confes-sions is valid that the church is to be in mission in the world, transform-ing it into a more just society as an implication of the sovereign claim of Christ over, and his love for, all creation.

Tensions within the PC(USA) and other denominations are occasioned by the differing perspectives and felt needs of subcultures representing, for example, differing racial backgrounds, economic strata, sexual orienta-tions, political affiliations, and theological commitments. A recognition and clarification of the reality and function of differing worldviews are es-sential. When tensions occasioned by worldview differences run high, there is the danger that people opposed to each other at the empirical or ideological level will doubt that they actually share the same ultimate,

167

religious commitment. Unless they each recognize the presence and power of their ideological worldviews, one may easily interpret the other's behavior as simply lacking in Christian commitment or motivated by ill will.

If people in a denomination can recognize that they do share the same ultimate religious commitment to the Christian, biblical story, then they have a common basis on which to build. On that foundation they will need to explore and work toward a common ideological perspective—a worldview that enables them commonly to interpret reality as Christians in twentieth-century America.

Surveys have indicated that the only circumstance of dialogue in which liberals and conservatives came close together was when they prayed together.[18] Prayer together was apparently a tacit recognition of the reality that all involved had one God and were one body. Survey data thus affirmed the thesis that reconciliation becomes possible when people acknowledge that they hold the same ultimate religious worldview. People can begin to trust one another when they are convinced that they believe in the same story that gives meaning to their lives.

Churches need to do what they are uniquely qualified to do—lead people into a vital experience of the living God. Churches need to provide a meaning in life that no other institution can provide as well—an ultimate religious worldview that brings people into touch with God, the final reality from which all else comes.

That does not mean that churches do nothing but provide a religious worldview, or that religion has no relationship to the rest of life. Indeed, a religion in touch with the ultimate reality of God is immediately relevant to all else. That makes it all the more important for denominational subcultures within the general American Protestant culture to nurture the ultimate religious worldview, elaborate it theologically, apply it in the culture, and be sensitive to all the possible experiential colorings of it.

Religious institutions need to be places where persons can claim the center that gives meaning in their individual lives and motivation for mission in the nation and the world. That is why mainstream churches need to develop a self-understanding and function that grounds people in the biblical tradition and enables them to cope with the modern world.

Claiming the Intellectual Center

The Mistaken Challenge

Some scholars have contended that the severe conflict within Presbyterianism illustrates the mainstream churches' preoccupation with the wrong challenge.[19] Mainstream Protestants have long memories. Many are still reacting to their more than half-century-old conflict with the fundamentalists. Milton Coalter, John Mulder, and Louis Weeks noted that "the preferential option for liberalism and the suppression of conservative alternatives are ironic in a denomination that takes pride in its openness and tolerance."[20] The stance of those on the left has clearly not been simply that of openness and tolerance, but rather a commitment to the values of the liberal/modernist worldview.

Ironically, research demonstrated that the real competition for those who were leaving mainstream churches was not conservatism but secularism.[21] While liberal Protestants did a good job of convincing their children of the dangers of fundamentalism, many of these same children left the mainstream churches for no religious affiliation at all.[22] The liberal Protestant critique of middle-class, family, and community values led their own young people away from belonging to the churches and into secular individualism.[23] As Roof and McKinney put it, "Liberal Protestantism's 'competition' is not the conservatives it has *spurned* but the secularists it has *spawned*."[24] The issue for young people in the 1980s was apparently, as it had always been, whether they could believe that religion is, as George Lindbeck once put it, "significantly" and "unsurpassably true."[25]

Research on the churchgoing patterns of the baby boomers shows that almost half of the young adults raised in mainline churches have left them.[26] Only a small percentage have gone to more conservative churches. Most have gone to no church at all. The researchers lay the blame squarely on the doorstep of mainline Protestant church leaders who "repeatedly chose openness and cosmopolitanism, and in doing so weakened their religious plausibility structure."[27]

The fundamental reason for young adults leaving the church was not denominational politics or the lure of other churches but a confusion over their religious beliefs. Sociologists Hoge, Johnson, and Luidens concluded in *Presbyterian Outlook:* "The main problem lies deeper, in the realm of beliefs—especially relativism, universalism and the scarcity of religious authority."[28] Almost everyone felt the need for meaning in life, but the majority of the boomers were confused about where to find meaning.

The liberal worldview espoused by the leadership of the church did not cause young people of the boomer and subsequent buster generation to embrace the church. Rather, they imbibed the liberal worldview and found that it enabled them to live with freedom in the secular world.[29]

169

A CENTRIST CRITICAL REALISM

It is time to look seriously at developing an intellectually centrist critical realism in the mainline churches. Reaction to the naïve Common Sense realism of the fundamentalists need not drive us into relativism. We can affirm truths that can be known adequately to guide human life without going to the extremes either of complete objectivity or of total subjectivity.

In the religious realm, critical realism assumes that there is a revelation from God. It comes in a very human, historically and culturally conditioned form. We do not know God directly or inerrantly. But we can know God and God's will for us adequately for the purpose of both our salvation and our responsibility for service to others. The Bible is like a map or model that points us in the right direction and gives us essential guidelines to follow as we make our human way in the world. It is not just one more human writing among others, but a divine norm by which we can judge other sources of information and guidance.[30]

That sort of approach to knowledge will seem too strict to suit the 10 percent on the far left of the Presbyterian spectrum. It will not seem solid enough to satisfy the 15 percent on the far right. But for the 75 percent in the middle it will be good news to know that there is a name for what they have been doing all along.

CENTRIST BIBLICAL INTERPRETATION

We have sources of authority and guidance. We need not start from scratch. The Bible gives us normative guidance and the confessions teach us how to interpret it in a way Reformed people have found helpful. And our Presbyterian churches in this country as recently as 1982 and 1983 have produced readable and responsible statements on biblical authority and interpretation that remain our current denominational policy.[31]

The simplest form of this policy is found in guidelines from the Reformed confessions drawn from our *Book of Confessions*. They are guidelines for interpreting scripture in matters of controversy. They are meant to be taken all together as a constellation of mutually correcting principles. They do not automatically and absolutely tell us which interpretation of a particular passage is correct. But they do provide a framework that will enable us to evaluate what is being asserted as biblical and make necessary judgments about its truth and usefulness.

We as a church have been so intent on creating social policy that we

170

have not bothered to let our members know that we have a biblical interpretation policy. That has been true even when studies have shown that
the chief cause of our conflicts is that we have no agreed-upon principles
of biblical interpretation.[32] We are so good at looking for the exceptions
that we have a hard time acknowledging that there are any rules.

CONVICTION AND CIVILITY

A critical realist can and should make two affirmations at the same time.
Regarding the truth, we should say with Martin Luther, "Here I stand. I
can do no other." And regarding our limited understanding, we respond
positively to the plea of Oliver Cromwell, "I beseech you, in the bowels of
Christ, think it possible you may be mistaken." Such is the human condition of living by faith and not by sight. This is the way we will constructively redefine "mainstream": by being critical of our own limited cultural
perspective, but being committed to the essentials of the Christian faith.

Some years ago I was making a presentation on the Reformed confessions to a gathering of Presbyterian ministers. I knew that some had an al-
lergic reaction to the notion of essential tenets of the faith. I was asserting
that confessions could be understood and used in different ways. To make
my point sound more sophisticated I used terms I had learned from an anthropologist friend of mine, Paul Hiebert. I said, "You can think of a confession as a bounded set or a centered set."

Before I could explain, a minister friend, Julian Alexander, exclaimed,
"Oh, you mean it can be a bird cage or a bird bath." Interested to learn
what he meant, I said, "Of course, tell us about that." His explanation was
most helpful. In a bird-cage approach the emphasis is on the boundaries.
You are either in the cage or you are out of it. Presumably, inside lay safety
and nourishment, and outside was wildness and danger. It is this view of
the confessions that leads to heresy hunts.

A bird bath also has boundaries, or all the water would trickle away. But
the attention is not on the boundaries. It is on the center, the nourishing
water of life.

Our task is to invite people to the center, where we have found nourishment in Jesus Christ. We can explain how Protestant and Reformed
theology have provided a framework that has helped us to stay in touch
with that nourishing center. And we must be clear that all for whom this
way of approaching the center is helpful and wholesome are invited. We
will learn from those who find a different approach useful. But we will not

171

go wandering off in search of every new way that is mentioned. We will tend our own garden and hope to make it attractive so that the water of life we have found there will be nourishing to others.

Until the 1960s, mainstream religious bodies and their conservative counterparts assumed a common, biblically based framework of values and moral ideals. Since then, liberals and conservatives have listed different sets of moral issues and offered different styles of moral decision making.

The Protestant community as a whole cannot even find a common way of framing the moral question in many disputed issues. The personal and public realms have become uncoupled. Mainstream church leaders have been activist and absolutist on what they considered central questions of public policy. But they have been hesitant in dealing with anything that appeared to be personal morality.

Conversely, for conservatives, on the one hand those issues that had exercised mainline Protestants in the 1960s and 1970s as matters of public debate are now relegated to the province of the "private sector" and the individual conscience—issues such as poverty, hunger, homelessness, the environment, and civil rights for minorities and women. On the other hand conservatives appear intent on publicly regulating what had previously been thought to be private matters, such as the place and form of prayer, what one reads and views, and how one expresses one's sexuality.

HOMOSEXUALITY AS THE PRESENTING PROBLEM

Mainstream Protestants can no longer escape a public discussion regarding that most private and personal of all moral matters, sexuality. The PC(USA) and most mainstream denominations are wrestling with the issue of homosexuality and will soon have to review their policy decisions. A mainstream denomination must develop a centrist policy that will enable its members to move with flexibility into the future.

The modern world is presenting us with realities in the sexual realm that we have not confronted as clearly in earlier times. Many known gay and lesbian persons today manifest gifts and graces for ministry—and more are acknowledging their sexual preferences. Our children are growing up in a world both more knowledgeable about variant forms of human sexuality and more accepting of them. It could be that the careful biblical exegesis that should characterize centrist Protestantism may not support a blanket and undifferentiated condemnation of all homosexual expression. Much is still to be determined before a wise decision can be made by the whole church on the matter of ordination of homosexuals. We need a centrist strategy that will allow us to live together while we learn more. Following the traditional policy of affirming community norms while granting individual exceptions could provide such a possibility.

The mainstream church must have a stance on homosexuality clearly different from that of our Christian brothers and sisters who are comfortable with a one-sided view to the left or to the right. Our task is both to preserve the biblical tradition and to enable people to cope with modernity. The open expression of faithful, loving, homosexual commitment by evidently Christian people is an aspect of modernity that we must bring into honest dialogue with the Christian tradition in order to offer a genuinely mainstream position.[33]

Morally, we must always find a way both to affirm the rights of individuals *and* to assure the integrity of the community. These must not be set in opposition to each other. In Presbyterianism the rights of the minority must be preserved while the majority is allowed to set policy. In this matter, as in all substantive questions, it is the majority in the middle who bear the representative responsibility for developing an acceptable approach.

FRAGMENTATION AND FIDELITY

The PC(USA) is functionally fragmented. It is as close to a formal fracturing as it has been since the 1930s in the north and the 1970s in the south. The decision to study the question of homosexual ordination for three years beginning in the middle of 1993 was a way of buying time. The question now before us is clear: Can we figure out a way of living together as one body? If not, we will divide into two or three competing denominations.[34]

My own commitment is clear. I still hear the words of my theological mentor in seminary saying: "If Christ is divided, who bleeds?"[35] I cannot contemplate schism with equanimity. I cannot predict what I would do in the uncertain future. But I know what I want and what I believe is needed. We Presbyterians need to remain one church.[36] If we cannot manage to overcome our present impasse, then the fragmentation of other formerly mainstream denominations cannot be far behind.[37] American Protestantism will take on a new character, and its configuration will be less like the days of Geneva, Wittenberg, and Canterbury than it will be like Bosnia, Croatia, and Serbia.

We need churches with a mainstream religious, theological, and ideological worldview. We need denominations that are loyal to their traditions and that communicate their riches into the ecumenical mix. We need Presbyterians who know what it means to be Reformed Protestants. And Presbyterians need to be expandingly inclusive of people of every ethnic and experiential background for whom the Presbyterian Church actually presents a worldview and a process of governance that fits them and will enable them to learn and grow and serve.

Musing from the Middle

I close with a personal statement. I wrote it on an airplane, a few years ago, after some Presbyterian meeting at which I was frustrated. I have not tried to update it for relevance. Perhaps I could state it better, but I think it represents who I am and what I want to say from somewhere deep inside me.

As one who has taught philosophy most of my adult life, I know that there are exceptions to every rule; there is more than one right way of doing most things; and there is probably more that we do not know than we do know—and what we do know, we know imperfectly. Most Presbyterians would understand and agree with these premises. That is less because we are religious than from life experience. Insofar as we are religious, we want to emphasize grace and mercy for those who fail, and hope for that same grace and mercy for ourselves.

When we affirm this set of premises, we give an uncertain message to the world. All the premises listed above are based on other premises that are implied. We need to state these implied premises for others and for ourselves.

First, if there are exceptions to every rule, that implies that there are rules. Those rules apply most of the time, in most situations, and they need to be stated. For example, when people cannot sustain a relationship of fidelity in marriage, we need to talk about forgiveness, restitution, and starting again. However, the rule is that the promises made in a marriage covenant need to be kept. That rule needs to be lifted up as a norm to which we are bound and to which we strive to adhere.

Second, if there is more than one right way of doing most things, it is also true that generally there is a best way of doing them. That way is revealed in scripture and tested in human experience. Alternative family arrangements, such as same-sex couples, men and women living together outside marriage, and communal living arrangements, may provide love, nurture, and stability. But for most people and most of society, one woman and one man living together, in faithfulness to their marriage covenant, is the best arrangement for human happiness and the raising of children.

Third, there is probably more we do not know than we do know, and certainly our knowledge is imperfect. But we do know some things in scripture confirmed by reason, tradition, and experience. Our knowledge of the basics of human life is adequate, though not perfect, for most of human life. If we always and only talk about the exceptions, people come to believe that anything goes and that there are no norms or standards. If we always emphasize our inadequacies, we disable and disempower people for living with confidence and capability in this world.

The Presbyterian Church since the 1960s has done three things. First, it has emphasized the exceptions rather than the rules and thus has conceded leadership in forming the values of society to more conservative bodies. Second, it has stressed alternative methods of Christian living and thus given the appearance of negating and rejecting traditional religious and family values. Third, it has made its treatment of all issues so complex and tentative that most people have turned elsewhere for positive guidance.

Therefore, without either denying or forsaking all that we know about exceptions, alternatives, and imperfections, the PC(USA) would be well advised to do the following:

1. Emphasize scripture as a revelation from God. Rightly interpreted, scripture provides a rule for our faith and life and gives norms to which we are called to relate.
2. Encourage stable patterns of Christian behavior in three ways: by interpreting alternatives in relation to the standard norms; by providing supports to enable people to succeed in living according to stable patterns of behavior; and by encouraging communal worship, disciplines of prayer, and the study of scripture.
3. Explain our views with simplicity, clarity, and conviction. We should communicate clearly with people of all societal situations and levels of education and in ways that will make sense cross-culturally. This involves teaching basic Christian truths, doing acts of mercy and kindness, and standing for Christian values over against idolatrous values and practices in society, government, and church.

Notes

Notes for Chapter 1—Worldview: A Source of Conflict

1. Ninian Smart, *Worldviews: Crosscultural Explorations of Human Beliefs* (New York: Charles Scribner's Sons, 1983), 5.

2. Milton J Coalter, John M. Mulder, and Louis B. Weeks, eds., *The Re-Forming Tradition: Presbyterians and Mainstream Protestantism* (Louisville: Westminster/John Knox Press, 1992), 24. (Hereafter *RT*.)

3. Martin Marty, "The Worlds the Fundamentalists Make," Clark Lecture II, delivered at Pomona College, Jan. 30, 1991.

4. Albert Wolters, *Creation Regained: Biblical Basics for a Reformational Worldview* (Grand Rapids: Eerdmans, 1985), 2–3.

5. Paul G. Hiebert, *Cultural Anthropology*, 2d ed. (Grand Rapids: Baker Book House, 1983), 356. Cf. Michael Kearney, *World View* (Novato, Calif.: Chandler and Sharp, 1984), 41: "The world view of a people is their way of looking at reality. It consists of basic assumptions and images that provide a more or less coherent, though not necessarily accurate, way of thinking about the world. A world view comprises images of Self and all that is recognized as not-Self, plus ideas about relationships between them."

Marguerite Kraft, *Worldview and the Communication of the Gospel: A Nigerian Case Study* (Pasadena, Calif.: William Carey Library, 1978), 4:

"Every culture has its own worldview, the central governing set of concepts and presuppositions that its society lives by. Robert Redfield described the worldview of a people as 'the way a people characteristically look outward upon the universe; . . . how everything looks to a people.'" Cf. Huston Smith, *Beyond the Post-Modern Mind* (New York: Crossroad, 1982), 132.

6. Charles H. Kraft, *Christianity in Culture: A Study in Dynamic Biblical Theologizing in Cross-cultural Perspective* (Maryknoll, N.Y.: Orbis Books, 1979) 45–46, suggests that the term "culture" in its technical sense was brought into English from the German *Kultur* in 1871 by the pioneer anthropologist E. B. Taylor.

7. Kraft, *Christianity in Culture*, 46.

8. Arthur Holmes, *Contours of a World View*, IFACS Studies in a Christian World View, 1 (Grand Rapids: Eerdmans, 1983), 32, comments that "everyone has the beginnings of a world view."

9. Kraft, *Christianity in Culture*, 53.

10. Smart, *Worldviews*, 6.

11. Paul G. Hiebert, *Cultural Anthropology* (Grand Rapids: Baker Book House, 1983), 371, states that "a worldview provides people with their basic assumptions about reality," cited in M. Kraft, *Christianity in Culture*, 4. See also Paul G. Hiebert, "Science, Theology, and Mission: The Implications of a Paradigm Shift" (Pasadena, Calif.: Fuller Theological Seminary syllabus, 1982), 16: "Because theories, paradigms and world views are not simply accumulations of facts, but conceptual systems for the interpretation of facts, disagreements lead to confrontation rather than to synthesis. In other words, the individual generally must choose one or the other. The shift from one to another is characterized by a 'conversion' or change in the paradigm or gestalt."

12. Clifford Geertz gives a "worldview" definition of religion: "A system of symbols which acts to establish powerful, pervasive and long-lasting moods and motivations in (human beings) by formulating conceptions of a general order of existence and clothing these conceptions with such an aura of factuality that the moods and motivations seem uniquely realistic." Quoted in Lucy Bregman, *Through the Landscape of Faith: Christian Life Maps* (Philadelphia: Westminster Press, 1986). Bregman understands that maintenance of such a symbol system is independent from a commitment to a formal religious system (p. 38).

13. Paul G. Hiebert, "The Missiological Implications of an Epistemological Shift," *TSF Bulletin* 8, no. 5 (May-June 1985): 13.

14. See John A. Hutchison, *Paths of Faith,* 4th ed. (New York: Mc-Graw-Hill, 1991), 5–6.

15. Hiebert, "Implications."Coined in the nineteenth century, the term "ideology" has many definitions and uses; see *Dictionary of the History of Ideas,* vol. 2 (New York: Charles Scribner's Sons, 1973), s.v. "ideology." I am using it for the sense that is common to most definitions, namely, that of a belief system that mobilizes people to action in the body politic, see *Harper Dictionary of Modern Thought,* ed. Alan Bullock and Oliver Stallybrass (New York: Harper & Row, 1977), s.v. "ideology."

16. Randy Frame, "Payback Time? Conservative Christians support GOP 'Contract' as profamily agenda takes a back seat," *Christianity Today* 39, no. 3 (Mar. 6, 1995): 42.

17. Ibid., 43.

18. Ibid., 46.

19. Jerry L. Van Marter, "Charges Fly at Second Reconciliation Meeting," *News Briefs, Presbyterian Church (U.S.A.)* (Dec. 9, 1994), 1–2.

20. Some church denominations, such as Mennonite and African-American, protest that the categorization of liberal and conservative or mainstream and evangelical churches does not provide a sufficiently nuanced understanding of American Protestantism.

A noteworthy effort is the project, Re-Forming the Center, directed by Douglas Jacobsen and William Vance Trollinger, Jr. of Messiah College. Conferences in 1994, 1995, and 1996 aim at moving "Beyond the Two-Party System of American Protestantism." This is a worthy endeavor which will yield a more varied understanding of American Protestantism.

My focus in this work is on understanding where the center is *within* the mainstream churches, not attempting to argue that they are at the center of American Protestantism.

21. *RT,* 278. The authors remark, regarding the PC(USA), "But the preferential option for liberalism and the suppression of conservative alternatives are ironic in a denomination that takes pride in its openness and tolerance."

22. Ibid., 23–24.

23. Ibid., 24.

24. Ibid., 53.

25. Ibid., 69–70.

26. Ibid., 70.

27. Ibid., 83. National polls reveal twice as many people identifying themselves as Presbyterians as appear on the church rolls of all the American Presbyterian denominations combined.

28. William R. Hutchison, ed., *Between the Times: The Travail of the Protestant Establishment in America, 1900–1960* (New York: Cambridge University Press, 1989), 19. (Hereafter *BT.*) See pages 304–5, where Hutchison remarks that this was a Protestant "decline" of such proportions "as to make twentieth-century realignments seem little more than mild, long-overdue adjustments." He argues that the "striking thing about the cultural authority of twentieth-century Protestantism is not its diminution but its persistence" in influence significantly out of proportion to its strength in the general American population.

29. *RT,* 38.

30. Robert Wuthnow, *The Restructuring of American Religion: Society and Faith Since World War II* (Princeton, N.J.: Princeton University Press, 1988), 21.

31. Wade Clark Roof and William McKinney, *American Mainline Religion: Its Changing Shape and Future* (New Brunswick, N.J.: Rutgers University Press, 1987), 236–37. (Hereafter *AMR.*)

32. I have been informed in this analysis by an unpublished paper by Dorothy C. Bass of Chicago Theological Seminary titled, "The American Religious Landscape: Relocating 'Mainline' Protestantism."

33. Martin E. Marty, "If It's Not 'Mainline,' What Is It?" *Christian Century,* 106, no. 33 (Nov. 8, 1989): 1031.

34. *RT,* 13.

35. A recent study that adds Lutheran and Reformed Church in America to the earlier six bodies is C. Kirk Hadaway and David A. Roozen, *Rerouting the Protestant Mainstream: Sources of Growth and Opportunities for Change* (Nashville: Abingdon Press, 1995), 13.

36. William R. Hutchison, "Preface: From Protestant to Pluralist America," in *BT,* xiii.

37. Ibid., viii. Hutchison comments that "the remarkable characteristic of the Protestant establishment, up to the 1960s and perhaps afterward as well, was not decline but persistence." Cf. *RT,* 39: "The Protestant attempt to Christianize American culture . . . succeeded to a remarkable degree."

38. Jack B. Rogers and Donald K. McKim, *The Authority and Interpretation of the Bible: An Historical Approach* (San Francisco: Harper & Row, 1979) (hereafter *AIB*), 235–47; see the bibliography indicated in the

footnotes. Cf. George Marsden, *Fundamentalism and American Culture* (New York: Oxford University Press, 1980), 14–16.

39. *RT,* 245.

40. Cf. ibid., 46.

41. See Martin E. Marty, *Modern American Religion,* vol. 2: *The Noise of Conflict, 1919–1941* (Chicago: University of Chicago Press, 1991), 198–205 on "The Faith of Modernism."

42. Cf. *RT,* 46.

43. Marty, 161, "It is best to understand Fundamentalism as a world-view among worldviews, one mode of looking at the world alongside others."

44. See William Joseph Weston, "The Emergence of the Idea of Religious Pluralism within the Presbyterian Church in the U.S.A., 1890–1940" (Ph.D. diss., Yale University, 1988).

45. Cf. *RT,* 47.

46. Ibid., 245.

Notes for Chapter 2—Separatism: Can We Have Unity in Diversity?

1. Richard N. Ostling, "Those Mainline Blues," *Time,* 133, no. 21, May 22, 1989, 94.

2. See Rick Nutt, "The Tie That No Longer Binds: The Origins of the Presbyterian Church in America," in *The Confessional Mosaic: Presbyterians and Twentieth-Century Theology,* ed. Milton J Coalter, John M. Mulder, and Louis B. Weeks (Louisville: Westminster/John Knox Press, 1990), 236–56. For the theological rationale behind the PCA split by one of the leading participants see Morton H. Smith, *Studies in Southern Presbyterian Theology* (Amsterdam: Jacob Van Campen, 1962).

3. For further details see Jack Rogers, "The Case of the Moderator's Conference on the Unity of the Church," unpublished paper, 1980.

4. See Susan Cyre, "PCUSA Funds Effort to Re-Create God," *Presbyterian Layman* 27, no. 1 (January/February 1994): 1, 4, 10–11.

5. *The New Encyclopaedia Britannica, Macropaedia,* vol. 15 (Chicago: Encyclopaedia Britannica, 1981), s.v. "Reformed and Presbyterian Churches." (Hereafter *NEB.*)

6. Sydney E. Ahlstrom, ed., *Theology in America: The Major Protestant Voices from Puritanism to Neo-Orthodoxy* (Indianapolis: Bobbs-Merrill, 1967), 26. (Hereafter *TA.*)

7. Bernard Brun, *The Timetables of History: A Horizontal Linkage of Peoples and Events* (New York: Simon and Schuster, 1982), 236. See *NEB,* vol. 8, s.v. "Henry of England."

8. *NEB,* vol. 15, s.v. "Puritanism." See also S. E. Ahlstrom, *A Religious History of the American People,* vol. 1 (Garden City, N.Y.: Image Books, 1975), 132. (Hereafter *RHAP.*)

9. *RHAP,* 131.

10. *NEB,* vol. 15, s.v. "Puritanism"; *TA,* 31.

11. Jack Rogers, *Presbyterian Creeds: A Guide to the Book of Confessions* (Philadelphia: Westminster Press, 1985), 140–59.

12. Robert T. Handy, *A Christian America: Protestant Hopes and Historical Realities* (New York: Oxford University Press, 1971), 6, claims that "with the Restoration of Charles II in 1660, the Anglicans regained control of the Church of England, and most Puritans were soon swept into separation." Winthrop S. Hudson, *Religion in America* (New York: Charles Scribner's Sons, 1965), 9, argues: "As the Calvinism of the early Puritans was not precisely the same as the Calvinism of Geneva, so the Puritanism of nineteenth-century America was not that of seventeenth-century England and it might more properly be described as Evangelicalism." S. E. Ahlstrom, "From Puritanism to Evangelicalism: A Critical Perspective," in *The Evangelicals: What They Believe, Who They Are, Where They Are Changing,* ed. David F. Wells and John B. Woodbridge (Nashville: Abingdon Press, 1975), 271, explains: "My argument in this essay will be that the term 'evangelicalism' (in the above described sense) does in fact refer to a fairly unified tradition. Though it has over the centuries undergone considerable change, it has nevertheless maintained its identity and looked back to its origins with considerable sympathy and respect. Its origins lie in that revolution in Christendom which the English Puritan movement intended to accomplish. Only in North America, however, where ancient traditions had very little social and economic footing, were the full implications of this revolution borne out."

13. Jack Rogers, "We Need a Balancing Act," *Presbyterian Survey* 76 (June 1986): 3–6.

14. George Marsden, *Fundamentalism and American Culture* (New York: Oxford University Press, 1980), 171.

15. Ibid., 174–75.

16. Ibid., 177.

17. Ibid., 117; *AIB,* 365.

18. Marsden, *Fundamentalism,* 262n.30.

19. *AIB,* 363.

20. Marsden, *Fundamentalism,* 180–81.

21. Ibid., 181; *AIB,* 363.

22. Marsden, *Fundamentalism,* 183–84.

23. For an earlier published version of this section, see Jack Rogers, "John Scopes and the Debate over Evolution," in *American Christianity: A Case Approach,* ed. Ronald C. White, Jr., Louis B. Weeks, and Garth M. Rosell (Grand Rapids: Eerdmans, 1986), 143–48.

24. C. Allyn Russell, *Voices of American Fundamentalism* (Philadelphia: Westminster Press, 1976), 183. (Hereafter *VAF.*)

25. Brandt Aymar and Edward Sagarin, *Laws and Trials that Created History* (New York: Crown, 1974), 124–25.

26. Marsden, *Fundamentalism,* viii, 189–91.

27. *AIB,* 366.

28. Ibid., 367.

29. Lefferts A. Loetscher, *The Broadening Church* (Philadelphia: University of Pennsylvania Press, 1957), 135.

30. *RT,* 125.

31. Ibid., 126.

32. *VAF,* 155–56; Loetscher, *Broadening Church* (Philadelphia: University of Pennsylvania Press, 1957), 148–49.

33. *VAF,* 156. Cf. Loetscher, *Broadening Church,* 151.

34. Jack Rogers, review of *Christianity and Liberalism* by J. Gresham Machen, in *American Presbyterians: Journal of Presbyterian History* 66, no. 4 (winter 1988): 308.

35. Quoted in ibid., 307.

36. Bradley J. Longfield, *The Presbyterian Controversy: Fundamentalists, Modernists, and Moderates* (New York: Oxford University Press, 1991), 45–53, 210–12, and 222–23.

37. Quoted in ibid., 220.

38. Quoted in ibid., 223.

39. Quoted in ibid., 216.

40. For an interesting parallel approach to this issue, see Thomas W. Gillespie, "Three Faces of Evangelism," *Presbyterian Communique* (fall/winter 1986/87): 1, 4, 10, and 16. Gillespie draws on the work of George Marsden "Reformed and American," in *Reformed Theology in America: A History of Its Modern Development,* ed. David F. Wells (Grand Rapids: Eerdmans, 1985), but uses different names for the three parties. Marsden refers to Doctrinalists, Pietists, and Culturalists. Gillespie prefers Confessionalists, Conversionists, and Culturalists. Both agree that the Doctrinalist or Confessionalist Old School party ceased to play a significant role in the PC(USA). What was left were the two halves of the

former New School: the social activist Culturalists and the evangelical Pietists or Conversionists. The situation in the PCUS was somewhat different. It was a primarily Old School church and continued to maintain more of those characteristics. In 1973 the PCUS experienced a schism in which 260 churches left to form the Presbyterian Church in America (PCA). The leadership of this movement self-consciously identified with Machen and the Old Princeton confessionalist party. See Nutt, "The Tie That No Longer Binds," 236–56. After 1973, the situation in the PCUS became more nearly like that in the Northern stream. Further struggles were between social activists and the more conversionist evangelicals. Southern conservatives, however, seemed much more adept at using polity to forward their cause than their Northern cousins.

41. Quoted in *AIB*, 366.

42. Quoted in Longfield, *Controversy*, 159.

43. Ibid.

44. William Joseph Weston, "The Emergence of the Idea of Religious Pluralism within the Presbyterian Church in the U.S.A., 1890–1940" (Ph.D. diss., Yale University, 1988), 189, quoted in Rogers, *American Presbyterians*, 308.

45. *AIB*, 368; Marsden, *Fundamentalism*, 192; *VAF*, 156–58, 209; Loetscher, *Broadening Church*, 150–55.

46. Harold J. Ockenga, "From Fundamentalism, Through New Evangelicalism, to Evangelicalism," in *Evangelical Roots*, ed. Kenneth S. Kantzer (New York: Thomas Nelson, 1978), 42.

47. Edwin S. Gaustad, "The Pulpit and the Pews," in *BT*, 22.

48. *Christianity Today* 39, no. 3 (Mar. 6, 1995): 27–28.

49. James I. Packer, "No Little Person," in *Reflections on Francis Schaeffer*, ed. Ronald W. Ruegsegger (Grand Rapids: Zondervan, 1986), 8.

50. *The Christian Activist*, A Schaeffer V Productions Newspaper, P.O. Box 909, Los Gatos, CA 95031 (Summer 1984), 1.

51. Kenneth Woodward, "Guru of Fundamentalism," *Newsweek* 100 (Nov. 1, 1982), 88.

52. Jack Rogers, "Francis Schaeffer: The Promise and the Problem," *Reformed Journal*, 27, no. 5 (May 1977): 14–15. Cf. Forrest Baird, "Schaeffer's Intellectual Roots," in *Reflections on Francis Schaeffer*, 54–58.

53. Rogers, "Francis Schaeffer," 14.

54. Baird, "Schaeffer's Intellectual Roots," 58–61; Rogers, "Francis Schaeffer," 15.

55. Rogers, "Francis Schaeffer," 14; Baird, "Schaeffer's Intellectual Roots," 59–61.

56. Baird, "Schaeffer's Intellectual Roots," 62.

57. Leo D. Lefebure, "Global Encounter," *Christian Century* 110, no. 26 (Sept. 22–29, 1993): 886–87.

58. David Briggs, "Spiritual leaders dream of bringing peace on earth," *Pasadena Star News* (Aug. 27, 1993), D6.

59. Lefebure, "Global Encounter," 889.

60. Larry B. Stammer, "Meeting of World Religions Leads to Ethics Rules," *Los Angeles Times*, (Sept. 5, 1993), A31.

61. Ibid.

62. Ibid.

63. Lefebure, "Global Encounter," 888–89.

64. *Presbyterian Outlook* 175, no. 34 (Oct. 4, 1993): 3.

65. Lefebure, "Global Encounter," 887.

66. Roland H. Bainton, *Here I Stand: A New Life of Martin Luther* (New York: New American Library, 1955), p. 144, comments: "The earliest printed version added the words, 'Here I stand, I cannot do otherwise.' The words, though not recorded on the spot, may nevertheless be genuine, because the listeners at the moment may have been too moved to write."

67. Oliver Cromwell, Letter CXXVI, "To the General Assembly of the Kirk of Scotland, 'or in case of their not sitting, To The Commissioners of the Kirk of Scotland," August 3rd, 1650, *Oliver Cromwell's Letters and Speeches with Elucidations by Thomas Carlyle,* Vol. II (New York: E.P. Dutton and Co., n.d.), p. 156.

68. Reinhold Niebuhr, *The Children of Light and The Children of Darkness: A Vindication of Democracy and a Critique of Its Traditional Defense.* New York: Charles Scribner's Sons, 1953.

69. *Book of Order* G-2.0200.

Notes for Chapter 3—Election as God's Chosen People: What Is the Church?

1. Denominational organization, especially at the General Assembly level, reflects shifting notions of the nature of the church. Craig Dykstra, vice president for religion of the Lilly Foundation, gave an address in 1990, "The Ecology of Denominational Organization," which has since been published. See Craig Dykstra and James Hudnut-Beumler, "The National

Organizational Structures of Protestant Denominations: An Invitation to a Conversation," in *The Organizational Revolution: Presbyterians and American Denominationalism,* ed. Milton J Coalter, John M. Mulder, and Louis B. Weeks (Louisville: Westminster/John Knox Press, 1992), 307–31.

2. *RT,* 42.

3. Cited in Mark A. Noll, Nathan O. Hatch, George M. Marsden, David F. Wells, and John W. Woodbridge, eds., *Eerdmans' Handbook to Christianity in America* (Grand Rapids: Eerdmans, 1983), 65. (Hereafter cited as *EHCA.)*

4. Ronald C. White, Jr., *Liberty and Justice for All: Racial Reform and the Social Gospel (1877–1925)* (San Francisco: Harper & Row, 1990), xvii and xxiii–xxiv.

5. Ibid., xxi.

6. Ibid., xviii.

7. Martin E. Marty, *Modern American Religion,* vol. 1: *The Irony of It All: 1893–1919* (Chicago: University of Chicago Press, 1986), 286.

8. Quoted in ibid., 288. See White, *Liberty,* xix.

9. Cited in *RT,* 186.

10. White, *Liberty,* 245.

11. William R. Hutchison, "The Protestant Agenda: Matters Arising," in *BT,* 93–94.

12. Marty, *Irony,* 269.

13. Ibid., 272–74.

14. Robert A. Schneider, "Voice of Many Waters: Church Federation in the Twentieth Century," in *BT,* 95–97.

15. Ibid., 105.

16. Ibid., 105–7.

17. Some have calculated that the PCUSA will cease to exist in 2025. See Douglas J. Brouwer, "Slipping," *Reformed Journal* 39, no. 3 (March 1989): 4.

18. See William McKinney and Wade Clark Roof, "Liberal Protestantism: A Sociodemographic Perspective," in *Liberal Protestantism: Realities and Possibilities,* ed. Robert S. Michaelsen and Wade Clark Roof (New York: Pilgrim Press, 1986), 37–50.

19. Robert Wuthnow, *The Restructuring of American Religion: Society and Faith Since World War II* (Princeton, N. J.: Princeton University Press, 1988), 88. For a more recent and detailed study of Presbyterian baby boomers see Dean R. Hoge, Benton Johnson, and Donald Luidens, *Van-*

ishing Boundaries: The Religion of Mainline Baby Boomers (Louisville: Westminster/John Knox Press, 1994).

20. See, e.g., "Biblical Authority and Interpretation: A Resource Document" (New York: Advisory Council on Discipleship and Worship, UPCUSA, 1982), 3–5.

21. M. Douglas Harper, "Congress on Renewal: 'Largest Presbyterian Gathering Ever!'" *The Open Letter* of the Covenant Fellowship of Presbyterians, January-February 1985, 1 and 5.

22. See *Findings:* Mission Design Consultations of the Presbyterian Church (U.S.A.), submitted to the Mission Design Committee of the General Assembly Council, January 1985, by the staff of the Research Unit of the Support Agency. (Hereafter *Findings.*)

23. Ibid., 31.

24. Ibid., 29.

25. This was first pointed out to me in an unpublished case study on the development of the structural design for mission by D. Scott Cormode, Fuller Theological Seminary, May 11, 1988.

26. See "Presbyterian Facts and Figures," *Presbyterian Survey* 78 (September 1988): 15–18, especially the bar graph on p. 16.

27. *RT,* 106.

28. Walter Brueggemann, "Disciplines of Readiness," Occasional Paper no. 1 (Louisville: Theology and Worship Unit, Presbyterian Church [U.S.A.], n.d.).

29. Jack Stotts, "Beyond Beginnings," Occasional Paper No. 2 (Louisville: Theology and Worship Ministry Unit, Presbyterian Church [U.S.A.], n.d.). Also in 1989, in an address to a gathering in St. Louis convened by evangelical Presbyterians, I suggested a third metaphor: that of the divided kingdoms of Israel and Judah. I argued that a potential misinterpretation of the metaphors of the exile and of the days of the judges would be to assume, with some of the sociologists of religion, that Presbyterian problems were largely imposed upon them by external circumstances. Or, worse yet, I feared that we might fall prey to the romantic delusion that Presbyterians were somehow like the genuinely marginalized racial ethnic churches or the minority church in South Africa, and that American Presbyterians were oppressed and virtuous in their decline. I used the metaphor of the divided kingdoms to remind my Presbyterian hearers that our weakness and disunity were due to our sins of competing with one another and denying the wholeness to which God had called us. James Andrews, the stated clerk of the General Assembly, was a respondent

to my address. He prefaced his remarks with the comment that no bureaucracy liked having either its methods or its motives questioned and jokingly but pointedly reminded me that in my role as associate for theological studies in the Theology and Worship Ministry Unit, I needed to remember that there was "no academic freedom in the bureaucracy." For the entire address, see Jack Rogers, "The Renewal of the Church," *Presbyterian Communique,* May/June 1989, 11–14.

30. *Is Christ Divided? Report of the Task Force on Theological Pluralism Within the Presbyterian Community of Faith* (Louisville: Office of the General Assembly, 1988). (Hereafter *Divided?*) Whenever I see that title, I think of an often repeated statement by one of my favorite seminary professors, "If Christ is divided, who bleeds?"

31. Ibid., 8.

32. Ibid., 54.

33. See Jack B. Rogers and Donald K. McKim, "Pluralism and Policy in Presbyterian Views of Scripture," in *The Confessional Mosaic: Presbyterians and Twentieth-Century Theology,* ed. Milton J Coalter, John M. Mulder, and Louis B. Weeks (Louisville: Westminster/John Knox Press, 1990), 37–58.

34. *AMR,* 79; see Dean R. Hoge, *Division in the Protestant House: The Basic Reasons Behind Intra-Church Conflicts* (Philadelphia: Westminster Press, 1976), 24.

35. See, e.g., Robert S. Wuthnow, "The Restructuring of American Presbyterianism: Turmoil in One Denomination," in *The Presbyterian Predicament: Six Perspectives,* ed. Milton J Coalter, John M. Mulder, and Louis B. Weeks (Louisville: Westminster/John Knox Press, 1990), 27–48. Wuthnow expands his thesis in *The Struggle for America's Soul: Evangelicals, Liberals, and Secularism* (Grand Rapids: Eerdmans, 1989). See also Hoge, *Division.*

36. Jack Rogers, "An Alternative to the 'Two-Church' Hypothesis," *Presbyterian Outlook,* 172, no. 19 (May 14, 1990): 9. Cf. Keith M. Wulff and John P. Marcum, "Cleavage or Consensus? A New Look at the Clergy-Laity Gap," in *The Pluralistic Vision: Presbyterians and Mainstream Protestant Education and Leadership,* ed. Milton J Coalter, John M. Mulder, and Louis B. Weeks (Louisville: Westminster/John Knox Press, 1992), 308–26. See the summary comment in *RT,* 236.

37. The terms "personal," "public," and "moderate middle," which I use to describe major attitudinal groupings within Presbyterianism, are adapted from categories developed by Martin E. Marty and used by other

historians and sociologists of American religion. Marty's terms are "private" and "public." For the application of these terms to Presbyterianism, see Hoge, *Division*, 24–25, where he quotes Marty's *Righteous Empire*. Others have used the term "Loyalist" for the middle group, which I believe only partly explains the ethos and motivation of those in the middle. See "Is This Party Private, or Can Anybody Join?" in *Context: A Commentary on the Interaction of Religion and Culture* 21, no. 4 (Feb. 15, 1989): 4–5.

38. Louis Weeks and William J. Fogelman, "A 'Two Church' Hypothesis," *Presbyterian Outlook,* 172, no. 12 (Mar. 26, 1990): 8–10.

39. *The Harper Dictionary of Modern Thought,* ed. Alan Bullock and Oliver Stallybrass (New York: Harper & Row, 1977), s.v. "Ideology."

40. Ibid.

41. *Beyond Establishment: Protestant Identity in a Post-Protestant Age,* ed. Jackson W. Carroll and Wade Clark Roof (Louisville: Westminster/ John Knox Press, 1993), 13. (Hereafter *BE*.)

42. Ibid., 15.

43. Cited in ibid.

44. Cited in ibid.

45. Ibid., 17.

46. Ibid., following Peter Berger.

47. Ibid., 18–19.

48. Ibid., 14.

49. Ibid., 346–47.

50. Ibid., 347.

51. Ibid., 348.

52. Ibid., 349.

53. See my editorial "Vision and Unity," *Presbyterian Outlook* 174, no. 19 (May 18, 1992): 8.

54. James M. Collie, "Where Have all the Leaders Gone?" *Presbyterian Outlook* 173, no. 4 (Feb. 4, 1991): 5, speaks of "often unknown, unaccountable, nonconstituent, categorically correct persons who fill our decision-making bodies." Cf. Donald W. McCullough, "The Diversity of Gifts," *Presbyterian Outlook* 173, no. 39 (Nov. 11, 1991): 6. He asserts: "To require governing bodies to have this or that group represented is rather like using chemotherapy on a cancer patient: a necessary use of poison that should be stopped as soon as possible."

55. "How Much Is Enough?" *Presbyterian Outlook* 174, no. 11 (Mar. 23, 1992): 9.

Notes for Chapter 4—Revivalism:
What Is the Role of Experience in Religion?

1. Conversation with me at the 1993 General Assembly.

2. Donald W. McCullough, "A Brief Affair or a New Marriage?" *Presbyterian Outlook* 175, no. 30 (Sept. 6, 1993): 9.

3. "The Readers' Outlook," *Presbyterian Outlook* 175, no. 35 (Oct. 11, 1993): 2. The magazine subsequently printed two articles challenging McCullough's view and two replies by him.

4. *EHCA,* 101.

5. *RT,* 42.

6. Maurice W. Armstrong, Lefferts A. Loetscher, and Charles A. Anderson, eds., *The Presbyterian Enterprise: Sources of American Presbyterian History* (Philadelphia: Westminster Press, 1956), 40.

7. *EHCA,* 106.

8. E.g., Winthrop S. Hudson, *Religion in America* (New York: Charles Scribner's Sons, 1965), 78–81.

9. Hudson, ibid., 81, attributes the birth of the denominational concept to the fact of the "Dissenting Brethren" at Westminster, which was then adopted by the circumstances of the Great Awakening. See further bibliography in note 26 on that page.

10. Ibid., 81–82.

11. Ibid., 77–78, 82.

12. G. F. Moran in *EHCA,* 130.

13. Garth M. Rosell, "Anne Hutchinson and the Puritans of Massachusetts Bay Colony," in *American Christianity: A Case Approach,* ed. Ronald C. White, Jr., Louis B. Weeks, and Garth M. Rosell (Grand Rapids: Eerdmans, 1986), 9–13.

14. See C. E. Jones, "Holiness Movement," in *Dictionary of Holiness and Charismatic Movements,* ed. Stanley M. Burgess and Gary B. McGee (Grand Rapids: Zonervan, 1988).

15. Donald W. Dayton, *Theological Roots of Pentecostalism* (Grand Rapids: Zondervan, 1987), 173–74. Dayton notes that these four themes permeated late nineteenth-century evangelicalism and fundamentalism. He argues that the network of "higher Christian Life" movements at the turn of the century constituted "a sort of pre-Pentecostal tinderbox awaiting the spark that would set it off" (174). These themes were found in muted form in the popular Reformed evangelicalism of the time as well (76).

16. Dayton, *Roots,* 176, asserts that this phenomenon "is a significant *novum* for the most part that truly does set Pentecostalism apart from the other 'higher Christian life' movements."

17. For a recent biography of Parham see James R. Goff, Jr., *Fields White unto Harvest: Charles F. Parham and the Missionary Origins of Pentecostalism* (Fayetteville: University of Arkansas Press, 1988). Goff concurs with Dayton that Pentecostalism was influenced by the preceding Wesleyan, Holiness, and Keswick and Reformed "Higher Life" groups (pp. 6–7).

18. The technical term for this experience of speaking in a known foreign language of which one has no prior knowledge is "xenoglossa," or "xenoglossia." "Glossolalia" is the more general term for speaking in tongues or the utterance of sounds, which constitute, or resemble, a language not known to the speaker. A second "charisma" or gift of interpretation is needed if such speech is to benefit the congregation who hears it. See R. P. Spittler, "Glossolalia," *Dictionary of Pentecostal and Charismatic Movements.*

19. Goff, *Parham,* 15–16.

20. See C. M. Robeck, Jr., "Azusa Street Revival," *Dictionary of Pentecostal and Charismatic Movements.*

21. Goff, *Parham,* 10, notes the work of Douglas J. Nelson, who argued that Seymour was the founder of a religious movement rooted in the genuine breakdown of racial and class barriers. Unfortunately, the interracial worship was of short duration; white Pentecostals later permitted racial segregation.

22. Goff, *Parham,* 9, dates the end of the revival in 1906. Robeck, "Azusa Street Revival," speaks of the end of the revival as "elusive." He states: "The culmination of the second international camp meeting sponsored by the AFM [Apostolic Faith Mission] in the Arroyo Seco between Los Angeles and Pasadena in April-May 1913, however, seems to provide an adequate terminus" (p. 31).

23. Robeck, "Azusa Street Revival," 34.

24. See *Los Angeles Times,* June 6, 1987, part II, p. 5. Cf. Robeck, "Azusa Street Revival," 35.

25. See Robeck, "Azusa Street Revival," and E. L. Blumhofer, "Assemblies of God," *Dictionary of Pentecostal and Charismatic Movements.* Cf. John Dart, "Pentecostal Fellowship to Form Racially Mixed Organization," *Los Angeles Times,* Jan. 22, 1994, B14.

26. Marty, *Modern American Religion,* vol. 1: *The Irony of It All: 1893–1919* (Chicago: University of Chicago Press, 1986), 283–86.

27. Cecil M. Robeck, Jr., "Pentecostals and the Apostolic Faith: Implications for Ecumenism," *Pneuma: The Journal of the Society for Pentecostal Studies,* 9, no. 1 (Spring 1987): 62–63.

28. John H. Gerstner, "The Theological Boundaries of the Evangeli-

cal Faith," in *The Evangelicals,* ed. David F. Wells and John D. Wood-bridge (Nashville: Abingdon Press, 1975), 34. Cf. George H. Williams and Rodney L. Peterson, "Evangelicals: Society, the State, and the Nation (1925–75)," in ibid., 221.

29. Harold J. Ockenga, "From Fundamentalism, Through New Evangelicalism, to Evangelicalism," in *Evangelical Roots,* ed. Kenneth S. Kantzer (New York: Thomas Nelson, 1978), 40.

30. Harold J. Ockenga, "Foreword," in Harold Lindsell, *The Battle for the Bible* (Grand Rapids: Zondervan, 1976), 11. Cf. Ockenga, "From Fundamentalism," 38, where he gives the date as 1947.

31. George Marsden, *Reforming Fundamentalism: Fuller Seminary and the New Evangelicalism* (Grand Rapids: Eerdmans, 1987). James Bradley, a professor of church history at Fuller Seminary in the 1980s, in his review of Marsden's book, argued that "The Repudiation of Fundamentalism" would have been a more apt title given the announced rejection of the separatist mentality characteristic of fundamentalism. See *Pneuma: The Journal of the Society for Pentecostal Studies,* 10, no. 1 (spring 1988): 67–72.

32. For information about Graham's life and ministry see, among others: David Lockhard, *The Unheard Billy Graham* (Waco, Tex.: Word, 1971); William McLoughlin, Jr., *Billy Graham: Revivalist in a Secular Age* (New York: Ronald Press, 1960); John Pollock, *Billy Graham: The Authorized Biography* (New York: McGraw-Hill, 1966) [hereafter *Authorized*]; John Pollock, *Crusades: 20 Years with Billy Graham* (Minneapolis: World Wide Publications, 1966).

33. Williams and Petersen, "Evangelicals," 226.

34. Pollock, *Crusades,* 54–57.

35. Charles W. Dullea, *A Catholic Looks at Billy Graham* (New York: Paulist Press, 1973), 27–28.

36. William Martin, *A Prophet with Honor: The Billy Graham Story* (New York: William Morrow and Co., 1991), 117.

37. McLoughlin, *Revivalist,* 56.

38. Williams and Petersen, "Evangelicals," 225–26; Pollock, *Authorized,* 96; Lockhard, *Unheard,* 150.

39. P. D. Hocken, "Charismatic Movement," *Dictionary of Pentecostal and Charismatic Movements,* 130–33.

40. Ibid., 133–37.

41. *Christian Century* 104, no. 15 (May 6, 1987): 430; *Los Angeles Times,* May 15, 1987, I-28.

42. *Christian Century* 104, no. 15 (May 6, 1987): 430.

43. *Los Angeles Times,* May 15, 1987, I-1.

44. *Los Angeles Times,* May 15, 1987, I-3.

45. *Reformed Journal* 37, no. 4 (April 1987): 3; *Los Angeles Times,* May 15, 1987, I-3.

46. *Christian Century* 104, no. 15 (May 6, 1987): 431.

47. Ibid.

48. Malcolm Gladwell, "Jerry Dumps George," *The New Republic* 195, Nov. 24, 1986, 15–16.

49. "One Step Closer to a Bid for the Oval Office," *Christianity Today* 30, no. 15 (Oct. 17, 1986): 39.

50. Anson Shupe, "The Reconstructionist Movement on the New Christian Right," *Christian Century* 106, no. 28 (Oct. 4, 1989): 882.

51. Rodney Clapp, "Democracy as Heresy," *Christianity Today* 31, no. 3 (Feb. 20, 1987): 21.

52. Pat Robertson, *America's Date with Destiny* (Nashville: Thomas Nelson, 1986).

53. *Los Angeles Times,* July 6, 1987, I-16; Jeffrey K. Hadden and Charles E. Swann, *Prime Time Preachers: The Rising Power of Televangelism* (Reading, Mass.: Addison-Wesley Publishing Co., 1981). 96. See also Hal Lindsey and C. C. Carlson, *The Late Great Planet Earth* (Grand Rapids: Zondervan, 1973).

54. *Los Angeles Times,* July 6, 1987, I-16.

55. Kenneth Woodward, "A Pentecostal for President," *Newsweek* 106, Oct. 14, 1985, 77.

56. *Los Angeles Times,* July 6, 1987, I-16.

57. Woodward, *Newsweek,* 106, Oct. 14, 1985, 77.

58. Jim Trotter, *Pasadena Star-News,* Mar. 29, 1987, A5.

59. *Omaha World-Herald,* Monday, July 20, 1987, 3.

60. "TV Preachers on the Rocks," *Newsweek* 112, July 11, 1988, 26–28.

61. Martin Marty review of Edith L. Blumhofer's *Restoring the Faith: The Assemblies of God, Pentecostalism, and American Culture* in *Christian Century* 111, no. 7 (Mar. 2, 1994): 233.

62. "Pentecostal Fellowship to Form Racially Mixed Organization," *Los Angeles Times,* Jan. 22, 1994, B14; and *Christian Century* 111, no. 32 (Nov. 9, 1994): 1040.

63. "Don't Count Out Televangelists, Researcher Says," *Los Angeles Times,* Nov. 20, 1993, B4. Cf. *Christianity Today* 39, no. 3 (Mar. 6, 1995): 42.

64. "God's Own Party: Evangelicals and Republicans in the '92 Election," *Christian Century* 110, no. 5 (Feb. 17, 1993): 175.

65. "'Purist' Right: Upward, Christian Soldiers," *Los Angeles Times,* Aug. 21, 1992, A13.

66. "Even Sensible Iowa Bows to the Religious Right," *Los Angeles Times,* Aug. 17, 1992, B5.

67. "Robertson's Lawyers," *Christian Century* 109, no. 30. (Oct. 21, 1992): 930.

68. See Susan Cyre, "PCUSA funds efforts to recreate God," *Presbyterian Layman* 27, no. 1 (Jan./Feb. 1994), 10.

69. Susan Cyre "Fallout Escalates over 'goddess' Sophia Worship," *Christianity Today* 38 (Apr. 4, 1994), 74.

70. Catherine Keller, "Inventing the Goddess," *Christian Century* 111, no. 11 (Apr. 6, 1994): 340.

71. *News Briefs* (Nov. 12, 1993), 9.

72. Keller, "Inventing," 341.

73. *News Briefs* (Nov. 12, 1993), 9.

74. Cyre, *Layman,* 11.

75. Ibid. The view that sex is revelatory of God is developing a theoretical base as well. For example, Christine E. Gudorf in her *Body, Sex, and Pleasure: Reconstructing Christian Sexual Ethics* (Cleveland: Pilgrim Press, 1994) is quoted as asserting "the primary experience of divinity itself, as well as of God's intention for the reign of God, is sexual. There is in sex, as in the Eucharist, the potential for participating in divinity." See the review by Jean Porter in *Christian Century* 112, no. 9 (Mar. 15, 1995): 307.

76. Joseph D. Small and John P. Burgess, "Evaluating 'Re-Imagining,'" *Christian Century* 111, no. 11 (Apr. 6, 1994): 343.

77. Cyre, *Layman,* 11.

78. Robert Wuthnow, *The Restructuring of American Religion: Society and Faith Since World War II* (Princeton, N.J.: Princeton University Press, 1988), 217.

79. C. Kirk Hadaway and David A. Roozen, *Rerouting the Protestant Mainstream: Sources of Growth and Opportunities for Change* (Nashville: Abingdon Press, 1995), 85.

80. Ibid., 81

81. Ibid., 82.

82. Ibid., 87.

83. Ibid., 48–51.

84. Martin E. Marty, "Tensions Within Contemporary Evangelical-

ism: A Critical Appraisal," in *The Evangelicals,* ed. David F. Wells and John D. Woodbridge (Nashville: Abingdon Press, 1975) 174–75.

85. Ibid., 178. On pp. 186–87 Marty declared that evangelicals and mainstream Protestants "have more in common than they have recognized." He predicted that "this will become even more evident as evangelicals come increasingly to the conclusion that modernist-liberal Protestantism of the 1920s was a deviation from nineteenth-century continuities and syndromes on the left just as the older fundamentalism was on the right."

Notes for Chapter 5—Common Sense: How Do We Interpret Scripture?

1. Edward W. Farley, "The Presbyterian Heritage as Modernism: Reaffirming a Forgotten Past in Hard Times," in *The Presbyterian Predicament: Six Perspectives,* ed. Milton J Coalter, John M. Mulder, and Louis B. Weeks (Louisville: Westminster/John Knox Press, 1990), 53.

2. Ibid., 52.

3. Ibid., 55–56.

4. Ibid., 61.

5. Ibid., 57 and 63.

6. Ibid., 61.

7. Ibid., 65.

8. Ibid. Farley's solution is a rigorous program of education for the young in the convictions of critical modernism.

9. See "The Case of Hume," in Jack B. Rogers and Forrest E. Baird, *Introduction to Philosophy: A Case Method Approach* (San Francisco: Harper & Row, 1981), 92–101.

10. For more detail see *AIB,* 235–48.

11. See, e.g., Henry F. May, *The Enlightenment in America* (New York: Oxford University Press, 1976) on the importance of Reid.

12. Garry Wills, *Inventing America: Jefferson's Declaration of Independence* (Garden City, N.Y.: Doubleday, 1978).

13. *RT,* 45.

14. *AIB,* 235–47, and the indicated bibliography. Cf. George Marsden, *Fundamentalism and American Culture* (New York: Oxford University Press, 1980), 14–16.

15. *RT,* 58–59.

16. Samuel Miller, *Brief Retrospect of the Eighteenth Century* (1803), 2:10–12, cited in John W. Stewart, "The Tethered Theology: Biblical Criticism, Common Sense Philosophy, and the Princeton Theologians, 1812–1860" (Ph.D. diss. University of Michigan, 1990), 240.

17. Lefferts Loetscher, *Facing the Enlightenment and Pietism: Archibald Alexander and the Founding of Princeton Theological Seminary* (Westwood, Conn.: Greenwood Press, 1983), 250.

18. Cited in Theodore Dwight Bozeman, *Protestants in an Age of Science: The Baconian Ideal and Antebellum American Religious Thought* (Chapel Hill, N.C.: University of North Carolina Press, 1977), 79.

19. Charles Hodge, *Systematic Theology,* vol. I (New York: Charles Scribner's Sons, 1871), 10.

20. Robert S. Michaelsen and Wade Clark Roof, "Introduction," in *Liberal Protestantism: Realities and Possibilities,* ed. Michaelsen and Roof (New York: Pilgrim Press, 1986), 3.

21. William R. Hutchison, *The Modernist Impulse in American Protestantism* (New York: Oxford University Press, 1982), 3.

22. Ibid., 3–4; Michaelsen and Roof, *Liberal Protestantism,* 4.

23. Hutchison, *Modernist Impulse,* 4; Michaelsen and Roof, *Liberal Protestantism,* 4.

24. Hutchison, *Modernist Impulse,* 4, speaks about the experience that lies behind scriptures and creeds; Michaelsen and Roof, *Liberal Protestantism,* 4, assert that "experience precedes words and words must always be reinvigorated through experience," citing Schleiermacher. C. Kirk Hadaway and David A. Roozen, *Rerouting the Protestant Mainstream: Sources for Growth and Opportunities for Change* (Nashville: Abingdon Press, 1995), 13, assert that the "theological heritage shared by the institutions of mainstream Protestantism is decidedly 'liberal.'" Their definition of liberalism closely aligns with the definitions given here, and also with an accepting nod to Schleiermacher (p. 78).

25. Hutchison, *Modernist Impulse,* 4; Michaelsen and Roof, *Liberal Protestantism,* 4. See Joseph C. Hough, Jr., "The Loss of Optimism as a Problem for Liberal Christian Faith," in Michaelsen and Roof, eds., *Liberal Protestantism,* 147: "religious liberalism refers to the sort of religious presence represented chiefly by the activist view of mission." He goes on to say that "this sort of religious presence is grounded theologically in a perspective most clearly represented by the Social Gospel in America, particularly . . . by Walter Rauschenbusch." Hough acknowledges that liberalism "as a theological movement in America preceded Rauschenbusch" (p. 265n.2).

26. Hutchison, *Modernist Impulse,* 8–11. Martin E. Marty, *Modern American Religion,* vol. 1: *The Irony of It All: 1893–1919* (Chicago: University of Chicago Press, 1986), 30. On page 257, Marty quotes Wash-

ington Gladden, one of the shapers of the social gospel movement, as insisting that "Christianity is no longer anti-natural; it is in the deepest sense natural."

27. Marty, *Irony*, 13.

28. Hutchison, *Modernist Impulse*, 7–10, discusses the attempt by some scholars to distinguish between "evangelical liberals" who began with revelation and then tried to adapt it to modern thought, and "modernistic liberals" who began with modern thought and then tried to fit what they could of Christianity into it. Such a distinction fails, Hutchison notes (9), because the principal commitment of liberalism is to overcome the distinction between religion and culture and to see them as one organic whole. The most recent works of scholarship on this period tend to follow Hutchison's lead. See, e.g., Bradley J. Longfield, *The Presbyterian Controversy: Fundamentalists, Modernists, and Moderates* (New York: Oxford University Press, 1991), 237–38 n8.

29. *AIB*, 180–84.

30. *RT*, 122.

31. *AIB*, 348–61.

32. Ibid., 360.

33. For a more detailed discussion see ibid., 348–61. For a recent summary see Longfield, *Presbyterian Controversy*, 22–23.

34. Harold Lindsell, *The Battle for the Bible* (Grand Rapids, Zondervan, 1976).

35. Ibid., 18. Cf. Jack Rogers, "Inerrancy," in *A New Handbook of Christian Theology*, ed. Donald W. Musser and Joseph L. Price (Nashville: Abingdon Press, 1992), 254–56.

36. Lindsell, *Battle*, 133.

37. Harold Lindsell, *The Bible in the Balance* (Grand Rapids: Zondervan, 1979).

38. Ibid., 320.

39. Ibid., 320–21. Unfortunately, this important statement in the book is garbled by an error in the first printing. It reads correctly if the first two lines of p. 320 are transposed with the first two lines of p. 321. In the last paragraph on p. 321, Lindsell offers an alternate suggestion: "Believers in the view that Scripture and the Word of God are synonymous can always use an alternate label such as *Orthodox Protestant* which I have already surfaced in this chapter."

40. "Taking a Stand on Scripture," advertisement in *Christianity Today* 22 (Dec. 30, 1977): 25. For news reports, see "Proinerrancy Draft

Their Platform," *Christianity Today* 23, no. 4 (Nov. 17, 1978): 36–37; "Scholars Consider Inerrancy in Chicago," *Presbyterian Journal* 37, no. 28 (Nov. 8, 1978): 4–5; "Inerrancy on the March," *Christian Century* 95, no. 38 (Nov. 22, 1978): 1126.

41. Available from the International Council on Biblical Inerrancy, P. O. Box 13261, Oakland, CA 94661. For official commentary on the statement, see R. C. Sproul, *Explaining Inerrancy: A Commentary* (Oakland, Calif.: International Council on Biblical Inerrancy, 1980).

42. Jack B. Rogers, "Biblical Authority and Confessional Change," *Journal of Presbyterian History* 59, no. 2 (Summer 1981): 135. Cf. Loetscher, *Facing,* 155f.; Edward A. Dowey, Jr., *The Knowledge of God in Calvin's Theology* (New York: Columbia University Press, 1965), 163; Robert Clyde Johnson, *Authority in Protestant Theology* (Philadelphia: Westminster Press), 58.

43. William E. Hordern, *A Layman's Guide to Protestant Theology,* rev. ed. (New York: Macmillan, 1968), 94.

44. Ibid., 130–31.

45. *RT,* 127. "Neo-orthodoxy resisted liberalism by asserting the centrality of scripture, and it opposed fundamentalism by arguing for the validity of biblical criticism."

46. Rogers, "Confessional Change," 135–36. Cf. Edward A. Dowey, Jr., "Tillich, Barth, and the Criteria of Theology," *Theology Today* 15 (Apr. 1958): 58.

47. Bob E. Patterson, *Reinhold Niebuhr* (Waco, Tex.: Word Books, 1977), 13.

48. Richard Wightman Fox, *Reinhold Niebuhr: A Biography* (San Francisco: Harper & Row, 1985), 214.

49. Ibid., 201–2.

50. Ibid., 234.

51. Ibid., 233–34.

52. Ibid., 238.

53. John A. Mackay, "Bonn 1930—and After: A Lyrical Tribute to Karl Barth," *Theology Today* 13 (Oct. 1956): 291.

54. Rogers, "Confessional Change," 136. *RT,* 128: "The triumph of neo-orthodoxy in American Presbyterian theology—and indeed in mainstream Protestantism—was complete by the 1950s and 1960s."

55. *RT,* 129.

56. Ibid., 130.

57. B. B. Warfield, *Revelation and Inspiration* (New York: Oxford University Press, 1927), 442.

58. Edward A. Dowey, Jr., chair of the committee that wrote the Confession of 1967, commented, "One would not guess from this Report that the Confession of 1967 was and is the only full-scale confessional achievement in any Reformed church in the world that shows the church both responding to and triumphing over the attacks on Scripture that were suffered for nearly two hundred years" ("A Critique of the Report on Biblical Authority and Interpretation, unpublished paper, June 23, 1982, 6).

59. Edward A. Dowey, Jr., *A Commentary on the Confession of 1967 and an Introduction to "The Book of Confessions"* (Philadelphia: Westminster Press, 1968), 100.

60. Jack Rogers, *Presbyterian Creeds: A Guide to the Book of Confessions* (Philadelphia, Westminster Press, 1985), 212–19. Cf. James H. Moorhead, "Redefining Confessionalism: American Presbyterians in the Twentieth Century," in *The Confessional Mosaic: Presbyterians and Twentieth-Century Theology*, ed. Milton J Coalter, John M. Mulder, and Louis B. Weeks (Louisville: Westminster/John Knox Press, 1990), 77–78.

61. *RT,* 128.

62. Jack B. Rogers and Donald K. McKim, "Pluralism and Policy in Presbyterian Views of Scripture," in Coalter, Mulder, and Weeks, eds., *Confessional Mosaic,* 40.

63. For my understanding of critical realism I am indebted to Paul Hiebert for many conversations and especially to his article, "Epistemological Foundations for Science and Theology," *TSF Bulletin* 8, no. 4 (March–April 1985): 5–10.

64. Farley, "Heritage," 64.

65. Ibid., 52.

66. Cited in Rogers and McKim, "Pluralism," 48.

67. Ibid., 51.

68. Ibid., 51.

69. Ibid., 44.

70. Ibid., 52.

71. Rogers and McKim, "Pluralism," 51–52. Both the former UPCUSA and the former PCUS reports are now available in one booklet, *Presbyterian Understanding and Use of Holy Scripture* and *Biblical Authority and Interpretation* (Louisville: Office of the General Assembly, Presbyterian Church (U.S.A.), 1992).

Notes for Chapter 6—Moralism:
What Are Our Moral Standards?

1. Minority Report of the Special Committee on Problem Pregnancies and Abortion, "God's Gift of Life." Reports to the 204th General Assembly (1992), Part I, Presbyterian Church (U.S.A.), Milwaukee, Wisconsin, June 2–10, 1992, 27.225.

2. *RT,* 45.

3. Catherine L. Albanese, *America: Religions and Religion* (Belmont, Calif.: Wadsworth, 1981), 258.

4. *RT,* 70–71. Cf. C. Kirk Hadaway and David A. Roozen, *Rerouting the Protestant Mainstream: Sources for Growth and Opportunities for Change* (Nashville: Abingdon Press, 1995), 22.

5. *RT,* 286–87.

6. Will Herberg, *Protestant—Catholic—Jew* (Garden City, N.Y.: Doubleday Anchor, 1960), 257–58, as quoted in *AMR,* 14.

7. Herberg, *Protestant—Catholic—Jew,* 234, quoted in *AMR,* 15.

8. Robert Wuthnow, *The Restructuring of American Religion: Society and Faith Since World War II* (Princeton: Princeton University Press, 1988), 61. William R. Hutchison, "Discovering America," in *BT,* 306, agrees that 'Mainline Protestantism' of this pre-1960s era served broadly to provide and articulate moral norms for American society, and that it has since abdicated that function or lost the power to perform it." He continues: "The pre-sixties Protestant establishment did offer a specifically religious—indeed quasi-ecclesiastical—matrix for common social values." R. Laurence Moore ("Secularization: Religion and the Social Sciences," in *BT,* 241–43) notes the efforts of social scientists to support a moral consensus.

9. King, *BT,* 134.

10. Wuthnow, *Restructuring,* 64.

11. Ibid., 114.

12. Stephen B. Oates, *Let the Trumpet Sound: The Life of Martin Luther King, Jr.* (New York: Harper & Row, 1982), 50.

13. Ronald C. White, Jr., *Liberty and Justice for All: Racial Reform and the Social Gospel (1877–1925)* (San Francisco: Harper & Row, 1990), 261–62.

14. Taylor Branch, *Parting the Waters: America in the King Years, 1954–63* (New York: Simon and Schuster, 1988), 128–29.

15. Oates, *Sound,* 65.

16. Ibid., 64–69; Branch, *Waters,* 128–39.

17. Branch, *Waters,* 141.

18. Oates, *Sound,* 71.

19. Silk, *BT,* 293–94.

20. R. Douglas Brackenridge, *Eugene Carson Blake: Prophet with Portfolio* (New York: Seabury Press, 1978), 91.

21. Oates, *Sound,* 220.

22. Ibid., 222.

23. Ibid., 230.

24. Brackenridge, *Blake,* 92.

25. Ibid., 92–96.

26. Oates, *Sound,* 254.

27. Ibid., 257–62.

28. Wuthnow, *Restructuring,* 145–46.

29. Ibid., 146.

30. Ibid.

31. Ibid.

32. Leonard Sweet, "Can a Mainstream Change Its Course?" in *Liberal Protestantism: Realities and Possibilities,* ed. Robert S. Michaelsen and Wade Clark Roof (New York: Pilgrim Press, 1986), 250.

33. Anne Motley Hallum, "Presbyterians as Political Amateurs," in *Religion in American Politics,* ed. Charles W. Dunn (Washington, D.C.: Congressional Quarterly Press, 1989), 63.

34. Ibid., 64.

35. Wuthnow, *Restructuring,* 254.

36. Ibid., 148–49.

37. *AMR,* 224 and 228.

38. Dinesh D'Souza, *Falwell Before the Millennium: A Critical Biography* (Chicago: Regnery Gateway, 1984), 80–81.

39. Erling Jorstad, *The Politics of Moralism* (Minneapolis: Augsburg, 1981), 73.

40. Ibid., 74.

41. "New Right Tops 1980 Religious News," *Christian Century* 97, no. 43 (Dec. 31, 1980): 1283.

42. Jim Wallis, "Recovering the Evangel," *Theology Today* 38, no. 2 (July 1981): 215.

43. Jerry Falwell, *Listen America!* (New York: Doubleday, 1986; reprint, New York: Bantam Books, 1981).

44. Jerry Falwell, *The Fundamentalist Phenomenon* (New York: Doubleday, 1981).

45. Martin Marty, "The New Christian Right," *1981 Britannica Book of the Year,* (Chicago: Encyclopaedia Britannica, 1981) (hereafter *EB, 1981*), 606.

46. Roy Larson, "Religion," *EB, 1981,* 595.

47. Erling Jorstad, *Evangelicals in the White House: The Cultural Maturation of Born Again Christianity, 1960–1981,* Studies in American Religion, 4 (New York: Edwin Mellen Press, 1981), 130. See also Gabriel Fackre, *The Religious Right and Christian Faith* (Grand Rapids: Eerdmans, 1982), 82: "The marks of the state of sanctification are indications of devotion to the political commitments of the Religious Right."

48. Samuel S. Hill and Dennis E. Owen, *The New Religious/Political Right in America* (Nashville: Abingdon Press, 1982), 46–48. On p. 48, the authors note that "Jerry Falwell argues that the state is responsible for punishing evildoers, both domestic and foreign, and that it has a special responsibility to punish 'the enemies of God.'"

49. Robert N. Bellah, Richard Madsen, William M. Sullivan, Ann Swidler, and Steven M. Tipton, *Habits of the Heart: Individualism and Commitment in American Life* (Berkeley, Calif.: University of California Press, 1985).

50. Alexis de Tocqueville, *Democracy in America,* 2 vols., tr. Francis Bowen, ed. Phillips Bradley (New York: Random House, 1945).

51. James M. Wall, "Tocqueville's 'Habits,' the 'Heart's' Freedom," *Christian Century* 102, no. 18 (May 22, 1985): 523.

52. Ibid.

53. Ibid.

54. AMR, 227.

55. Ibid., 226.

56. Cited in Jack B. Rogers and Donald K. McKim, "Pluralism and Policy in Presbyterian Views of Scripture," in *The Confessional Mosaic: Presbyterians and Twentieth-Century Theology,* ed. Milton J Coalter, John M. Mulder, and Louis B. Weeks (Louisville: Westminster/John Knox Press, 1990), 46.

57. Donald K. McKim, "Biblical Interpretations in Presbyterian Statements on Sexuality," *Church and Society* 80, no. 2 (November/December 1989): 92–108.

58. See, e.g., Marion L. Soards, "The Biblical Understanding of Homosexuality," *ReNews: A Publication of Presbyterians for Renewal* (Febru-

ary 1993), 6–1 through 6–4; James A. Sanders, "Care to Consider: Theological/Biblical Issues of Homosexuality," an unpublished paper prepared for Church and Society Subcommittee of San Gabriel Presbytery, June 1993.

59. See, e.g., Charles R. Ehrhardt, "Divorce Versus Homosexuality," *Monday Morning,* Apr. 19, 1993, 8.

60. "Presbyterian Church (U.S.A.) Sexual Misconduct Policy and Its Procedures," *Minutes of the 205th General Assembly (1993) of the Presbyterian Church (U.S.A.),* Part I: *Journal,* p. 570. The original, groundbreaking research in this area was done by Richard Allen Blackmon at the Graduate School of Psychology of Fuller Theological Seminary, in a 1984 Ph.D. dissertation titled "The Hazards of Ministry." In a survey of 300 ministers in four denominations in Southern California, 37 percent reported having engaged in sexual behavior inappropriate for a minister and over 12 percent reported having intercourse with a church member other than their spouse. Presbyterians in the survey were slightly lower in the first category (34 percent) but higher in the second (26 percent). A national study conducted by the Professional Ethics Group of the Center for Ethics and Social Policy at the Graduate Theological Union in Berkeley and funded by the Lilly Endowment indicated that 25 percent of clergy had had some kind of sexual contact with a parishioner and 10 percent have had an affair with a parishioner. See "Clergy and Sexuality," *Christian Century* (7 March 1990): 240.

61. See David Finkelhor, *Child Sexual Abuse* (New York: Free Press, 1984); and Roland Summit, "Beyond Belief: The Reluctant Discovery of Incest," in *Sexual Assault and Abuse,* ed. Mary D. Pellauer, Barbara Chester, and Jane Boyajian (San Francisco: Harper & Row, 1987), 172–197.

62. Marie M. Fortune, *Is Nothing Sacred? When Sex Invades the Pastoral Relationship* (San Francisco: Harper & Row, 1989). See also Peter Rutter, *Sex in the Forbidden Zone: When Men in Power—Therapists, Doctors, Clergy, Teachers, and Others—Betray Women's Trust* (Los Angeles: Jeremy P. Tarcher, 1989).

63. Marie M. Fortune in a presentation to the PC(USA) Task Force on Human Sexuality, June 21, 1990.

64. Personal conversations with clinical psychologists familiar with such cases.

65. "Storm Clouds Gathering over Coming Report of the Task Force on Human Sexuality," *ReNews: A Publication of Presbyterians for Renewal* (December 1990), n.p.

66. For one such expression see Ray S. Anderson, "Human Rights and Human Sexuality — Discrimination or Differentiation?" unpublished paper presented to the Church and Society Subcommittee of the Presbytery of San Gabriel, June 1993.

67. Presbyterian Panel Survey, done for the General Assembly Special Committee on Human Sexuality but omitted from its 1991 report to the PC(USA) General Assembly. Available in the Research Division of PC(USA) in Louisville.

68. "Body and Soul: A New Look at Human Sexuality and the Church," *Church and Society* (November/December 1989), 1–112.

Notes for Chapter 7—Millennialism: What Is Our Future Hope?

1. Jeffrey Sheler, "The Christmas Covenant," *U.S. News and World Report*, 117 (Dec. 19, 1994), 62–71, quoted in *Current Thoughts and Trends* (February 1995), 4.

2. *RT*, 46–47. Coalter et al. treat postmillennialism as the exclusive property of liberalism and assign premillennialism to the fundamentalists. That is true after the decisive division between fundamentalists and modernists in the 1920s, but before that time both groups shared a cultural optimism that comported well with postmillennialism.

3. Edwin Scott Gaustad, *A Religious History of America* (New York: Harper & Row, 1966), 151.

4. See Charles Hodge, *Systematic Theology*, Vol. III, (New York: Charles Scribner's Sons, 1871), 271, where Hodge refers to postmillennialism as "the common doctrine of the Church."

5. George Marsden, *Fundamentalism and American Culture* (New York: Oxford University Press, 1980), 46.

6. Ibid., 54.

7. Timothy P. Weber, "Dispensationalism," in *A New Handbook of Christian Theology*, ed. Donald W. Musser and Joseph L. Price (Nashville: Abingdon Press, 1992), 127.

8. Marsden, *Fundamentalism*, 61–62.

9. Bradley J. Longfield, *The Presbyterian Controversy: Fundamentalists, Modernists, and Moderates* (New York: Oxford University Press, 1991), 20–21. For more detail on the distinguishing features of dispensationalism, see Clarence B. Bass, *Backgrounds to Dispensationalism: Its Historical Genesis and Ecclesiastical Implications* (Grand Rapids: Baker Book House, 1960), 13–47. (Hereafter *BD*.)

10. Marsden, *Fundamentalism,* 118–20.

11. Quoted in *BD,* 19. See also David A. Reiter, "The Quiet Clash of Reformed and Dispensational Theologies in the Presbyterian Congregation and Strategies for Ministry," San Francisco Theological Seminary: Unpublished D.Min. Dissertation Project, 1995.

12. For a brief description of each of the seven dispensations see Charles C. Ryrie, *Dispensationalism Today* (Chicago: Moody Press, 1965), 57–64.

13. Weber, "Dispensationalism," 126.

14. William M. King, "The Reform Establishment," in *BT,* 128.

15. Quoted in Robert A. Schneider, "Church Federation in the Twentieth Century," in *BT,* 117.

16. King, "Reform Establishment," 132.

17. Dennis N. Voskuil, "Reaching Out: Mainline Protestantism and the Media," in *BT,* 77–80.

18. Mark Silk, "The Rise of the 'New Evangelicalism,'" in *BT,* 292.

19. Ibid., 293.

20. Ibid., 292–93.

21. Brackenridge, 128–29.

22. Ibid., 128.

23. Ibid., 132.

24. Ibid., 131–32.

25. Ibid., 137.

26. Ibid., 128.

27. Ibid., 137–38.

28. Ibid., 141. Other denominations joined the consultation: Evangelical United Brethren and Disciples of Christ (1962), African Methodist Episcopal Church and Presbyterian Church in the U.S. (1965), African Methodist Episcopal Zion Church (1966), and Christian Methodist Episcopal Church (1967), 142.

29. Quoted in Erling Jorstad, *The Politics of Moralism: The New Christian Right in American Life* (Minneapolis: Augsburg Publishing House, 1981), 93.

30. Quoted in ibid., 93–94.

31. *EB, 1981,* 605.

32. Ibid.

33. Rodney Clapp, "Democracy as Heresy," *Christianity Today* 31, no. 3 (Feb. 20, 1987): 17 and 21.

34. Ibid., 22.

35. Anson Shupe, "The Reconstructionist Movement on the New Christian Right," *Christian Century* 106, no. 28 (Oct. 4, 1989): 881.

36. Clapp, "Democracy," 18; Shupe, "Movement," 881.

37. Clapp, "Democracy," 18; Shupe, "Movement," 881.

38. Clapp, "Democracy," 18–20.

39. Ibid., 19–20.

40. Ibid., 21.

41. Shupe, "Movement," 882. For a "secular" view of Reconstructionism see "Prophets of a Biblical America," Vol. CCXIII, no. 71, *The Wall Street Journal,* Apr. 12, 1989, A14.

42. *Newsweek* 100 (Nov. 1, 1982), 88.

43. *Eternity* 33, no. 1 (Jan. 1982), 19.

44. *Newsweek* 100 (Nov. 1, 1982), 88.

45. *The Other Side* (September 1984): 36.

46. Quoted in Jeffrey K. Hadden and Charles E. Swann, *Prime Time Preachers: The Rising Power of Televangelism* (Reading, Mass.: Addison-Wesley Publishing Co., 1981).

47. Tim LaHaye, *The Battle for the Mind* (Old Tappan, N.J.: Revell, 1980), 46–48.

48. Quoted in Hadden and Swann, *Prime Time,* 86.

49. See Paul W. Kurtz, *A Secular Humanist Declaration* (Buffalo, N.Y.: Prometheus Books, 1980).

50. *Christian Century* 99, no. 30 (Oct. 6, 1982): 972.

51. *Christianity Today* 28, no. 9 (June 15, 1984): 70.

52. Sidney Blumenthal, "The Religious Right and Republicans," in *Piety and Politics: Evangelicals and Fundamentalists Confront the World,* ed. by Richard John Neuhaus and Michael Cromartie (Washington, D.C.: Ethics and Public Policy Center, 1987), 284.

53. *Los Angeles Times,* Mar. 29, 1986, I-A, 7.

54. Ibid.

55. See Larry Jones and Gerald T. Sheppard, "The Politics of Biblical Eschatology: Ronald Reagan and the Impending Nuclear Armageddon," *TSF Bulletin* 8, no. 1 (September–October 1984): 16–17; John Dart, "Armageddon — Reagan's Ideas Debated," *Los Angeles Times,* Nov. 3, 1984), Part I, 7.

56. John Walvoord, *Armageddon, Oil, and the Middle East Crisis* (Grand Rapids: Zondervan, 1974).

57. Geraldine Baum, "Has Time Run Out?" *Los Angeles Times,* Feb. 7, 1991, E2.

58. Jorstad, *Politics* 49–50.

59. See, e.g., "History Has Seen Many Apocalyptic Scenarios," *Los Angeles Times,* Mar. 13, 1993, B4.

60. Pat Robertson, *The New Millennium: 10 Trends That Will Impact You and Your Family by the Year 2000* (Dallas: Word, 1990), 312–13.

61. Ibid., 318.

62. John R. Muether, "The Theonomic Attraction," in *Theonomy: A Reformed Critique,* ed. William S. Barker and W. Robert Godfrey (Grand Rapids: Zondervan, 1990), 251.

63. Ibid., 252–257.

64. Silk, *BT,* 295 96.

65. Robert Wuthnow, *The Restructuring of American Religion: Society and Faith Since World War II* (Princeton, N.J.: Princeton University Press, 1988), 12.

66. Ibid., 161.

67. Ibid., 130–31, 219.

68. Benton Johnson, "Winning Lost Sheep: A Recovery Course for Liberal Protestantism," in *Liberal Protestantism: Realities and Possibilities,* ed. Robert S. Michaelsen and Wade Clark Roof (New York: Pilgrim Press, 1986), 224–25. Cf. *AMR,* 46.

69. *RT,* 14. Cf. C. Kirk Hadaway and David A. Roozen, *Rerouting the Protestant Mainstream: Sources for Growth and Opportunities for Change* (Nashville: Abingdon Press, 1995) 23–30.

70. Martin E. Marty, "Mainline or Mainstream?," *Christian Century* 106, no. 38 (Dec. 13, 1989): 1183.

71. Johnson, "Winning," 229.

72. AMR, 250.

73. Glenn T. Miller, "Professionals and Pedagogues: A Survey of Theological Education," in *Altered Landscapes: Christianity in America, 1935–1985,* ed. David W. Lotz, Donald W. Shriver, Jr., and John F. Wilson (Grand Rapids: Eerdmans, 1989), 203–8.

74. Ibid., 208.

75. John M. Mulder and Lee A. Wyatt, "The Predicament of Pluralism: The Study of Theology in Presbyterian Seminaries Since the 1920s," in *The Pluralistic Vision: Presbyterians and Mainstream Protestant Education*

and *Leadership,* ed. Milton J Coalter, John M. Mulder, and Louis B. Weeks (Louisville: Westminster/John Knox Press, 1992), 69.

76. Wuthnow, *Restructuring.* 302.

77. Ibid., 241.

78. *AMR,* 75.

79. "Is the End Still Near?" *Los Angeles Times,* July 30, 1992, E1–3.

80. "Is the End Still Near?" *Los Angeles Times,* July 30, 1992, E1.

Notes for Chapter 8—Worldview: A Resource for Reconciliation

1. There are many calls for a return to the center. See, e.g., Robert H. Bullock, Jr., "A Church in Search of Its Center and Its Boundaries," *Presbyterian Outlook,* 175, no. 24 (June 21, 1993): 12: "As one immerses oneself in the meetings of General Assembly in recent years, one realizes how incredibly diverse the church is now—how many theologies there are which compete with one another, how far apart are the most divergent worldviews in the mix. One wonders if indeed it can hold together." Cf. Robert D. Taylor, "A Case for the Centrist Position," *Presbyterian Outlook* 175, no. 36 (Oct. 18, 1993): 7. Not all are convinced. Robert M. Davidson, a former General Assembly moderator, wrote a letter to the editors published under the heading, "What's So Holy about the Center?" (*Presbyterian Outlook* 175, no. 28 [Aug. 2–9, 1993]: 2).

2. *BE,* 11, where Martin Marty coined the phrase, and 346–47, where editors Carroll and Roof use it in another way. I have added my own expansion of the term.

3. *BE,* 347–49.

4. "Loving One Another," *Presbyterian Outlook* 174, no. 14 (Apr. 20, 1992): 8, puts it in the darkest light: "Each individual, each organized group is seeking victory over all the others — a kind of Hobbesian war of all against all."

5. See Kyle A. Pasewark and Garrett E. Paul, "Forming an Emphatic Christian Center: A Call to Political Responsibility," *Christian Century* 111, no. 24 (Aug. 24, 1994): 780–83.

6. *Book of Order,* ch. 2.

7. See, e.g., "Conservative Christian Blocs Thriving Nationwide," *San Francisco Chronicle,* Sept. 13, 1993, A1, A6, and A7.

8. Jack B. Rogers and Forrest E. Baird, *Introduction to Philosophy: A Case Method Approach* (San Francisco: Harper & Row, 1981), 8–10.

9. Leander E. Keck, *The Church Confident* (Nashville: Abingdon Press, 1993).

10. Ibid., 21–22.

11. Ibid., 22n10.

12. Subtitled, *Reinventing the Congregation for a New Mission Frontier* (Washington, D.C.: Alban Institute, 1991).

13. James Wall, "Tocqueville's 'Habits,' the 'Heart's' Freedom," *Christian Century* 102, no. 18 (May 22, 1985): 523.

14. Martin Marty, "Filling in the Gaps of Liberal Culture," *Christian Century* 106, no. 33 (Nov. 8, 1989): 1019.

15. Ibid., 1022.

16. *RT,* 248–73.

17. There is considerable skepticism in the church regarding real change as evidenced by the editorial statement in *Presbyterian Outlook:* "It was the consensus of most observers [to the 1993 General Assembly] that the order and priorities of the leadership in Louisville remain, within the new structure, virtually unchanged. The General Assembly Mission budget distributes less money, but distributes it in virtually the same proportions as it did last year." See "Faith Seeking Stalemate," *Presbyterian Outlook* 175, no. 26 (July 5–12, 1993): 10.

18. Robert Wuthnow, *The Restructuring of American Religion: Society and Faith Since World War II* (Princeton, N.J.: Princeton University Press, 1988), 217.

19. *RT,* 279.

20. Ibid., 278.

21. *AMR,* 241–42.

22. Wuthnow, *Restructuring,* 88–89. William H. Willimon stated, "We provided our children with a theological rationale for embracing secularism." Cited in C. Kirk Hadaway and David A. Roozen, *Rerouting the Protestant Mainstream: Sources for Growth and Opportunities for Change* (Nashville: Abingdon Press, 1995), 46.

23. *AMR,* 46.

24. Ibid., 242.

25. Ibid., 241.

26. "Why Baby Boomers Leave Church Is Studied," *Presbyterian Outlook* 174, no. 28 (Aug. 3–10, 1992): 5. In this study by Dean Hoge, Benton Johnson, and Donald Luidens "boomers" refers to young adults between the ages of 33 and 42. For more detail see Wade Clark Roof, *A Generation of Seekers: Baby Boomers and the Quest for Spiritual Style* (San Francisco: HarperCollins, 1993). Roof describes the attitudes of 76 million men and women born between 1946 and 1964.

27. "Boomers," 5.

28. Ibid.

29. For further development of the "lay liberalism" of the baby boomers see Dean R. Hoge, Benton Johnson, and Donald A. Luidens, *Vanishing Boundaries: The Religion of Mainline Protestant Baby Boomers* (Louisville: Westminster/John Knox Press, 1994). For a statistical analysis of the religious attitudes of the next younger generation see George Barna, *The Invisible Generation: Baby Busters* (Glendale, Calif.: Barna Research Group, 1992).

30. See *AIB, passim,* for the historical concept of "accommodation" in biblical interpretation which is similar to critical realism in philosophy.

31. "Presbyterian Understanding and Use of Holy Scripture and Biblical Authority and Interpretation" (Louisville: Office of the General Assembly, Presbyterian Church (U.S.A.), 1992).

32. Report of the Committee on Pluralism to the 1978 General Assembly of the United Presbyterian Church.

33. For an earlier and more detailed treatment of this topic see my essay "Sex, Philosophy, and Politics: How and What the Church Must Decide in the Debate over Ordination of Homosexuals," in *Homosexuality in the Church: Both Sides of the Debate,* ed. Jeffrey S. Siker (Louisville: Westminster/John Knox Press, 1994), 161–77.

34. *Calvin: Institutes of the Christian Religion,* ed. John T. McNeill, tr. Ford Lewis Battles, Library of Christian Classics, 21 (Philadelphia: Westminster Press, 1960), 4.1.2. "The Church is called 'catholic,' or 'universal,' because there could not be two or three churches unless Christ be torn asunder [cf.1 Cor. 1:13]—which cannot happen!"

35. President Addison Hardie Leitch of Pittsburgh-Xenia Seminary.

36. I agree with President J. Randolph Taylor of San Francisco Theological Seminary, who said, "There is no priority, no moral commitment that is more important than the unity of the church" (*Presbyterian Outlook* 175, no. 24 [June 21, 1993]: 13).

37. United Methodists, American Baptists, and Episcopalians all reviewed their position on ordination of homosexuals in recent years. All maintained the present stance against ordination of homosexuals but all continued to study it. The Lutherans have begun a study process leading to a vote in 1995. Of the mainstream denominations only the United Church of Christ admits avowed, sexually active gay and lesbian persons into its ministry. See "Church Allows Gay Ministers, *Pasadena Star-News,*

Aug. 3, 1991, B-9. Cf. Gayle White, "Episcopalians Stand Pat on Homo-sexuality," *Christian Century* 108, no. 23 (Aug. 7–14, 1991): 740–41; "Two Protestant Groups Will Put Sexuality to the Test," *Los Angeles Times,* June 29, 1991, F19; and "ABC on Sexuality," *Christian Century* 108, no. 22 (July 24–31, 1991): 713.

Index